PAT BROWN, MBA

Financial Literacy For Doctors

"From Residency to Retirement: A Complete Guide to Money for Medical Professionals"

ABRAM · 47 · BROWN

First published by AbramBrown47 2025

First edition

ISBN: 978-1-967737-28-4

This book was professionally typeset on Reedsy.
Find out more at reedsy.com

Contents

Author's Preface

Financial Literacy For Doctors

Before we dive into numbers, strategies, or financial frameworks, let me start with this:

This book is built on respect.

Respect for what it takes to become a doctor.

Respect for the years of school, the residency grind, the emotional weight, the long hours, the sacrifices—both seen and unseen.

And respect for the deep, life-changing impact you have on people every single day.

I've worked with professionals from all walks of life, but over the years, I've developed a deep personal and professional connection to those in medicine. Today, I proudly serve as a **Board Trustee for a hospital**, and that role has given me an even deeper understanding of the critical, complex, and often overwhelming world that doctors live in.

From that vantage point, I've seen the **excellence** you bring to your patients.

But I've also seen the **lack of support** you're given when it comes to something just as vital: **your financial life.**

Despite your intelligence, discipline, and capacity for learning, most of you were never taught the basics of money management.

Not in undergrad.

Not in medical school.

Not during residency.

And certainly not while trying to build a life amid debt, call shifts, career changes, or private practice pressures.

That's why I wrote this book.

Not to impress you—but to equip you.

Whether you're early in your career or years into practice, this book is designed to help you do what you do best: make informed, high-impact decisions under pressure. Except now, those decisions aren't about patients—they're about your future.

We'll cover everything:

- Understanding your contract
- Navigating taxes
- Investing wisely
- Protecting your income
- Building long-term wealth
- Planning for life after medicine

No jargon. No pitch. No judgment. Just clear, actionable guidance written by someone who knows what it's like to support high performers—and who cares deeply about seeing professionals like you win, both personally and financially.

And with that, I want to take a moment to dedicate this book to the people who shaped me:

To my **mother**, whose love, strength, and quiet guidance lit the path.

To my **father**, who taught me by example what consistency and character look like.

To my **wife Cassandra**, my partner, encourager, and biggest supporter.

To my daughters, **Peyton (in California)** and **Ryan (in New York)**—you are my motivation, my legacy, and my joy.

And to my **brother**, who's always been in my corner, even in the hardest seasons.

This book is part of that legacy.

Now it's in your hands—to guide you, challenge you, and hopefully, empower you to take full ownership of your financial future.

Because you didn't come this far just to earn a paycheck.

You came this far to **build a life**—on your terms.

Let's get started.

— Pat Brown, MBA

Why This Book Was Written

Let's be honest—this book shouldn't have to exist.

Doctors are some of the most highly trained, highly educated professionals in the world. You go through undergrad, medical school, residency, fellowships, board exams, and years of intense on-the-job learning. You're taught how to diagnose rare conditions, perform complex procedures, and lead care teams in high-stress environments.

But despite all of that education...

you were never really taught how to manage money.

- Not how to read a contract.
- Not how to navigate debt.
- Not how to plan for taxes, protect your income, or build long-term wealth.

And that's a problem.

Because while you're trained to take care of others, no one trained you to take care of **yourself—financially**.

That's why this book was written.

I've spent more than 20 years in financial services helping people—from young professionals to seasoned executives—understand how money works and how to make it work for them. Along the way, I've worked with many doctors. I've sat across the table from residents with $300,000 in debt and no idea where to start. I've counseled attending physicians making six figures who felt like they were still living paycheck to paycheck. And I've helped senior physicians figure out what retirement really looks like after a lifetime of giving their all to others.

I have the honor of serving as a **Board Trustee for a hospital**, where I've gained an even deeper understanding of the emotional, physical, and financial demands placed on doctors today.

And it became crystal clear:

You need—and deserve—a guide that speaks your language and fits your life.

Not a textbook.

Not a sales pitch.

But a clear, practical, real-world playbook that shows you how to take control of your financial future.

This book was written:

- To simplify financial concepts that often get overcomplicated
- To give you tools and steps you can act on immediately
- To help you avoid mistakes that cost other doctors years of progress
- And to empower you to make decisions with clarity, confidence, and purpose

Whether you're a med student, a new resident, a practicing physician, or a department head, this book was created with your journey in mind. Because you've sacrificed too much to live in financial confusion or chaos.

You were called to heal, serve, and lead.

Let's make sure you can also **build, protect, and grow**.

That's why this book was written.

Let's begin.

How to Use This Book

Financial Literacy for Doctors is not a textbook — it's a practical guide, written by a financial literacy advocate, designed to meet you where you are in your financial journey. Whether you're a medical student just trying to understand loan options or a seasoned attending looking to optimize retirement, this book is meant to grow with you.

This Book Is Modular — Not Linear

You don't have to read it cover to cover (though you certainly can). Each chapter is structured as a standalone topic, so you can jump to whatever's most relevant in your life right now.

If you're:

- **In medical school** → Start with chapters on student loans, budgeting, and understanding the financial roadmap ahead.
- **In residency or fellowship** → Focus on chapters about debt management, disability insurance, and building early money habits.
- **An early-career attending** → Dive into income breakdowns, contracts, investing basics, and lifestyle planning.
- **Mid-career or a practice owner** → Explore chapters on tax strategies, business ownership, practice valuation, and wealth building.
- **Preparing for retirement or slowing down** → Check out chapters on exit planning, estate considerations, and life after medicine.

Use the **table of contents** as your menu. Skim, highlight, dog-ear, or annotate as needed.

This Book Is Financial Literacy — With a White Coat On

Most finance books aren't written for people who've delayed their income for over a decade, carry hundreds of thousands in student debt, and work 60+ hour weeks under emotional and physical strain.

This one is.

We address topics unique to physicians:

- The emotional toll of burnout and how it affects money
- Delayed gratification and how it shapes lifestyle inflation
- Private practice vs. employment trade-offs
- How physicians really get paid — RVUs, call pay, and all
- Non-clinical income options that still use your degree

We also cover the universal financial truths — budgeting, investing, credit, taxes — through the lens of your career as a doctor.

This Book Is a Resource, Not a Rulebook

There's no one-size-fits-all path to financial wellness. You won't find shame, guilt, or rigid formulas here. Instead, you'll find:

- Examples from real physician lives
- Case studies and scenarios you can relate to
- Frameworks that can adapt to your goals
- Practical, jargon-free explanations

Use this book to **make informed decisions**, not to chase someone else's idea of wealth. Your goals may be early retirement, part-time work, practice ownership, charitable giving, or just peace of mind. All are valid.

Take Action, Not Just Notes

Knowledge is great — but action creates change. At the end of many chapters, you'll find:

- Checklists
- Reflection questions
- Step-by-step guides

Use them. Write in the margins. Start that emergency fund, schedule that disability insurance consult, or finally make the call to your student loan servicer. Tiny steps today = major freedom tomorrow.

Stay Connected

The journey doesn't end with the last chapter. Financial literacy is a lifelong process — and it evolves as your life, goals, and career change.

To stay current:

- Visit **www.FinancialLiteracyForDoctors.com** for updated resources, new tools, and expert interviews.
- Join the conversation with other financially-minded doctors.
- Subscribe to updates and bonus materials that supplement this book.

Final Thought

This book was written because doctors deserve better financial guidance — guidance that acknowledges your sacrifices, your potential, and your real life. Use this book not just to manage your money, but to build the life you imagined when you first put on that white coat.

Now turn the page and take your next step toward financial clarity, confidence, and freedom.

The Financial Literacy Gap in the Medical Community

There's a widespread belief—both inside and outside the profession—that doctors are "set for life" as soon as they land their first big attending job. After all, you're highly educated, in demand, and earning what most people would consider a great salary.

But here's what most people don't realize:

Income doesn't equal understanding.

And **education doesn't always mean financial literacy.**

The truth is, the medical community is facing a quiet but serious crisis—**a financial literacy gap that affects doctors at every stage of their career.**

You can complete over a decade of advanced education, be entrusted with people's lives, and make six or seven figures—yet still feel completely lost when it comes to money.

I've worked with many physicians over the years—residents drowning in debt, attendings unsure where their money is going, specialists feeling trapped by golden handcuffs, and even senior doctors realizing too late that they missed key opportunities to build wealth.

And I've seen one thing hold true across all those experiences:

You were never taught how to manage your money.

How the Gap Happens

The financial literacy gap in medicine isn't about intelligence. Doctors are some of the brightest minds in any industry. It's not about discipline, either—you don't get through med school without that. It's about **exposure,**

education, and priorities.

Here's why the gap exists:

- **Medical training doesn't include personal finance.**
- Medical school curricula are laser-focused on preparing you to diagnose, treat, and lead in clinical settings—but almost nothing is offered in terms of real-world financial education. No one teaches you how to interpret a contract, how compound interest works, how to manage variable income, or what to look for in a disability insurance policy.
- **You're taught to delay everything.**
- In medicine, there's a constant message of "just wait." Delay gratification. Sacrifice now, earn later. By the time you finally start making real money, you feel like you're behind—and that pressure leads to quick spending, lifestyle creep, and financial decisions made without a plan.
- **You're surrounded by high earners—but not high learners.**
- Many doctors make a good living, but few talk openly about how they manage that income. There's a lot of pride in the profession—and not a lot of space to admit when you're unsure. That silence allows the gap to persist.
- **You don't have time to catch up.**
- Long hours, high stress, and administrative overload make it easy to ignore your finances altogether—until there's a crisis or a major career shift. By then, fixing the problem can be expensive or painful.

Why This Gap Matters

The consequences of this financial literacy gap are serious—and not just for your wallet.

- It leads to **stress** that affects your health, your family, and your work.
- It limits your **options** when you want to change jobs, start a practice, or reduce hours.

- It delays or derails **retirement**, even for high earners.
- And it can put your legacy and long-term goals at risk—because no one builds wealth by accident.

Too many doctors live paycheck to paycheck—even on six-figure salaries—because they never learned how to turn income into **freedom.**

And that freedom matters. It's the ability to walk away from a toxic job. To take a sabbatical. To retire early. To spend more time with family. To practice medicine on your terms.

Bridging the Gap

The good news? This gap is real—but it's also **fixable**.

Financial literacy isn't a matter of being perfect with money. It's about building the awareness, knowledge, and systems to make confident decisions at every stage of your career.

That's what this book is here to do.

Whether you're a med student trying to stretch every dollar, a resident navigating debt, an attending ready to invest, or a senior physician thinking about retirement, this book is your roadmap. A straight-up, practical guide to help you understand and take ownership of your financial future—without needing to become a financial expert.

You already know how to lead in the OR, the clinic, the lab, or the classroom.

Now let's make sure you know how to lead in your **financial life** too.

Because as much as you've given to your patients and your profession, **you owe it to yourself** to close the gap—and build a future that works for you, not just because of you.

Inspired by a Broader Mission

This book isn't just a standalone resource. It's part of something bigger—a growing financial literacy platform designed to reach people where traditional education has too often left them behind.

Over the years, I've seen firsthand how brilliant, talented, hard-working people—from student-athletes to high-earning professionals—end up confused, overwhelmed, or even paralyzed when it comes to money. Not because they're careless. Not because they're greedy. But because **no one ever taught them how to manage their finances with clarity and confidence.**

That realization led me to create a financial literacy ecosystem built around **access, relatability, and relevance.** It's not about lecturing. It's about equipping.

What started with student-athletes—young adults navigating sudden NIL income, pressure, and expectations—has expanded to serve professionals across industries, including:

- **College coaches** navigating inconsistent income and contract negotiations
- **Attorneys and doctors** dealing with high earnings but limited financial planning
- **Parents and families of athletes** trying to guide their children through life-changing opportunities
- **Pro athletes** in need of long-term planning beyond the highlight reel
- **Communities of color and underserved populations** who've often been excluded from traditional financial education spaces

Each group faces different challenges, but the gap is the same:

No one ever handed them the playbook.

And that's what this platform exists to do—**provide the playbook.**

Why Doctors? Why Now?

As I built financial literacy content and programs for athletes and coaches, I kept hearing the same thing from physicians I knew and worked with:

> *"I make good money, but I don't really know what to do with it."*
> *"I wish someone taught this stuff in med school."*
> *"I feel like I should be further along financially than I am."*

Then, serving as a **Board Trustee for a hospital**, I gained a new level of perspective and respect for what physicians go through every day—professionally, emotionally, and financially.

I saw how deeply committed doctors are to their patients and how little support they receive when it comes to protecting their income, managing burnout, preparing for career shifts, or planning their legacy.

So I wrote this book.

Not as a one-size-fits-all manual, but as part of a larger movement—to bring financial literacy **to the people who need it most, in the language they understand, and in the format that fits their lives.**

This Book Is Part of a Bigger Vision

Financial Literacy For Doctors is one chapter in a broader body of work that includes:

- **Financial Literacy For NIL**
- **Financial Literacy For Student-Athletes**
- **Financial Literacy For College Coaches**
- **Parents of Student Athletes**

- **Financial Literacy For Attorneys**
- **Financial Literacy For The Culture**
- **Financial Literacy For Pro Athletes**
- *And more coming soon...*

Each resource is designed to meet people where they are—with humility, practical tools, and a commitment to making financial literacy a lifelong skill, not just a buzzword.

Because financial peace of mind shouldn't be a privilege—it should be part of your foundation.

The Goal

To provide a clear, non-intimidating, and action-oriented financial roadmap for doctors at every stage of their career.

Let's face it—most financial advice out there either feels too generic, too technical, or too overwhelming to apply to real life. Especially when "real life" for you means long shifts, unpredictable schedules, and a career that never really slows down.

You didn't get into medicine to become a financial planner.

But that doesn't mean you shouldn't have a **solid plan.**

The goal of this book is simple:

To give you a **clear**, **non-intimidating**, and **action-oriented** financial roadmap—one that works whether you're a med student just trying to stay afloat, a resident drowning in debt, an attending managing new income, or a senior physician planning your exit strategy.

You won't find confusing jargon or one-size-fits-all formulas here.

What you will find is:

- Real talk about money—without the guilt or shame
- Practical steps you can take, no matter your current situation
- Insight on how to make smarter financial decisions without having to become an expert
- Tools to help you protect your income, reduce stress, and build lasting wealth
- Confidence to navigate your career with purpose—financially and personally

Whether you're earning $50,000 or $500,000 a year, this book is designed to meet you **where you are** and help you move toward where you want to be.

Because every doctor deserves more than just a paycheck.

You deserve **freedom**, **options**, and **peace of mind**—now and in the future.

And it starts here.

Part 1: The White Coat Years – Med School & Residency

You've made it this far—and that's no small thing.

Getting into medical school was an accomplishment. Surviving it is another. Residency? That's a whole different challenge. These years are full of sacrifice: sleep, time, relationships, sometimes even your own health. You're constantly pouring into others—learning, adapting, grinding.

But while you're gaining clinical skills and medical knowledge, there's one area that continues to be overlooked:

your financial health.

And make no mistake: just because you're early in your career doesn't mean money shouldn't be a priority. In fact, this stage—the White Coat Years—is one of the **most important times** to build strong financial habits.

Why?

Because the way you handle your finances now, when you're earning less and managing debt, sets the foundation for how you'll manage money when you're earning more. If you can learn to plan, save, and stay aware during these tight years, you'll be miles ahead once your income increases.

Unfortunately, most medical students and residents are:

- **Drowning in student loans**
- **Unsure how to budget with irregular or limited income**
- **Overwhelmed by credit card debt**

- **Too exhausted to even think about investing or insurance**
- **Surrounded by peers who are equally unsure but too proud to admit it**

And through it all, you're being told:

"Don't worry—you'll make good money later."

"Just focus on training for now."

"You'll figure it out after residency."

But here's the truth: **you can't afford to wait.**

These years may be lean, but they're also **teachable, transformative years**—where smart, small decisions compound into real-life freedom down the line. You don't need to have everything figured out. You just need to take steps in the right direction.

In This Section, You'll Learn:

- How to build a simple, realistic budget—even on a residency paycheck
- What to do about student loans (and what not to panic over)
- How to build an emergency fund—even if it's just a few hundred dollars
- Why your credit score matters and how to protect it
- Whether you should get disability or life insurance now
- How to set up your first investment account (yes, it's possible)
- And how to develop the mindset that will help you stay focused and financially grounded during this demanding phase

These chapters won't add more pressure to your life. They're built to **lighten the mental load** by helping you take control of your finances, one decision at a time.

So take a deep breath.

You've made it to med school or residency—that means you're smart, disciplined, and capable.

Now it's time to apply those same qualities to your money.

Chapter 1: Financial Survival in Medical School

B*uilding Smart Habits Before the Paychecks Start Rolling In*

You're in medical school—the dream is becoming real. You've got the white coat, the schedule, the sleepless nights, and maybe even your first clinical rotation under your belt. But while you're deep in anatomy, pharmacology, and OSCE prep, there's another critical subject no one is officially teaching you: **money management**.

And make no mistake, medical school is not just academically intense—it's financially demanding. This is where many physicians first fall behind financially, even before they've earned a single dollar as an attending. It's not due to carelessness, but due to a lack of preparation, understanding, and most of all—access to practical financial education.

In this chapter, we'll walk through the key aspects of surviving med school **financially**, not just academically—so you don't start your career from a deeper hole than you have to.

Understanding the Cost of Medical Education

Before you can manage the financial journey, you need to know what you're really dealing with. Medical school is expensive—**often staggeringly so.**

According to the Association of American Medical Colleges (AAMC), the average cost of attendance for a four-year medical program is around **$250,000 to $330,000**, including tuition, fees, and living expenses. Some programs cost even more, especially if you attend a private institution or live in a high-cost city.

But that's not all. If you took out loans during undergrad, you're likely entering medical school with debt already on your back. Now, you're borrowing more money—most of which starts accruing interest the moment you sign.

The sticker price is one thing. The **true cost** is what it turns into over time when interest and poor planning enter the equation.

Student Loans: Know What You're Borrowing

Let's break down the common types of student loans medical students typically rely on:

1. Subsidized Loans

- These are offered based on financial need.
- **Interest does not accrue while you're in school** or during deferment periods.
- These loans are limited in availability and are more common in undergrad.

2. Unsubsidized Loans

- The most common for med students.
- Interest starts accruing **immediately**—even while you're still in school.
- Offered regardless of financial need.
- You don't need to make payments while enrolled, but the debt grows in the background.

3. Grad PLUS Loans

- Federal loans that cover costs beyond unsubsidized limits.
- Higher interest rates and fees.
- Also accrue interest immediately.
- Easier to qualify for than private loans.

4. Private Loans

- Offered through banks or credit unions.
- Interest rates vary based on credit and lender.
- Often less flexible when it comes to deferment, forbearance, or income-driven repayment options.
- May require a co-signer.

5. Loan Consolidation

- Combines multiple federal loans into one.
- Can simplify payments and extend terms.
- Does **not** lower interest rates; it takes the weighted average.
- You may lose access to some original borrower benefits.

The takeaway? **Understand what you're borrowing, when interest starts, and what your options are.** You're not just taking out loans—you're taking on future obligations.

Budgeting on Borrowed Money

Let's be real: budgeting in med school can feel pointless when you're living off loans. But here's why it matters more than ever:

You're borrowing every dollar you spend.

Every coffee, every takeout order, every new iPad—if you're not paying for it with outside income, it's being added to a loan that's gaining interest right now.

Let's say you borrow $100,000 at a 6.8% interest rate during med school. If you don't touch that loan for four years, the balance will be closer to $129,000 when you graduate—without spending an extra penny.

A budget doesn't just track spending—it helps you borrow less.

Quick budgeting tips for med students:

- Know your financial aid disbursement schedule—plan around those lump sums.
- Break expenses down into monthly targets: rent, groceries, transportation, etc.
- Use tools like Mint, You Need a Budget (YNAB), or even Google Sheets to track cash flow.
- Avoid credit card debt at all costs—this is high-interest debt stacked on top of your loans.
- Don't compare your lifestyle to classmates. Everyone's borrowing differently.

Budgeting now creates the discipline you'll need later when you're earning six figures.

Scholarships, Grants & Side Income

Contrary to popular belief, you don't have to rely only on loans. There are legitimate ways to **reduce borrowing** or supplement your income.

Scholarships & Grants:

- **AAMC, AMA, local medical societies**, and specialty-specific organizations offer scholarships.
- Search early and often—many go unclaimed due to lack of awareness.
- Some schools offer internal "need-based" or "service-based" scholar-

ships mid-program.

Public Service Loan Forgiveness (PSLF):

- If you plan to work in academic medicine, non-profit hospitals, or public institutions, **federal loans may be forgiven** after 10 years of qualifying payments.
- Enroll in an income-driven repayment plan (IDR) and **certify your employment annually**.

Side Hustles (within reason):

- Tutoring MCAT or undergrad science courses
- Research assistant roles
- Freelance writing, editing, or medical content creation
- Peer mentoring or note-sharing platforms

Be careful not to overextend—your **education and mental health** come first. But small income streams can reduce your loan dependence over time.

Planning Ahead: Interest Accrual & Capitalization

Interest accrual is one of the most misunderstood (and dangerous) aspects of student debt.

Here's what you need to know:

- On **unsubsidized and Grad PLUS loans**, interest starts accruing the moment the loan is disbursed.
- That interest continues to build during school, deferment, and grace periods.
- When your grace period ends and repayment begins, the **interest is**

capitalized—meaning it's added to your principal balance.
- You now pay **interest on your interest.**

This is how $200,000 in loans can quietly become $250,000+ before your first attending paycheck.

How to minimize the impact:

- **Make interest-only payments during school** if you can—even small amounts help.
- **Know your grace periods** and repayment start dates.
- Keep good records. Your future self will thank you for knowing what you owe, to whom, and when.

Final Thoughts

Med school is a grind—mentally, physically, emotionally, and yes, financially. But the habits and awareness you build now will serve you for life.

This chapter wasn't about solving everything. It was about giving you clarity. You don't need to be perfect with money—you just need to be **intentional**.

Even while living on borrowed funds, you can start thinking like the future physician you're becoming: one who makes confident, informed decisions that benefit the "you" five, ten, and thirty years down the line.

Because once you get through school, the real paychecks will come.

And when they do—you'll be ready.

Chapter 2: Residency = Real Pay, Real Pressure

How to Make Progress Without Losing Control

Residency is often the first time a medical student feels like a "real doctor." You're in the hospital. You've got a badge. You've got responsibility. And—finally—you're getting paid.

But the reality of that "real paycheck" quickly sets in.

Residency pay might look like a lot on paper compared to the $0 income of med school, but after taxes, loan notices, long shifts, and rising costs of living, it can feel like you're stuck in neutral financially—**grinding hard with little to show for it.**

This chapter is about helping you take control, even in a season where time is short, income is tight, and pressure is high.

Because no, you may not be able to max out investment accounts or pay off six figures in loans right now—but you *can* build the habits and foundation that will carry you through the rest of your career.

Making the Most of a Modest Income

Residency salaries typically range from $55,000 to $70,000 a year, depending on location and program year. That might sound reasonable—until you remember:

- Taxes will take 20–30%

- Rent in a medical hub city could eat 30–50% of your net income
- Your loans are still growing in the background
- You're expected to maintain a "professional" appearance
- And oh yeah—you need to sleep, eat, commute, and occasionally live a little

The key? Don't aim for luxury right now. Aim for **momentum.**

Residency isn't about "winning" with money—it's about **not falling behind** any more than you have to.

Your goal is simple:

Live below your means. Keep your expenses low. And build systems that make it easier to succeed when your income eventually increases.

Loan Deferment, Forbearance & Income-Driven Repayment (IBR, PAYE, REPAYE)

Let's talk about your biggest financial weight: student loans.

You generally have three choices during residency:

1. Deferment/Forbearance

- These options allow you to *pause* payments, but **interest still accrues** (especially on unsubsidized and Grad PLUS loans).
- Over time, that interest capitalizes—meaning you'll end up owing interest on your interest.
- This option provides short-term relief but is the **most expensive** long-term.

2. Income-Driven Repayment Plans (IDRs)

If you want to make progress—even in small amounts—consider an IDR plan.

- **IBR (Income-Based Repayment)**: Caps payments at 10–15% of discretionary income.
- **PAYE (Pay As You Earn)**: 10% of income, with forgiveness after 20 years. Good for those with high debt-to-income ratio.
- **REPAYE (Revised Pay As You Earn)**: Also 10%, but includes interest subsidies—meaning the government may cover part of your unpaid interest each month.

Why IDR Plans Matter in Residency:

- You're likely earning too little to make full standard payments.
- IDR payments keep your loans from ballooning uncontrollably.
- **If you plan to pursue Public Service Loan Forgiveness (PSLF), these years count—**but only if you're making qualifying payments on an IDR plan while working for a nonprofit hospital or academic institution.

> 📌 *Bottom line:* ***Enroll in an IDR plan early.*** *It protects your budget, helps with long-term planning, and may open doors to forgiveness programs.*

Creating Your First Real Budget

This is your first consistent paycheck—and your first chance to take full control of how money moves in and out of your life.

Budgeting doesn't mean restriction. It means **freedom with a plan.**

How to Start:

1. **Track your income and expenses for one month.** You can't manage what you don't measure.
2. **Break down expenses into essentials, variable, and future goals.**

- Essentials: rent, utilities, groceries, gas
- Variable: eating out, clothing, subscriptions
- Future goals: debt payments, savings, travel, gifts

1. **Use the 50/30/20 framework** (if possible):

- 50% needs
- 30% wants
- 20% savings/debt repayment

1. **Use tools** like YNAB, Mint, or a simple spreadsheet. Don't overcomplicate it.

Resident Budgeting Tips:

- Live with roommates or in affordable housing if possible
- Meal prep and limit delivery/takeout—it adds up
- Keep credit card balances at zero
- Don't "flex" to match what attendings or peers are doing
- Automate your savings and bill payments

Think of budgeting like managing a patient load—when things are organized and monitored, the outcomes improve.

Building an Emergency Fund—Even if It's Small

An emergency fund is your **financial immune system.** It protects you when life hits with an unexpected bill, car trouble, family situation, or health issue.

As a resident, you may not be able to set aside thousands right away. That's okay. Start small, but **start now**.

Goal: $500–$1,000 to start

Eventually aim for 3–6 months of essential expenses

Where to keep it:

- High-yield savings account
- Separate from your checking account to avoid accidental spending
- Not invested in stocks—this is *not* a growth account, it's your "break-glass-in-case-of-emergency" stash

Saving $50–$100 a month might feel minor now, but that's the same discipline you'll use later to save $1,000 or more a month.

And when—not if—life throws a financial curveball, you'll be ready.

Why You Must Start Learning About Investing Early

You don't need to max out retirement accounts during residency.

But you *do* need to start **understanding** investing.

Here's why:

- **Time is your greatest financial asset.** The earlier you start investing, the more compound interest can work in your favor. Even a $50/month contribution matters.
- You'll soon face a flood of options: Roth IRAs, 403(b)s, 457(b)s, HSAs,

brokerage accounts, mutual funds, index funds, etc. Don't wait until you're earning six figures to start learning.
- Many residents think, "I'll invest once I make more." But once that happens, lifestyle inflation kicks in—and investing gets pushed back again.

Start here:

- Open a Roth IRA (if eligible based on your income)
- Read basic investing books or follow financial educators
- Learn the difference between **stocks, bonds, index funds, ETFs, and target-date funds**
- Know what "compound interest" actually means—run the numbers and watch how time builds wealth

Even if you're not ready to invest yet, the *knowledge* you build now is the foundation for smart decisions later.

Final Thoughts

Residency is the beginning of your professional life—but it's also a continuation of your financial education. The pressure is real, the pay is limited, but the opportunity to build smart habits is powerful.

Remember:

- You don't need to pay off all your loans today.
- You don't need to invest like a millionaire.
- You just need to be aware, intentional, and consistent.

Start where you are. Use what you have. Build forward with focus.

Because the goal isn't just to become a doctor—it's to become a doctor **who's financially free**.

And that journey starts here.

Chapter 3: Fellowship & Sub-Specialization Years

The Balancing Act Between Career Progress, Family Life, and Financial Focus

By the time you enter fellowship, you've already sacrificed years of your life to the pursuit of becoming a physician. You've gone through med school, survived residency, and now you're doubling down to pursue your specialty.

And while your clinical expertise is growing, so are the financial pressures—and often, **so is your fatigue.**

These are the years where burnout meets ambition. Where your skills are sharp, but your energy is fading. And financially, it can feel like you're standing still while everyone around you—your non-medical peers, classmates, or even family members—seems to be "moving on" in life.

You're not alone in that feeling.

This chapter is about helping you manage this unique chapter with clarity. You may not have full earning power yet, but you *do* have the ability to make strategic financial moves that will pay off down the road.

Let's talk about how.

Managing "Training Fatigue" While Staying Financially Focused

By now, the novelty of "I'm a doctor" has likely worn off. You've been grinding for years, and your bank account might still look more like a grad student than a highly trained professional.

This is when many fellows mentally check out of financial planning. You're tired, busy, and hyper-focused on becoming the best at your subspecialty. And rightfully so.

But here's the hard truth:

If you let fatigue become financial apathy, you'll lose even more time—and compound even more debt.

Instead, find **simple, sustainable systems** that allow you to stay financially engaged without needing to micromanage every dollar.

Examples:

- **Automate your bills and savings** each month
- Use a budgeting app to track high-level trends without daily input
- Check in on your loans and credit quarterly—not daily
- Create a "financial dashboard" once a month: income, expenses, savings, debt
- Set one financial goal per quarter (e.g., build $1,000 in savings, learn about Roth IRAs, compare disability insurance plans)

This is about **consistency, not complexity**.

Balancing Family Planning and Financial Goals

The fellowship years are often when life outside medicine starts to accelerate:

- You may be getting married, or newly married

- You may be thinking about starting a family—or already juggling young kids
- You might want to buy a home, relocate, or travel before starting your attending role

Every one of those life decisions comes with a price tag. That's not a reason to delay them—but it *is* a reason to align them with your financial priorities.

A few financial questions to consider:

- Are we ready for the financial commitment of children (childcare, parental leave, insurance, housing)?
- Can we save for a wedding *without* racking up credit card debt or personal loans?
- Should we rent or buy during fellowship? (In most cases, **renting is safer** due to short timelines and market unpredictability.)
- Have we talked about joint accounts, budgeting, and managing debt together as a couple?

> *Pro tip: A healthy financial plan during fellowship isn't about saying* no *to everything—it's about knowing what you're saying* yes *to.*

Should You Moonlight? Pros, Cons, and Tax Impact

Many fellows consider moonlighting as a way to boost income—and understandably so. You've got the skills, the license, and the drive to earn more. But moonlighting comes with trade-offs you'll want to weigh carefully.

Pros of Moonlighting:

- Extra income to pay down debt or build savings
- More autonomy and confidence in clinical decision-making
- Can help cover childcare, relocation, or future transition costs
- Sometimes leads to job offers post-fellowship

Cons of Moonlighting:

- Less rest = higher risk of burnout or medical error
- Reduced time for research, studying, or family
- Some programs restrict or prohibit moonlighting—check your contract
- You're 1099—meaning **you're on the hook for self-employment taxes**

Tax Considerations:

- Most moonlighting gigs don't withhold taxes, so you'll need to **set aside 25–30% of your income** for federal and state taxes
- Keep detailed records of income and expenses
- Consider paying quarterly estimated taxes to avoid IRS penalties
- Talk to a CPA about writing off eligible expenses (malpractice premiums, travel, CME, etc.)

Moonlighting can be a game-changer—but only if you treat it like a business, not a bonus.

When and How to Buy Life & Disability Insurance

Fellowship is one of the **best times** to lock in both disability and life insurance. Why? Because:

1. You're young and (typically) healthy
2. Rates are lower
3. You can get coverage **before your income jumps**, protecting future earning potential
4. Waiting until you're older or have medical issues can lead to higher premiums or exclusions

Disability Insurance: Your Most Important Policy

You've invested hundreds of thousands of dollars into your career. Disability insurance protects that investment if illness or injury prevents you from working.

Look for:

- **Own-occupation coverage** (especially for your specific specialty)
- Non-cancelable and guaranteed renewable
- Riders for future purchase options as your income increases
- Residual/partial disability riders (if you can work part-time but lose income)

Life Insurance: Protecting Your People

Even if you're single with no kids, life insurance is worth considering if:

- You have co-signed loans or family members who depend on you
- You're about to get married or start a family
- You want to lock in low rates while healthy

Term life insurance is affordable and sufficient for most doctors during early-to-mid career stages.

Example: A healthy 30-year-old can often get $1 million of term life coverage for $30–$50/month.

Final Thoughts: Build Your Bridge to Attending Life

Fellowship is the final stretch before your income increases dramatically. But the foundation you lay during this phase will determine how ready you are when that moment arrives.

This is your chance to:

- Streamline your spending
- Learn how to handle increased earnings
- Build financial trust with your spouse or partner
- Establish protection for your future family
- Start your investing journey—however small

You don't need to have everything figured out right now.

But you *do* need to stay intentional.

The decisions you make in these years—about money, protection, and priorities—can put you in position to not just survive, but **thrive** the moment you take your first attending role.

The finish line is in sight. Let's make sure you cross it financially prepared—not just clinically trained.

Chapter 4: Your First Attending Job

The Paycheck Feels Real—But So Does the Pressure

You did it. After years of medical school, residency, and maybe even fellowship—you're now officially an attending physician. The title is real, the paycheck is bigger, and the expectations just went up.

This is the moment many doctors have dreamed of: financial independence, the ability to support a family, maybe even catch up on lost time and missed experiences. But with this exciting new chapter comes the most financially impactful decisions of your career—starting with how you evaluate and negotiate your very first attending job.

This chapter will walk you through what to look for, what to avoid, and how to resist the urge to "spend like a doctor" just because you finally can.

Evaluating Compensation Packages

Not all job offers are created equal—and not all dollars are equal either. One of the biggest mistakes new attendings make is looking only at **base salary** while ignoring the rest of the financial picture.

Here's what to evaluate in a compensation package:

1. Base Salary

- This is your guaranteed income, typically paid as a fixed annual amount.
- Compare it to your specialty's average by region and setting (hospital vs. private).

- Consider whether the salary is fixed or transitions to productivity-based after a period of time.

2. RVUs (Relative Value Units)

- Often used in productivity-based compensation models.
- You're paid based on how much work (measured in RVUs) you generate.
- Understand the **conversion factor**: how much they pay per RVU and how many RVUs are expected.

Example: If your contract says you'll earn $50 per RVU with an expectation of 5,000 RVUs, that's $250,000/year.

- Ask about what counts toward RVUs—do teaching, admin time, or certain procedures get counted?

3. Signing Bonus

- Often ranges from $5,000 to $50,000 depending on specialty and location.
- **Ask if it's taxed upfront and if there's a payback clause** if you leave before a certain period.

4. Relocation Assistance

- Can cover moving costs, temporary housing, and license transfer fees.
- Often structured as a reimbursement—be sure to save receipts.
- Check if it's considered taxable income.

5. Benefits

- Health, dental, vision insurance
- Retirement plans (401a, 403b, 457b—ask about match!)
- Malpractice insurance: Is it occurrence-based or claims-made (do you need tail coverage)?
- CME stipend and time
- Paid vacation, parental leave, and holidays
- Disability and life insurance

Don't just compare offers by salary—compare total compensation, lifestyle fit, and long-term growth.

Choosing Between Hospital Employment, Private Practice, or Academic Medicine

Each setting offers different benefits, challenges, and long-term implications.

Hospital Employment

- **Pros:** Steady salary, administrative support, predictable hours in some fields, benefits package
- **Cons:** Less autonomy, productivity pressures, potential burnout in larger systems

Private Practice

- **Pros:** Entrepreneurial opportunity, autonomy, partnership potential
- **Cons:** Business responsibilities, overhead costs, variable income, more financial risk

Academic Medicine

- **Pros:** Teaching/research opportunities, prestige, more time for mentorship
- **Cons:** Typically lower pay, slower salary growth, more committees/a dministrative duties

Your choice will depend on your values: stability vs. flexibility, money vs. mission, autonomy vs. structure. There's no wrong answer—but **know what you're signing up for.**

Understanding Taxes: From Trainee to Full-Time Earner

As a resident or fellow, you likely got a tax refund or paid very little. Once you become an attending, everything changes.

Key Tax Considerations:

- **You'll likely move into a higher tax bracket** (24–35% federal for many attendings).
- Signing bonuses and moonlighting income may not have had enough taxes withheld—expect a tax bill.
- You may need to start making **quarterly estimated tax payments**, especially if you have side income.
- Maximize your **retirement plan contributions** (401a, 403b, 457b) to lower taxable income.
- Consider working with a **CPA who has experience with physicians**—they understand deductions, income types, and strategy.

Pro tip:

Keep a buffer of $3,000–$5,000 in a high-yield savings account during your first year just in case you owe more than expected in taxes.

Lifestyle Inflation: Avoiding the "Doctor Trap"

You've lived lean for years. You've sacrificed time, energy, and probably your social life. Now, it's tempting to reward yourself—with a new car, a luxury apartment, lavish vacations, or a home purchase that stretches your budget.

But here's the trap: You feel rich... before you *actually are* rich.

Many new attendings fall into the habit of spending their paycheck before it hits their account. The lifestyle expands right along with the income—and suddenly, they're living paycheck to paycheck again, just on a higher level.

What to do instead:

- Keep your fixed costs low for the first 1–2 years
- Build an emergency fund of at least 3–6 months
- Max out Roth IRA and workplace retirement contributions
- Avoid large purchases (cars, homes, weddings) until you've fully settled into your income and understand your cash flow
- Choose *one* splurge—then stay disciplined elsewhere

> *The goal is to grow your* ***net worth****, not just your wardrobe or social media feed.*

Final Thoughts: The Foundation for Long-Term Wealth

Your first attending job is more than just a career milestone—it's the beginning of your financial transformation. You finally have the income to make serious progress, but the decisions you make in the first 12–24 months will set the tone for your next decade.

So ask the hard questions. Read the fine print. Think long term.

This is your chance to go from surviving to thriving—not just professionally, but financially.

Because financial peace isn't about how much you earn—it's about what you do with it.

Chapter 5: Understanding Contracts and Negotiation

What You Sign Can Shape Your Career—Read It Like Your Future Depends on It

By the time you're offered your first attending position—or even your second or third—there's a good chance that your focus is on salary, location, and how soon you can start practicing. But tucked inside that offer letter or formal employment agreement are pages of legal language that can dramatically affect your **income**, **autonomy**, and **career trajectory** for years to come.

This chapter is about helping you slow down, zoom in, and approach your employment contract with the seriousness it deserves.

Because let's be clear:

Employment contracts are not a formality.

They're a roadmap—and if you don't understand it, you might be walking into a situation you'll regret later.

Let's break it down.

How to Read and Negotiate an Employment Contract

Before you negotiate, you need to understand what you're actually agreeing to. Every physician contract will look a little different depending on your specialty, employer, and region—but most include several standard components.

Key Contract Elements to Review:

1. **Position and Duties**

- What exactly are you expected to do?
- Are clinical, research, teaching, and administrative duties clearly outlined?
- Are there expectations for weekend/holiday coverage?

1. **Compensation**

- Is it base salary only? Or productivity-based (RVUs or collections)?
- How often is it reviewed or adjusted?
- Are there signing bonuses, relocation stipends, or retention bonuses?

1. **Incentives and Benefits**

- Is there a quality bonus or performance-based pay?
- What's included in your benefits: health, retirement match, disability, malpractice, CME?

1. **Term and Termination**

- How long is the contract?
- What is the notice period to terminate the agreement (for you and them)?
- Are there any automatic renewal clauses?

1. **Restrictive Covenants**

- This includes non-compete clauses and more (we'll cover this below).

Negotiation Tips:

- **Always negotiate—respectfully.** You don't have to accept the first offer.
- Focus on *total value,* not just salary—ask about signing bonuses, moving support, call schedule, and CME.
- If you're told something verbally ("don't worry, we're flexible"), ask for it in writing.
- Don't negotiate alone—**get expert help**.

> ***Reminder:*** *Everything is negotiable before you sign. Very little is afterward.*

What to Look for in Restrictive Covenants (Non-Competes)

One of the most misunderstood—and most damaging—sections in a physician contract is the **restrictive covenant**, often called a **non-compete clause**.

What It Means:

A non-compete prevents you from practicing within a certain **geographic area** and **time period** if you leave the employer.

Example: You may be prohibited from working within 20 miles of your current hospital for 12–24 months after departure.

Why It Matters:

This clause can:

- Limit your options if things go wrong
- Force you to relocate
- Delay your ability to earn in your specialty

- Impact your family, especially if you've bought a home or have children in school

What to Do:

- Ask for the radius and time period to be reduced (e.g., 5–10 miles instead of 20+)
- Exclude certain hospitals or practice types
- Remove the clause entirely if you're in a saturated urban area (where it may be unenforceable anyway)
- Know your state's laws—some states are tightening limits on physician non-competes

Don't assume "it won't be enforced." Protect your options up front.

Malpractice Coverage: Occurrence vs. Claims-Made

Many physicians sign contracts without fully understanding their malpractice coverage—and end up stuck with surprise costs later.

There are two main types of malpractice insurance:

1. Occurrence-Based

- Covers any incident that **occurred** while you were insured, regardless of when the claim is filed.
- **No tail coverage needed.**
- Preferred by most physicians, but often more expensive for employers.

2. Claims-Made

- Only covers claims **filed** while you're insured under the policy.
- If a claim is filed after you leave, you need **tail coverage** to protect yourself.

- Tail coverage can cost **100–250% of your annual premium**—often **$20,000 to $50,000+** depending on specialty.

What to Ask:

- What type of malpractice insurance is provided?
- If it's claims-made, **who pays for tail coverage**—you or the employer?
- What is the coverage limit and carrier?
- Will I have a say in settlement decisions?

Malpractice protection isn't a checkbox—it's your **financial shield**. Don't overlook it.

Why You Need a Healthcare Attorney to Review Your Agreement

This might be the most important advice in this chapter:

Hire an experienced healthcare attorney to review your contract.

Not your cousin who practices real estate law. Not your friend from undergrad who just passed the bar. You need someone who knows **physician employment law**—someone who's seen hundreds of contracts and can catch the small clauses that create big problems.

A healthcare attorney can:

- Spot vague or predatory language
- Help you understand what's typical (and what's not) in your specialty or region
- Assist in drafting revisions or redlining terms
- Coach you on how to negotiate without losing an offer
- Protect your rights, your license, and your future

This is a **one-time cost** (typically $500–$2,000) that can save you **tens of thousands of dollars**, protect your reputation, and give you long-term peace of mind.

Think of it this way: You'd never let a patient undergo surgery without reviewing their chart.

Don't sign a life-changing contract without reviewing yours.

Final Thoughts: Contracts Aren't Just Paper—They're Strategy

Your first contract isn't just about what you get paid—it's about how much control you have, how protected you are, and how free you'll be to make choices in the years ahead.

Read it. Question it. Protect yourself.

Because once the ink is dry, the power shifts.

This is your career, your livelihood, and your future.

Make sure the contract honors that.

Chapter 6: Building a Solid Foundation

Turning Income Into Stability, Security, and Long-Term Wealth

After years of training and delayed gratification, you're finally earning a strong income. The urge to enjoy that money is real—and you deserve to celebrate. But here's the truth:

Earning a high income isn't the same as building wealth.

Without a solid financial foundation, your six-figure salary can disappear just as quickly as it came. That's why this chapter is about turning your income into a long-term game plan—one that balances enjoying your success today while preparing for the decades ahead.

This is where financial momentum is made. Let's build it.

Setting Up Automatic Savings and Investments

If there's one simple habit that separates financially successful doctors from stressed-out ones, it's this:

Automate everything.

When you set your money up to move automatically—before you ever see it in your checking account—you bypass willpower and start building wealth on autopilot.

Where to automate:

- **Emergency savings**: Send a portion of each paycheck to a high-yield savings account
- **Retirement contributions**: Through your employer's 401(k), 403(b), or 457(b)
- **IRA contributions**: Set monthly or quarterly transfers to a Roth or Traditional IRA
- **Brokerage investments**: Automate monthly contributions to index funds or ETFs

You're already working 60+ hours a week. You shouldn't have to remember to move money around. Let your systems do the work.

Start small. Stay consistent. Scale as your income grows.

Paying Off Student Loans Strategically

Most doctors finish training with **six-figure student loan debt**—and there's no one-size-fits-all approach for paying it off. But you *do* need a strategy.

Step 1: Know what you owe

- Federal vs. private
- Interest rates
- Current repayment plan
- PSLF eligibility if working at a nonprofit

Step 2: Choose your repayment path

Option A: Public Service Loan Forgiveness (PSLF)

- Available for those working in nonprofit hospitals or academic

medicine
- Make 120 qualifying payments on an income-driven repayment plan
- Tax-free forgiveness at the end
- Be sure to **certify employment annually** and keep accurate records

Option B: Aggressive Payoff

- Best for those in private practice or high-earning roles with no forgiveness eligibility
- Consider **refinancing** to a lower interest rate if you're no longer pursuing PSLF
- Use a "debt avalanche" approach—pay off highest-interest loans first

Pro tip:

Don't rush to pay off low-interest loans at the expense of saving and investing. Balance is key. You can pay down debt *and* build wealth at the same time.

Maxing Out Retirement Accounts

You'll never regret starting early—and you'll always wish you started sooner.

Key Retirement Accounts for Physicians:

1. 401(k) or 403(b)

- Employer-sponsored retirement accounts
- Often offer matching contributions (free money—always take it!)
- 2024 contribution limit: **$23,000** (plus $7,500 catch-up if 50+)

2. 457(b)

- Additional tax-deferred plan available to many physicians in hospitals and academic institutions
- Contribution limits are separate from the 401(k)/403(b)—a powerful combo
- Be cautious: some 457(b)s are "non-governmental," meaning funds could be at risk if the employer faces financial trouble

3. Roth IRA

- Fund with after-tax dollars
- Tax-free growth and withdrawals in retirement
- Income limit to contribute directly: ~$146,000 single / ~$230,000 married
- If over the limit, consider the **Backdoor Roth IRA strategy**

4. Health Savings Account (HSA)

- Only if enrolled in a high-deductible health plan
- Triple tax advantage: deductible contribution, tax-free growth, tax-free withdrawals for qualified health expenses
- Can be used like a stealth retirement account if invested and saved long-term

Set your retirement accounts to auto-contribute, even if it's just a few hundred a month at first. Time is more valuable than timing.

High-Yield Savings Accounts & Taxable Brokerage Accounts

You need more than just retirement accounts to build a flexible financial life.

High-Yield Savings Accounts (HYSA)

- Where your **emergency fund** should live
- Pays interest (typically 4–5x more than traditional savings accounts)
- FDIC-insured, easy to access but separate from checking

Use your HYSA for:

- 3–6 months of expenses
- Upcoming purchases (wedding, vacation, home repairs)
- Quarterly estimated tax payments if you have side income

Taxable Brokerage Accounts

- No income or contribution limits
- No withdrawal penalties
- Ideal for long-term investing outside of retirement accounts

Use for:

- Building wealth beyond retirement
- Saving for early retirement or financial independence
- Funding big goals (home down payment, kids' college, sabbaticals)

Choose **low-cost index funds or ETFs** to keep it simple and tax-efficient.

The Importance of Financial Advisors Who Understand Physicians

You've spent years training to treat complex conditions—and you'd never want your patients relying on a generalist for specialized care.

The same applies to your finances.

A physician's financial life is different:

- High delayed income followed by sudden jumps in pay
- Massive student loan debt
- Complex compensation (RVUs, bonuses, call pay)
- Career uncertainty and geographic moves
- Risk of burnout and early retirement considerations

What to look for in a financial advisor:

- **Fiduciary duty**: Legally required to act in your best interest
- **Fee-only**: Avoid commission-based "advisors" who sell products
- Experience with physicians or medical professionals
- Can help with tax planning, investing, retirement, insurance, and student loans
- Transparent, easy-to-understand advice

> *Interview multiple advisors. Ask about credentials (like CFP®), services, and how they get paid.*

Even if you manage things yourself early on, eventually you'll want a **trusted team**—just like you'd want in a care setting.

Final Thoughts: Think Systems, Not Stress

This chapter wasn't about becoming a financial expert. It was about helping you **lay the foundation** so your money can start doing the heavy lifting.

You don't need to do everything at once—but you do need to do *something*.

- Automate your savings
- Pay down debt with intention
- Max out accounts when you can
- Protect your income
- Get guidance when it matters

You've already built a career rooted in discipline and excellence. Now it's time to build a financial life that reflects that same strength.

Because this isn't just about making a living—it's about building a life of choice, freedom, and long-term peace.

Chapter 7: Insurance Essentials for Doctors

Protecting What You've Worked So Hard to Build

You've spent years training, sacrificing, and investing in your career. You've built a high-income skill set, taken on massive responsibility, and you're finally earning what you deserve.

But here's the reality:

The higher your income and the more you have to lose, the more you need to protect.

Insurance isn't exciting, and it's often misunderstood. But for physicians, it's absolutely essential. One illness, lawsuit, or accident can derail everything you've built if you're not covered properly.

In this chapter, we'll break down the six core areas of insurance that every doctor needs to understand—and help you build a coverage strategy that protects both your income and your peace of mind.

Disability Insurance: Own-Occupation vs. Any-Occupation

Your greatest asset as a physician is your ability to earn income. Disability insurance protects that income if injury or illness prevents you from working.

But not all disability insurance is created equal.

Two Main Types:

1. Own-Occupation Disability Insurance

- **Definition**: Pays benefits if you can't work in **your specific medical specialty**, even if you can work in another profession.
- **Best for physicians**—especially those in procedure-based specialties.
- Example: If you're a surgeon and can't operate due to hand tremors, an own-occupation policy would still pay benefits even if you teach or consult.

2. Any-Occupation Disability Insurance

- Pays only if you're unable to work **in any occupation** for which you're reasonably qualified.
- Often less expensive but **much harder to qualify for benefits**.
- Not recommended for doctors.

Key Riders to Consider:

- **Future purchase option** (lets you increase coverage as income grows)
- **Residual/partial disability** (covers loss of income if you can work part-time)
- **Non-cancelable and guaranteed renewable** (locks in your premium and coverage terms)

Rule of thumb: Get coverage ***during residency or fellowship*** *when you're young and healthy—it's cheaper and easier to qualify.*

Life Insurance: Term vs. Whole Life (and Avoiding Bad Policies)

Life insurance provides a safety net for your loved ones if something happens to you. But many physicians get sold the wrong type of policy by commission-driven salespeople.

Term Life Insurance

- **Simple, affordable coverage** for a set number of years (e.g., 20 or 30 years)
- Best for most doctors, especially those with young families or significant debt
- Example: $1 million in 20-year term coverage for a healthy 35-year-old could cost $30–$50/month

Whole Life (or Permanent) Insurance

- Combines insurance with a cash value investment component
- Expensive, complex, and often **over-sold to physicians**
- May have a place in advanced estate planning, but not for most early-career doctors

What to Do:

- If someone depends on your income, you need **term life insurance**
- Coverage amount = 10–15x your annual income
- Shop around using independent brokers—not insurance companies that only offer one product
- Avoid mixing insurance and investing unless you're working with a fee-only planner

Malpractice Insurance: Types, Tail Coverage, and Policy Limits

Every physician needs malpractice coverage—but many don't fully understand what they're signing up for.

Two Main Types:

1. Occurrence-Based

- Covers any incident that happened during the time you were covered, **regardless of when the claim is filed**
- More expensive, but you don't need to buy tail coverage when you leave

2. Claims-Made

- Covers incidents **only while the policy is active**
- If you leave or switch jobs, you'll need to purchase **tail coverage** to protect against future claims
- Tail coverage can cost 1–2x your annual premium—**$20,000 to $50,000+** depending on your specialty

What to Ask:

- Is the policy **claims-made or occurrence-based**?
- If claims-made, **who pays for tail coverage**—you or the employer?
- What are the **policy limits**? (Typical: $1 million per claim / $3 million aggregate)
- Does it include **legal defense costs**?

Malpractice isn't just about lawsuits—it's about protecting your license, career, and financial future.

Home & Auto: Proper Coverage and Bundling

As your net worth increases, so does your exposure to lawsuits, property damage, and liability.

Home Insurance

- Be sure your policy covers **replacement cost**, not just current value
- Add **riders** for high-value items (jewelry, electronics, collectibles)

Auto Insurance

- Choose **high liability limits**—at least 100/300/100
- Add **uninsured/underinsured motorist protection**

Bundling

- Many companies offer discounts if you bundle home and auto policies
- More importantly, make sure coverage limits reflect your **real risk as a high-income earner**

Umbrella Insurance: Why Doctors Are High Liability Targets

Physicians are often viewed as **deep pockets**—even if you're early in your career. If someone sues you for damages beyond your auto or home policy's coverage limits, you could be personally liable.

Umbrella Insurance

- Provides **additional liability coverage** beyond home and auto
- Kicks in once your other coverage is exhausted
- Typically sold in $1 million increments
- Affordable: $1 million of coverage may cost $150–$300/year

If you're earning six figures or more, ***you need an umbrella policy.*** *It protects your assets and your future income.*

Insurance Planning for Your Spouse and Children

You're not the only one who needs coverage. If your family relies on your spouse's income, or they contribute meaningfully in non-financial ways (like childcare), you need to consider protecting **both sides** of the household.

Spouse:

- If they earn income: Get **term life insurance** to replace that income
- If they manage the home or care for children: Still consider term life to cover the cost of replacement help if needed
- Check **health insurance options** if you rely on them for coverage

Children:

- You don't need a large life insurance policy for kids—but a **small rider** ($10,000–$25,000) can help cover funeral costs and provide peace of mind
- Focus instead on **saving for their future** through 529 plans or custodial accounts

Final Thoughts: Protection Is Power

Insurance is often viewed as boring, complicated, or optional. But for physicians, it's none of those things.

It's **essential**. It's **strategic**. And it's the only thing standing between your family's future and an unexpected crisis.

The best time to get covered is **before** you need it.

The second-best time is **now**.

Make it a priority. Review your policies. And when in doubt, work with a trusted advisor who can help you navigate it all with confidence.

Because your career is about saving lives.

Let's make sure you protect the one you've worked so hard to build.

Chapter 8: Investing and Building Wealth

How to Turn Your Income into Long-Term Freedom

Most physicians spend years learning how to earn a paycheck—but almost no time learning what to do with it once it arrives.

Here's the reality: **Income makes you rich today. Investing makes you wealthy tomorrow.**

The problem is, many doctors are high earners who never learn the *rules of the game* when it comes to investing. That's how so many physicians can earn millions over their careers—yet still feel unsure, stressed, or completely unprepared for retirement.

This chapter is about helping you break that cycle.

We're not here to turn you into a Wall Street trader. We're here to give you a simple, clear investing roadmap—built for your lifestyle, your time constraints, and your long-term goals.

Let's dive in.

Asset Allocation: Stocks, Bonds, Real Estate, and Cash

The foundation of any successful investment strategy is **asset allocation**—how you divide your money across different types of investments to balance risk and reward.

1. Stocks (Equities)

- Ownership in companies
- Higher risk, higher potential return
- Best for long-term growth (especially for retirement accounts)
- Accessible through mutual funds, index funds, and ETFs

2. Bonds (Fixed Income)

- Loans to companies or governments that pay you interest
- Lower risk, lower return than stocks
- Help balance portfolio volatility
- Useful for income or preservation as you near retirement

3. Real Estate

- Can be active (owning rental property) or passive (REITs or syndications)
- Potential for appreciation, cash flow, and tax benefits
- Riskier without due diligence
- A common physician wealth-building strategy (covered more below)

4. Cash

- Savings accounts, money markets, CDs
- Minimal risk and return
- Use for emergency funds and short-term goals—not long-term investing

Your mix depends on your goals, time horizon, and risk tolerance—but as a physician in your 30s or 40s, a ***growth-heavy portfolio*** *(70–90% stocks) is typically appropriate for long-term investing.*

Passive vs. Active Investing

Passive Investing

- Invests in the overall market using index funds or ETFs
- Low-cost, low-maintenance, and historically effective
- Example: S&P 500 index fund
- Perfect for busy professionals who want simplicity and reliable long-term growth

Active Investing

- Trying to beat the market by picking stocks or timing trades
- Higher fees, higher risk, lower probability of long-term outperformance
- Requires time, research, and emotional control

> *Research shows passive investors consistently outperform most active investors* ***over time****—especially after fees.*

As a physician, you're busy. Let the market work for you while you focus on your career. Passive investing is not boring—it's *smart.*

Avoiding Investment Scams and Bad "Doctor Deals"

Doctors are high earners—and unfortunately, **prime targets for financial predators.**

You'll be approached with:

- "Guaranteed" returns
- Real estate partnerships
- Private equity "insider" investments
- Life insurance policies disguised as investment vehicles

- Startups with "huge upside" but no track record

Some of these may be legit—but many are high-risk, overpriced, or outright scams.

Red flags:

- Pressure to act fast
- No clear way to exit the investment
- Vague or overly complex explanations
- Non-transparent fees
- Promises of "risk-free" returns

What to do:

- Never invest in something you don't understand
- Get a second opinion from a **fee-only fiduciary advisor**
- Beware of advisors who also sell products—they're often incentivized to sell, not guide
- Remember: **If it sounds too good to be true, it is**

You trained too long and worked too hard to gamble your future away on hype.

Tax-Efficient Investing

Doctors face a double challenge: high income and high tax brackets. That's why **tax efficiency matters** in your investment strategy.

Key Tools:

1. Tax-Advantaged Accounts

- **401(k), 403(b), 457(b):** Pre-tax contributions = immediate tax savings
- **Roth IRA:** Post-tax contributions = tax-free withdrawals
- **HSA:** Triple tax advantage if used for healthcare or saved for retirement
- **529 Plan:** For tax-free education savings

Max these out *before* investing in taxable accounts.

2. Taxable Brokerage Accounts

- Fully flexible, but taxable
- Use **tax-efficient index funds** or ETFs
- Hold investments longer than 1 year to benefit from long-term capital gains rates
- Use **tax-loss harvesting** if working with an advisor or robo-advisor platform

3. Asset Location Strategy

- Put tax-inefficient assets (like bonds) in tax-advantaged accounts
- Keep tax-efficient assets (like index funds) in taxable accounts

> *Every dollar you save in taxes is a dollar that keeps compounding for you—not the IRS.*

Real Estate as a Long-Term Wealth Strategy

Many physicians are drawn to real estate—and for good reason. It can generate **cash flow**, offer **appreciation**, and provide **generous tax benefits** when structured correctly.

Common Ways to Invest in Real Estate:

- **Direct ownership:** Single-family rentals, duplexes, small multifamily
- **Real estate syndications:** Passive investments in large-scale projects
- **REITs (Real Estate Investment Trusts):** Publicly traded funds of real estate assets—like mutual funds for property

Pros:

- Monthly income
- Appreciation over time
- Leverage (using other people's money to grow wealth)
- Depreciation and tax deductions (real estate investors can reduce their taxable income significantly)

Cons:

- Requires capital and time
- Risk of bad tenants, market downturns, or vacancies
- Legal and tax complexity (especially if you're not working with a team)

> *Real estate can be a powerful diversification tool—but it's not passive unless you treat it like a business and* ***hire smart help****.*

Final Thoughts: Let Your Money Work as Hard as You Do

You spent years training your brain to save lives. Now it's time to train your money to create freedom.

- Automate your investments
- Diversify across assets and accounts
- Stay consistent through market ups and downs
- Avoid high-fee "doctor deals" that prey on your income

- Invest not just for retirement—but for **choices, independence, and peace of mind**

Wealth isn't built in big leaps. It's built one smart, intentional step at a time. **Start now. Keep going. And let compounding do the rest.**

Chapter 9: Credit, Debt, and Leveraging Your Financial Profile

C*ontrol Your Debt—Don't Let It Control You*

Debt is a part of almost every physician's story. Between undergrad, med school, car payments, mortgages, and the occasional business or practice loan, doctors are often juggling multiple financial obligations long before they've reached their full earning potential.

And while debt can feel heavy—or even shameful—it doesn't have to be.

Debt, when managed wisely, can be a powerful financial tool. But when ignored or misunderstood, it can limit your freedom, restrict your choices, and delay your goals.

This chapter is about making sure *you* stay in control.

We'll explore how to build credit, understand your credit score, and use debt as leverage—not as a trap. Whether you're fresh out of training or deep into your career, these are skills every physician needs to master.

Building and Maintaining Excellent Credit

Your credit score is like your financial GPA. It determines your ability to borrow, your interest rates, and sometimes even your ability to rent a home, secure a mortgage, or obtain certain professional licenses.

The 5 Factors That Impact Your Credit Score:

1. **Payment History (35%)** – Pay your bills on time, every time.
2. **Credit Utilization (30%)** – Keep credit card balances below 30% of their limits.
3. **Length of Credit History (15%)** – The longer your accounts have been open, the better.
4. **Credit Mix (10%)** – A variety of loans (credit cards, auto loans, student loans, mortgage) shows responsible use.
5. **New Credit Inquiries (10%)** – Too many hard inquiries in a short time can lower your score.

Tips to Build and Maintain Great Credit:

- Always pay at least the minimum on time—set up auto-pay
- Keep old accounts open (unless they have high fees)
- Limit new applications to when truly needed
- Review your credit report **annually** at AnnualCreditReport.com

A good credit score (typically 720 and above) unlocks lower interest rates and better financial options across the board.

Understanding Credit Scores and Reports

You have three major credit reports: **Experian, Equifax, and TransUnion.** These are the reports lenders use to assess your creditworthiness. You're entitled to one free report from each bureau every year.

What to check for:

- Accounts that aren't yours (fraud or reporting error)
- Incorrect balances or missed payments
- Closed accounts that should still be open (or vice versa)

If you find an error, dispute it directly with the bureau in writing and follow up with documentation.

Also check your **FICO Score** (used by most lenders) and **VantageScore** (used by some free tools like Credit Karma). They may differ slightly, but both give you a snapshot of how you're doing.

When (and How) to Use Debt Strategically

All debt is not created equal. There's **destructive debt** (like high-interest credit cards), and there's **strategic debt**—used thoughtfully to grow your net worth or smooth out life transitions.

Examples of Strategic Debt:

- **Mortgages** with favorable terms, building equity while preserving cash
- **Low-interest student loans** while saving and investing simultaneously
- **Business/practice loans** to start or grow a private practice
- **Real estate leverage** in investment properties, when done carefully

Key rules:

- Always know the **interest rate** and **total repayment amount**
- Have a clear **repayment plan** before borrowing
- Don't use future income as an excuse for overextending today
- Avoid co-signing loans unless you're prepared to take full responsibility

Strategic debt creates options. Unmanaged debt creates stress.

How to Refinance Student Loans (and When Not To)

Student loan refinancing is a hot topic among doctors—and for good reason. It can lower your interest rate and save you thousands. But **it's not for everyone**.

When Refinancing Makes Sense:

- You have **private loans** with high interest rates
- You're no longer pursuing **Public Service Loan Forgiveness (PSLF)**
- You have **stable income** and strong credit
- You're confident you won't need the flexible protections of federal loans (like forbearance or income-driven repayment)

When NOT to Refinance:

- You're working at a **nonprofit hospital** and pursuing PSLF
- You may qualify for federal loan forgiveness or income-based repayment
- You're unsure about future employment or financial stability

Tips:

- Shop multiple lenders for the best rate
- Look for **no origination fees** or prepayment penalties
- Choose a fixed rate if you're risk-averse
- Some lenders offer rate discounts for auto-pay or loyalty

Refinancing can be a smart move—but it's a **point of no return** for federal loan benefits. Know the trade-offs.

Managing Personal and Professional Debt (e.g., Practice Loans)

As your career evolves, you may take on **new forms of debt**—like opening a private practice, buying into a partnership, or expanding your clinical offerings.

Personal Debt to Watch:

- **Car loans** – Keep monthly payments under 10–15% of take-home pay
- **Credit cards** – Pay in full each month; interest rates are too high to carry balances
- **Mortgages** – Buy less house than you can technically "afford"

Professional Debt (Practice Loans, Equipment Financing):

- Only take on practice debt with a **clear ROI**
- Hire a financial advisor or accountant to assess the viability of the investment
- Don't let lenders overextend your practice with more debt than it can service
- Understand whether the loan is personally guaranteed—meaning **you** are responsible, not just the practice entity

Key Concept: Debt-to-Income Ratio

- This is what banks and lenders use to evaluate your borrowing ability
- Try to keep your total monthly debt payments **below 36% of your gross monthly income**

> *Borrow like a business owner, not just a doctor with access to credit. Know your numbers.*

Final Thoughts: Debt Doesn't Define You—But It Can Direct You

Debt is neither good nor bad—it's a tool. And like any tool, its usefulness depends on how you use it.

- Build strong credit.
- Review your reports.
- Use debt thoughtfully.
- Refinance when it makes sense.
- Avoid chasing the image of wealth at the expense of your real financial health.

You've already proven you can manage complexity in medicine. Now apply that same focus to your money.

Because the goal isn't to avoid debt—it's to **master it.**

Chapter 10: Advanced Planning as a Senior Physician

Leadership, Legacy, and the Financial Moves That Define Your Final Act

By the time you reach the senior stage of your career—whether as a chief of staff, medical director, department chair, or private practice partner—you've likely achieved a level of financial stability and professional credibility that few others can match. You've put in the years, earned the respect, and shaped care systems and the next generation of physicians.

But this phase of your career brings a **different set of financial decisions**—ones that are less about how to make money and more about **how to maximize, protect, and eventually exit** with clarity.

This is the "second half" of your financial game—and how you play it determines the lifestyle, flexibility, and legacy you'll leave behind.

Chief of Staff, Partner, or Medical Director: How Compensation Shifts

Moving into leadership doesn't just change your title—it often reshapes how you're compensated. Your income may become a blend of base salary, performance incentives, bonuses, and administrative stipends.

Common Shifts in Compensation Structure:

- **Less RVU-based pay, more fixed salary or incentive packages** tied to department goals or system performance
- **Leadership stipends** for roles like Medical Director or Chair (can range from $10K to $50K+)
- **Profit-sharing or partnership distributions** in private practices
- **Greater access to institutional deferred comp plans** or executive retirement benefits

It's critical to understand exactly **how you're being paid, what's taxable,** and whether performance bonuses are achievable or unrealistic.

> *Pro tip: If bonuses are tied to metrics, ask to see past years' performance data—don't assume they're guaranteed.*

Equity, Profit Sharing, and Business Ownership

If you're in private practice or leadership at an independent hospital group, **equity and profit sharing** may become part of your compensation package.

This can be a powerful wealth-building tool—but it requires a business mindset.

Equity & Partnership Buy-Ins:

- Understand **buy-in cost**, ownership percentage, and **return on investment**
- Ask for **historical financials** to see how profitable the business really is
- Know what happens when you leave or retire—**how and when do you cash out?**

Profit Sharing:

- Often distributed quarterly or annually
- Can vary widely based on productivity, expenses, and collections
- Make sure you understand **the formula** and **your role in driving results**

Equity can create significant upside—but it can also create liability. Don't buy in without doing your due diligence.

Deferred Compensation Plans and Defined Benefit Pensions

At this stage, you may have access to **advanced retirement vehicles** beyond the typical 403(b) or 401(k). Understanding and using them wisely can set you up for long-term security.

Deferred Compensation Plans (457(f), 409A, SERPs):

- Allow you to defer a portion of your income to be paid later (usually at retirement or separation)
- Often **non-qualified**, meaning funds may be at risk if the employer becomes insolvent
- Payouts can come with **big tax hits**—work with a CPA to plan withdrawal timing

Defined Benefit Pensions:

- Rare in private settings, but still offered by some universities and large hospitals
- Provide a **guaranteed income stream** in retirement based on years of service and salary history
- Ensure you understand **vesting schedules** and **benefit calculations**

These tools can dramatically reduce your retirement tax burden—but only if coordinated with your other income streams.

Making Financial Decisions for Your Group or Department

As a senior physician, you may now influence how money is managed for **more than just yourself**—perhaps for a whole department or practice. That responsibility comes with new considerations:

- Budgeting for staff, technology, and clinical operations
- Negotiating contracts for your team
- Deciding on profit-sharing structures or partner buy-in arrangements
- Creating or revising retirement benefit options for your group
- Advocating for compensation parity, fair call distribution, or CME funding

You've become a steward—not just of medicine, but of the institution's financial culture. Treat it with care.

Preparing for Potential Burnout or Exit Planning

Senior physicians are at increased risk for burnout—particularly those balancing patient care with leadership, administrative tasks, and family life. Planning ahead gives you options **before** you feel trapped or depleted.

Key Exit Planning Questions:

- If I stopped working tomorrow, how long could I support my lifestyle?
- Am I financially able to reduce my hours, shift roles, or consult instead of practice full-time?
- Have I planned a **retirement glide path** (gradual reduction in work)?
- Do I have disability coverage and succession plans if I'm forced to stop working early?

- Have I reviewed my estate plan in the past 3–5 years?

Burnout is real—but it's not just emotional. It's financial too. ***Options create freedom. Freedom creates peace.***

Final Thoughts: Finish Strong—On Your Terms

You've already won the game in many ways. Now it's time to **win the endgame**—not just with titles and accolades, but with a financial strategy that gives you **freedom, dignity, and options** in the years to come.

This is the season to:

- Maximize your compensation
- Protect your wealth
- Mentor the next generation
- Prepare for transitions
- Create a legacy—both financially and professionally

Whether you retire at 55, shift to part-time at 65, or teach until 75, the goal is the same:

Leave when you want, how you want, with your finances—and your future—fully intact.

You've taken care of others for decades. Let's make sure you're taking care of yourself, too.

Chapter 11: Estate Planning for High-Earning Professionals

Leave More Than a Legacy—Leave a Plan

As a high-earning physician, you've spent your life taking care of others—your patients, your family, your team. You've built a career that matters, saved money, bought a home (maybe a few), paid down your student loans, and possibly even started investing for future generations.

But here's the question no one wants to ask—yet everyone should:

If something happened to you tomorrow, would your family know what to do next?

This chapter isn't about death. It's about direction.

Estate planning is not a task for the ultra-wealthy—it's a necessity for *anyone* with people depending on them, assets they care about, or a legacy they want to protect.

As a physician, your income and assets often grow faster than your planning. That's why now—not someday—is the time to get clear, get organized, and get protected.

Creating Wills, Trusts, and Healthcare Directives

1. A Will

- A will is the legal document that outlines your wishes for how your assets should be distributed after your death.
- It also names **an executor** (the person responsible for carrying out your wishes) and **guardians for your children**, if applicable.
- Without a will, your estate is subject to **state intestacy laws**, which may not reflect your intentions.

2. A Living Trust

- A **revocable living trust** lets you transfer ownership of your assets into a legal entity while you're alive—and control them just like you do now.
- Upon your death, your trustee distributes the assets without going through **probate** (the court process that can be expensive and public).
- Trusts are especially useful for high earners, business owners, and those with **multiple properties or complex family dynamics**.

3. Healthcare Directives

- Includes a **living will** (your medical wishes if you're incapacitated) and a **healthcare proxy** or **durable power of attorney** (someone you trust to make decisions if you cannot).
- These documents prevent confusion and family conflict during emotionally difficult times.

Estate planning isn't about control. It's about ***clarity****—for you and for those you love.*

Setting Up Guardianship for Children

If you have children under 18, naming a legal guardian in your will is one of the most important decisions you'll make.

- Choose someone who shares your values and parenting philosophy.
- Talk to them first—**don't surprise them with the responsibility.**
- Name **backup guardians** in case your first choice is unable or unwilling.
- Be clear about financial resources—who will raise your children vs. who will manage the money may be two different people (and that's okay).

You don't have to be wealthy to need guardianship plans—you just need to be a **parent who cares** about what happens next.

Tax Planning for Generational Wealth

Doctors often hit income levels that come with **higher estate tax exposure**—especially when you include real estate, retirement accounts, life insurance, and business equity.

While the federal estate tax exemption is high (currently over $13 million per person as of 2024), state estate taxes can kick in at **much lower thresholds** in places like New York, Massachusetts, and Oregon.

Ways to Reduce Future Estate Taxes:

- Use the **annual gift exclusion** to move wealth tax-free
- Fund **529 plans** for children or grandchildren
- Create **irrevocable trusts** to remove assets from your taxable estate
- Consider **life insurance trusts** to avoid having large death benefits taxed as part of your estate
- Use **spousal portability** and marital deduction strategies for married

couples

Tax planning isn't about loopholes—it's about **using the rules wisely to create opportunity for the next generation.**

Philanthropy, Donor-Advised Funds, and Legacy Giving

Many physicians feel a strong desire to give back—to their alma mater, their hospital foundation, their faith institution, or their community. Estate planning is the perfect opportunity to align **your values with your wealth**.

Legacy Giving Options:

- **Donor-Advised Funds (DAFs)** – Think of it like a charitable checking account. You fund it now, get an immediate tax deduction, and recommend grants over time.
- **Charitable Remainder Trusts (CRTs)** – Provides income to you now, then donates the remainder to a nonprofit after your death.
- **Charitable Bequests** – A simple clause in your will or trust directing a portion of your estate to a cause or organization you care about.
- **Naming a nonprofit as a beneficiary** on a retirement account or life insurance policy

*Legacy isn't just what you leave behind—it's **what you build into the future.***

Why Estate Planning Protects Your Family—Not Just Your Wealth

Doctors often delay estate planning because they're busy, overwhelmed, or unsure where to start. But if you have assets, a partner, children, a home, or even just personal preferences—you already have an estate. The only question is whether it's been planned for.

Estate Planning Prevents:

- Expensive probate delays
- Unintended beneficiaries (ex-spouses, distant relatives, the state)
- Family conflict and legal disputes
- Gaps in care or access if you're incapacitated
- Unnecessary tax burdens on your heirs

Estate planning isn't morbid—it's a **gift** to your loved ones. It removes uncertainty in the hardest moments. It tells the people you care about: *"I thought about you. I prepared for you. I protected you."*

Final Thoughts: It's Not Just for Someday—It's for Now

No one wants to think about the worst-case scenario. But doctors know better than most that life can change in a moment.

Estate planning doesn't make you morbid. It makes you **mature, wise, and deeply responsible.**

- Create your will
- Set up a trust if needed
- Name your children's guardians
- Talk to an estate attorney
- Review your beneficiary designations annually
- Have the hard conversations now, while you still can

This chapter isn't about endings. It's about peace, protection, and preparation.

Because one day—hopefully many, many years from now—what you built will outlive you.

Let it be intentional. Let it be generous. Let it be yours.

Part 2: Entering the Field – From First Job to Financial Growth

You made it.

After years of schooling, training, testing, sleepless nights, and patient notes written at 2 a.m.—you're finally getting that first real paycheck. It's a big moment. The white coat still fits, but now you're entering a different kind of world: the professional one. With that first attending job or post-fellowship role comes responsibility, pressure... and significantly more money than you've likely ever earned.

Here's the good news: **you have options now.**

You can afford to do things you've put off—pay down debt, travel, buy nicer things, maybe even help family or start saving for a home.

Here's the challenge: **you also have decisions to make.**

And if you're like most new doctors, no one trained you to make them.

This is where things get real.

Because once that first direct deposit hits, the pressure to "catch up" kicks in fast:

- You've delayed gratification for years, so it's tempting to start spending big.
- You want to start attacking those student loans, but you're not sure of the smartest way to go about it.
- You hear you should invest, but no one taught you how.
- You're offered benefits, retirement plans, maybe even signing bonuses—

but you're not sure what you're looking at.
- And maybe for the first time, people are asking you for financial help or treating you like a walking ATM.

In other words: **more income doesn't automatically mean less stress.**

In fact, it can mean more confusion—if you don't have a plan.

That's what this section is for.

The Goal of Part 2:

To help you **make the most of your new income**, avoid common traps, and build a solid foundation for long-term growth—not just short-term satisfaction.

Because this stage of your life isn't just about earning more. It's about making **your money work for you**, not the other way around.

In This Section, You'll Learn:

- How to create a financial plan for your first attending job
- What to do with student loans now that you're earning more
- How to approach budgeting when your income finally expands
- The basics of investing (and how to actually get started)
- What benefits to look for—and what questions to ask when reviewing your offer
- How to avoid lifestyle inflation and financial comparison traps
- How to set healthy boundaries with family, friends, and "financial expectations"
- Why your financial habits in these early earning years will shape your next 30+

This is one of the most important stretches of your financial life.

It's where doctors either begin to build real wealth—or unintentionally create golden handcuffs that keep them stuck in stress, debt, and financial uncertainty despite a high income.

You've already proven you can handle the hard stuff.

Now it's time to use those same skills—discipline, precision, long-term thinking—to make your money work as hard as you do.

Chapter 12: Planning With Your Spouse

B*ecause Wealth Isn't Just Built Alone—It's Built Together*

Medicine may be a solo journey in training, but in life, it rarely is. Whether your partner is also in healthcare, works in another field, or manages your home and family full-time, **your financial life is shared**. And like any strong relationship, success comes from clarity, communication, and collaboration.

Too often, financial conversations are reactive—sparked by a big purchase, an unexpected bill, or a tough life event. But the healthiest financial households? They plan together **on purpose**, not just when they have to.

This chapter is your roadmap for doing just that.

Financial Conversations Every Medical Couple Should Have

Start with this: *Have we ever truly sat down to talk about money—not just the bills, but the big picture?*

Whether you're engaged, newly married, or decades into partnership, these questions matter:

Key Conversations to Have:

- What are our **shared financial goals**—in 1 year, 5 years, and 20?
- How do we each feel about debt, saving, and spending?
- What are our individual **money mindsets**—and where did they come from?

- Are we combining finances fully, partially, or keeping them separate?
- What does "financial security" look like to us as a couple?

These questions aren't about right or wrong—they're about understanding. Even if one of you is the "money person," **both partners need visibility** into the overall plan.

Pro tip: Schedule a recurring "money date" each month or quarter to check in, update goals, and stay aligned.

Protecting Your Spouse Financially in the Event of Your Disability or Death

As a physician, your income likely makes up a significant portion—if not the majority—of your household's financial engine. That's why **protecting your spouse** financially in the event of an accident, illness, or death is non-negotiable.

1. Disability Insurance

- If you're unable to work, disability insurance replaces a portion of your income (typically 60–70%)
- Choose **own-occupation** coverage and add riders like future increase options
- Consider your spouse's needs if you were to be out of work for years—or permanently

2. Life Insurance

- If your spouse depends on your income, term life insurance provides essential protection
- Calculate needs based on outstanding debts, future living expenses, childcare, education costs, and time off for grieving

- Don't forget **stay-at-home spouses**—their work has replacement value too

3. Legal Planning

- Wills, trusts, power of attorney, and healthcare directives ensure your spouse has authority and clarity during crisis
- Keep all policies and documents updated, accessible, and **communicated**—they should know what exists and where to find it

Love isn't just provision. It's preparation.

Coordinating Benefits, Insurance, and Retirement

If both partners work—especially if both are in medicine—you may be juggling multiple workplace benefits, retirement accounts, and insurance options.

Steps to Coordinate Effectively:

- Review each partner's **health insurance**—which plan is better for your family?
- Choose **one flexible spending account (FSA)** or **dependent care account** to avoid tax issues
- Coordinate **disability and life insurance** so there's no coverage gap
- Maximize **both retirement plans** (401(k), 403(b), 457(b), etc.)—or use one to save more aggressively
- Track beneficiaries across all accounts and update them regularly

You're not just managing your own plan—you're designing a **household financial system**.

Financial Roles and Responsibilities in Your Household

Every couple divides responsibilities differently. Some are 50/50, others follow more traditional roles. What matters most is that **you agree on the structure—and revisit it regularly**.

Suggested Roles to Clarify:

- Who pays the bills and handles day-to-day finances?
- Who manages long-term planning—investments, taxes, insurance?
- Who tracks savings, retirement goals, and big purchases?
- Who communicates with professionals (advisors, accountants, estate attorneys)?
- Do we both have access to all accounts, passwords, and documents?

If one person is handling most of the financial tasks, the other should still be **informed and involved**. Transparency builds trust, and both partners need to be equipped in case of emergency.

Managing Dual Careers, Stay-at-Home Spouses, and Blended Families

Every family structure brings unique dynamics. Let's break down some of the most common situations:

Dual-Career Couples

- Talk about how to handle big decisions: moving for jobs, work-life balance, who earns more
- Avoid "lifestyle inflation wars"—just because you both earn a lot doesn't mean you have to spend a lot
- Decide how to split shared expenses (proportionally or equally?) and what to save for jointly

Stay-at-Home Spouses

- Their contribution is real and valuable—even if unpaid
- Ensure they're financially protected: life insurance, access to credit, savings in their name
- Retirement planning: Consider spousal IRAs or employer contributions in joint financial plans

Blended Families

- Communicate openly about existing obligations: alimony, child support, prior financial plans
- Set clear expectations around estate planning and inheritance
- Consider creating **separate trusts** for each branch of the family, especially if children from different relationships are involved

> *Every family has its own playbook. What matters is that* ***you write it together.***

Final Thoughts: Partnership Is the Foundation of Financial Peace

Whether you're married, engaged, cohabiting, or building a family, financial alignment is one of the most important parts of a successful relationship.

You don't have to agree on every purchase or share every account.

But you *do* need to communicate, collaborate, and create a plan that works for both of you.

Because when life gets busy—and it will—your financial peace as a couple will depend not just on your income, but on your **intentionality**.

Talk. Plan. Protect. And keep showing up—for each other, and for your future.

Chapter 13: Planning for Life After Medicine

Designing a Future That's Purposeful, Peaceful, and Financially Secure

After years—maybe decades—of caring for others, teaching students, leading teams, and building a professional legacy, many physicians begin to ask themselves a new set of questions:

When is it time to step away? Will I have enough? What will life look like after the last patient note is signed?

Retirement isn't just about leaving medicine. It's about entering a chapter that you've been preparing for your entire career, even if you didn't realize it. This isn't just a financial decision—it's also deeply personal and emotional.

This chapter is your bridge from full-time medicine to the life that comes after. Whether you're five years away or already picturing the beach, the mountains, or the grandkids, these insights will help you plan with clarity and purpose.

When to Retire: Financial vs. Emotional Readiness

There are two sides to the retirement equation:

1. Financial Readiness

- Do you have enough saved and invested to maintain your lifestyle for the rest of your life?
- Have you accounted for inflation, rising healthcare costs, and long-term care?
- Are your debts paid off—or manageable within your retirement income?
- Have you maximized your retirement vehicles (403(b), 457(b), IRAs, pensions)?

2. Emotional Readiness

- Do you have a plan for your time, identity, and purpose outside of medicine?
- Are you retiring *to* something—or just *from* something?
- Are you ready to let go of the white coat and what it represents?
- Have you talked with your spouse or partner about expectations for post-retirement life?

> *Retirement isn't an escape. It's a* ***transition****—one that works best when you're emotionally and financially aligned.*

How Much Is Enough? Determining Your "Number"

Your "number" is the amount of money you'll need to support your lifestyle, without the paycheck.

A simple way to estimate it:

1. Determine your **annual spending goal** in retirement

- Most physicians need 60–80% of pre-retirement income

1. Subtract any guaranteed income (Social Security, pensions, annuities)
2. Multiply the difference by **25–30** to reflect 25–30 years of retirement (based on the 4% rule)

Example:
If you plan to spend $180,000/year and expect $40,000/year from Social Security and pension:
$180,000 - $40,000 = $140,000 gap
$140,000 x 25 = $3.5 million retirement nest egg needed

That's a starting point—not a rule. Talk to a financial advisor to refine it based on:

- Healthcare expenses
- Life expectancy
- Legacy and giving goals
- Risk tolerance

The more clearly you define your number, the more confidently you can make decisions around work, savings, and when to step away.

Income Streams in Retirement: Social Security, Annuities, Investments

Your retirement income should come from multiple, coordinated sources—so you're not relying on just one bucket.

1. Social Security

- Can start as early as age 62, or as late as 70 (delayed benefits increase 8% per year after full retirement age)
- For high earners, the benefit is capped, but still valuable as a predictable income stream

- Consider tax implications—up to 85% of Social Security benefits may be taxable based on total income

2. Annuities

- Provide guaranteed income for life or a set period
- Useful to cover essential expenses (housing, food, healthcare)
- Beware of high fees and commission-based sales—consult a fee-only advisor
- Consider SPIAs (Single Premium Immediate Annuities) for simplicity

3. Investments

- 401(k), 403(b), 457(b), IRAs, brokerage accounts
- Use a drawdown strategy based on your goals and tax situation
- Withdraw from taxable accounts first to preserve tax-deferred growth
- Required Minimum Distributions (RMDs) begin at age 73 for most retirement accounts

> *Pro tip: Diversify your tax buckets—have money in **taxable, tax-deferred, and tax-free accounts** for flexibility.*

Downsizing, Second Homes, and Cost of Living Considerations

Your home—and where you choose to live—has a major impact on your retirement budget and lifestyle.

Downsizing

- Selling a larger home can unlock equity and reduce ongoing costs
- Consider maintenance, property taxes, and mobility/future care needs
- Some physicians downsize in stages: main residence → condo or

townhome → senior community

Second Homes

- A vacation home can be a source of joy—or a financial and logistical headache
- Factor in maintenance, property management, insurance, taxes, and travel
- Renting it out part-time can offset costs, but comes with tax and time implications
- Ask: *Will we use it enough to justify owning it?*

Geographic Flexibility

- Cost of living can vary drastically by state—so can state income and estate taxes
- Some physicians retire to lower-tax states (e.g., Florida, Texas) for tax efficiency
- Think about access to healthcare, family, and community—not just sunshine

> *Your retirement lifestyle isn't just about how much you've saved—it's about* ***how and where you live.***

Final Thoughts: The Rest of Your Life Deserves as Much Planning as the First

You've spent a career planning treatment plans, OR schedules, and patient care. You've made thousands of decisions with clarity and precision.

Now it's time to apply that same intentionality to your own life.

- Start by defining what a meaningful, fulfilling retirement looks like to you

- Clarify your "enough" number
- Create income streams that feel stable and sustainable
- Make lifestyle choices that support—not stress—your financial goals
- Involve your spouse, your advisor, and your heart in the planning process

Because life after medicine isn't the end of your purpose—it's the **beginning of the freedom you worked so hard to earn**.

Let's make sure it's everything you want it to be.

Chapter 14: Exit Planning for Practice Owners

Turning a Lifetime of Work into a Smooth Transition and Strong Finish

If you've built your own private practice, you already know the level of commitment, risk, and reward that comes with ownership. You weren't just a physician—you were an entrepreneur, leader, manager, mentor, and problem-solver.

But now, whether retirement is on the horizon or you're simply ready for a new chapter, a major question looms:

What happens to the practice when you leave?

Exit planning isn't just about selling a business. It's about **protecting your legacy**, your patients, your staff—and securing the financial reward that comes from everything you've built.

This chapter will help you think through the personal, legal, financial, and ethical layers of stepping away from your practice with intention and clarity.

Selling or Passing On a Private Practice

You essentially have two main exit options as a practice owner:

1. Sell the Practice

- To another physician
- To a hospital or health system
- To a private equity group
- To a group of partners already in the practice

2. Pass It On

- To a family member in medicine
- To a junior associate or partner
- Through a **buy-in/buy-out agreement** gradually over time

The key is planning early—**at least 3–5 years before your intended exit**—so you can shape the practice into a business that's attractive, valuable, and easy to transfer.

> *Start by asking:* Who do I want to serve my patients after I leave—and what kind of legacy do I want to leave behind?

Valuation, Buyer Selection, and Transition Planning

Business Valuation

You'll need a formal valuation to determine what your practice is worth. This takes into account:

- Revenue and profitability (3–5 years of financials)
- Patient volume and referral sources
- Contracts with payers
- Location, equipment, and staff
- Goodwill and reputation

Pro tip: Work with a professional appraiser or healthcare CPA to get a fair and accurate valuation. Don't rely on rules of thumb alone.

Buyer Selection

Choose a buyer who:

- Has the clinical skills and leadership to continue care
- Understands your patient population and business model
- Is financially qualified—or backed by a firm that is
- Will honor your legacy, staff, and community

You may consider seller financing, especially with younger buyers—just make sure legal protections are in place.

Transition Planning

A well-managed transition usually takes **6 to 18 months**. Key steps include:

- Notifying patients and referral sources
- Training or mentoring the new physician(s)
- Transferring billing, licensing, and credentialing
- Ensuring continuity of care and protecting HIPAA compliance

A smooth transition builds trust—with the buyer, your staff, and your patients.

Taxes, Succession, and Retirement Accounts Tied to the Practice

Exiting your practice isn't just about receiving a check—it's about **structuring the exit in a tax-efficient and strategic way.**

Tax Considerations

- The **structure of your business (LLC, S-Corp, C-Corp)** will impact how proceeds are taxed
- **Asset sale vs. stock sale** can affect both buyer and seller taxes
- Proceeds from the sale may be taxed as capital gains or ordinary income
- Use tax planning to minimize your liability—especially in a high-income year

Succession Planning

- Have a written succession plan that outlines how decisions will be made, who assumes leadership, and how the transfer of ownership unfolds
- Include buy-sell agreements and key-man insurance, if applicable
- Update legal documents regularly (including your estate plan)

Retirement Accounts

If you've used a **practice-sponsored retirement plan** (e.g., solo 401(k), SEP IRA, or defined benefit plan), you'll need to:

- Roll funds into an IRA or another qualified plan
- Discontinue or transfer administration
- Finalize employee benefits and distributions per ERISA guidelines

Work closely with a financial advisor and tax attorney to ensure a clean, compliant, and optimized exit.

Protecting Patients and Staff in Your Transition

Your practice may be your asset—but your patients and staff are your **legacy**.

For Your Patients:

- Provide **clear, advance communication** about your departure and their continued care
- Introduce them to the new physician if possible
- Transfer medical records securely and legally
- Maintain continuity of care—especially for chronic or complex cases

For Your Staff:

- Be transparent about the sale and timing
- Offer retention bonuses or phased transition plans if appropriate
- Help the buyer assess staff roles, strengths, and compensation
- Provide strong recommendations and references if some employees move on

> *The way you exit affects not just your wealth—but your reputation. Make it count.*

Final Thoughts: Exit With Grace, Clarity, and Confidence

You didn't just build a business. You built something meaningful—a place where lives were healed, jobs were created, and a community was served.

Now it's time to pass the torch, and **reap the financial rewards** of your investment, effort, and vision.

- Start early
- Seek expert guidance
- Protect what you've built
- Take care of the people who made it possible
- And make the next chapter just as intentional as the first

You've done the hard work. Now it's time to exit on your terms—with purpose, pride, and peace.

Chapter 15: Staying Active Without the Grind

How to Design a Fulfilling Next Chapter Without Clocking 60 Hours a Week

Retirement from medicine doesn't have to mean stepping away completely. For many physicians, the idea of "retirement" doesn't mean doing nothing—it means **doing something meaningful, flexible, and on your terms**.

Whether it's part-time work, mentorship, volunteering, or entirely new ventures, many doctors find the sweet spot in **semi-retirement**—a place where they still contribute, still earn, and still grow—without the stress, schedule, and burnout of full-time clinical life.

This chapter is about designing that next phase. You've earned the right to slow down, but that doesn't mean you're ready to stop completely.

Let's talk about how to stay active without the grind.

Teaching, Consulting, Board Service, and Locums Work

There are plenty of ways to put your skills to work that **don't require a full clinical load**.

1. Teaching

- Academic medicine, adjunct faculty roles, or clinical preceptorship
- Teach residents, med students, or nurse practitioners in community settings
- Create online courses or contribute to continuing medical education (CME) content
- Benefit: Flexible, intellectually stimulating, and high-impact

2. Consulting

- Offer expertise to healthcare startups, hospital systems, or legal teams
- Specialties like informatics, compliance, product development, and expert witness work are in high demand
- Set your own rates and hours—projects can be short-term and highly profitable
- Tip: Join a consulting network or build a niche brand based on your expertise

3. Board Service

- Serve on hospital boards, non-profit boards, or corporate advisory panels
- Adds meaning, professional engagement, and in some cases, compensation
- You'll need to understand fiduciary responsibility and time commitment—but it's often manageable and rewarding

4. Locum Tenens (Locums) Work

- Temporary clinical assignments in various locations
- Great for travel flexibility and maintaining clinical skills
- Choose how much or how little you want to work

- Locums pay is often competitive, and travel/housing is frequently covered

*Semi-retirement isn't about stepping away—it's about stepping into **a version of your work that works for you.***

Financial Strategies for a Semi-Retired Lifestyle

Just because you're not working full-time doesn't mean you should stop planning financially. A **semi-retired lifestyle** brings its own set of opportunities and challenges.

Key Financial Considerations:

- **Health Insurance**: If you're not yet eligible for Medicare, consider COBRA, ACA marketplace plans, or joining a spouse's coverage
- **Income Planning**: Balance part-time income with withdrawals from retirement accounts—strategize to avoid jumping tax brackets
- **Tax Efficiency**: Semi-retirement is a great time to convert traditional retirement assets to Roth IRAs, since income may be lower
- **Keep Saving**: You can still contribute to IRAs, HSAs, and solo 401(k)s if you have earned income through consulting or locums
- **Social Security Timing**: Consider delaying benefits to increase your monthly payment—especially if other income supports your lifestyle

*The key is to **build flexibility** into your plan—so you can scale up or down depending on your interests and energy.*

Volunteer Work and Medical Missions

Many physicians find their deepest fulfillment in retirement through **service**.

Opportunities:

- Domestic free clinics or mobile health units
- Global health missions through organizations like Doctors Without Borders, Medical Teams International, or faith-based groups
- Local mentorship, youth education, or public health initiatives
- Board membership or fundraising for medical nonprofits

Before committing to medical missions abroad, make sure:

- Your licenses and malpractice coverage are valid for international work
- You're physically fit for the demands of travel and service
- You research organizations with strong infrastructure and ethical standards

> *Volunteering allows you to continue healing, teaching, and giving—without the paperwork, bureaucracy, or billing.*

Lifestyle Design in Retirement

Money alone won't make retirement fulfilling. What will?
Intention, purpose, community, and health.

Ask Yourself:

- What brings me energy now that I'm no longer in full-time practice?
- How do I want to spend my days—structured or spontaneous?
- Who do I want to spend more time with?
- What did I put off during my career that I now have time to pursue?

Maybe it's:

- Learning a language

- Traveling off-season
- Writing a book or starting a podcast
- Starting a garden or mentoring future physicians
- Spending uninterrupted time with grandchildren, friends, and faith

Consider:

- Downsizing or relocating for lifestyle—not just cost
- Balancing relaxation with structure to maintain identity and rhythm
- Reconnecting with hobbies, passions, or a cause you care about

> *This isn't the end of your story—it's a **brand-new chapter**. Write it with as much purpose as you did the rest of your career.*

Final Thoughts: Freedom Without Emptiness

You don't have to trade your entire identity to walk away from full-time work.

With good planning, you can retire *from the grind*—without retiring from meaning, income, connection, or contribution.

The goal isn't to do nothing. The goal is to do what **matters most to you**, with people you care about, on a schedule you actually enjoy.

You've given so much to the profession. Now it's time to give something to yourself.

Welcome to the best of both worlds: **a semi-retired life that's full—without being full-time.**

Chapter 16: Choosing the Right Financial Planner

Because Who You Trust with Your Money Matters

As a physician, you've spent your life mastering complexity. You've trusted mentors, consulted specialists, and relied on your training to make life-saving decisions. Managing your finances shouldn't be any different.

But choosing the right financial planner can be overwhelming. Titles, certifications, sales pitches—it's not always clear who is working in your best interest and who is selling a product.

This chapter will give you the clarity to choose a financial professional who aligns with your goals, your lifestyle, and the unique demands of your profession.

Credentials That Matter

Not all financial advisors are held to the same standards. Some have minimal training, while others have rigorous education and fiduciary responsibilities. Here are the designations worth understanding:

CFP® (Certified Financial Planner):

This is one of the most respected and comprehensive credentials. A CFP is trained in investments, retirement, tax planning, insurance, and estate planning, and must pass a difficult exam and adhere to ethical standards.

CFA (Chartered Financial Analyst):

Focused heavily on investment management, a CFA is an excellent choice for doctors with complex portfolios or those interested in asset management. Less focused on holistic planning.

ChFC (Chartered Financial Consultant):

Similar in scope to the CFP, though slightly less recognized. Still a solid credential with broad financial knowledge.

Fiduciary (not a credential, but a standard):

A fiduciary is legally and ethically obligated to act in your best interest at all times. Some advisors act as fiduciaries only part of the time—look for one who is fiduciary 100 percent of the time.

Fee-Only vs. Commission-Based vs. Fee-Based

How an advisor is paid can dramatically influence the quality and objectivity of their advice. Understanding these models is crucial:

Fee-Only:

These advisors are compensated directly by you. They don't earn commissions or incentives for selling products. This structure eliminates many conflicts of interest and encourages advice that aligns with your needs. Fee-only advisors are often fiduciaries.

Commission-Based:

These individuals earn their money by selling financial products like annuities, insurance, or investment funds. While they may offer some guidance, their business is ultimately driven by product sales. Conflicts of interest can be significant.

Fee-Based:

A hybrid of the two. These advisors charge fees and may also earn commissions. While not inherently unethical, fee-based arrangements require scrutiny and clear disclosure.

If you're unsure how someone is paid, ask. A trustworthy advisor will explain their fee structure in writing—clearly and without hesitation.

Essential Questions to Ask a Financial Advisor

Before you hire a planner, ask these questions:

1. Do you specialize in working with physicians or high-income professionals?
2. Your profession brings unique financial challenges and opportunities. Your advisor should understand them.
3. Are you a fiduciary at all times?
4. Don't settle for an answer like "most of the time." You want a clear, unqualified "yes."
5. How do you charge for your services?
6. Ask for specifics—flat fee, percentage of assets under management, hourly rate, or commissions. Transparency is critical.
7. What is your investment philosophy?
8. Do they rely on evidence-based, long-term strategies or promise to beat the market? Their answer should be grounded in research and discipline.
9. Can you walk me through a sample financial plan?
10. This will show you how they approach planning—whether it's comprehensive or simply focused on investing.
11. Do you help with taxes, estate planning, student loans, and insurance?
12. Comprehensive advisors add the most value by addressing your full financial life—not just your portfolio.
13. Where is my money held, and who has custody of the assets?
14. Your funds should always be held at a secure, third-party custodian (like Fidelity or Charles Schwab), not the advisor's firm.

Red Flags to Watch For

Even without a finance degree, you can spot concerning behavior. Be cautious if:

- The advisor is vague or evasive about fees
- They push products early in the relationship (like annuities or life insurance)
- They avoid giving you written documentation
- They are not transparent about whether they are a fiduciary
- They promise guaranteed or unusually high investment returns
- They don't seem to understand the realities of a physician's financial life

You deserve someone who treats your goals with the same care and precision you offer your patients.

When to Change Advisors

Sometimes the advisor you started with is not the advisor you need now. If any of the following apply, it may be time to reevaluate:

- Your financial life has become more complex, but their service hasn't evolved
- You're unclear on what you're paying—or what you're getting in return
- You're not getting proactive advice or ongoing planning
- The advisor focuses on selling products, not solving problems
- They don't seem to listen or understand your long-term goals

An advisor should be your advocate—not just your broker. If the relationship no longer feels like a partnership, it's okay to move on.

Final Thoughts

You wouldn't refer your patients to someone you don't trust or respect. The same standard should apply when choosing your financial guide.

Work with someone who brings clarity, experience, and empathy—not just credentials. Look for professionalism, transparency, and a long-term mindset.

You've trained too hard, worked too long, and built too much to leave your financial future to chance.

Choose wisely. Your peace of mind—and your legacy—depend on it.

Chapter 17: Working With a CPA Who Understands Doctors

Because You Deserve More Than Just a Tax Return

As a physician, your financial life isn't simple. Between W-2 income, 1099 moonlighting gigs, business ownership, student loans, and multi-state licensing, your taxes are more complex than most.

That's why working with a qualified Certified Public Accountant (CPA) who understands doctors is not just helpful—it's essential.

A good CPA isn't just someone who files your taxes. They're a long-term financial ally who helps you **plan, protect, and optimize** your income throughout your entire career.

Key Roles a CPA Plays in a Physician's Financial Life

1. **Tax Filing**
2. At a minimum, your CPA should ensure your federal and state returns are accurate, timely, and compliant. But if that's *all* they're doing, you're not getting your money's worth.
3. **Strategic Tax Planning**
4. Beyond filing, a CPA helps you minimize taxes legally through deductions, credits, timing strategies, and entity structuring (especially for business owners or side hustlers).
5. **Audit Protection**
6. Should you ever be audited by the IRS, a CPA can represent you,

respond to inquiries, and help defend your return. A CPA with experience in physician tax issues can ensure your records are in order and reduce the risk of red flags.

7. **Proactive Advice Throughout the Year**
8. The best CPAs meet with you *before* tax season to recommend strategies—not just after the fact. These may include quarterly tax estimates, deductions related to CME, home offices, equipment, or charitable giving strategies.

Why Your CPA Should Understand Physician-Specific Financial Issues

Your tax professional should understand not just the tax code, but also the **real-life income patterns** and financial decisions that affect doctors.

Topics Your CPA Should Be Familiar With:

- **Income-Based Repayment Plans and PSLF**
- For early-career doctors, your tax return determines your student loan payments. A smart CPA can help manage AGI (adjusted gross income) to lower your payments if you're pursuing forgiveness.
- **Moonlighting and Locums Income (1099)**
- If you earn non-W-2 income, your CPA should help you set up estimated tax payments, track business deductions, and consider whether to form an entity (like an LLC or S-Corp).
- **Business or Practice Income**
- For practice owners, your CPA should advise on business structure, retirement plan options, employee tax considerations, and profit-sharing strategies.
- **Multi-State Licensing and Work**
- Many physicians earn income in more than one state. Your CPA should be experienced in handling **multi-state tax filings**, reciprocal agreements, and residency rules.

- **Retirement Planning Contributions**
- They should coordinate with your financial advisor on pre-tax retirement savings strategies and help time contributions for maximum benefit.
- **Charitable Giving and Donor-Advised Funds**
- Doctors are often philanthropic. Your CPA can guide you on tax-efficient ways to give, especially during high-income years.

Questions to Ask When Hiring a CPA

Before hiring a CPA, make sure they understand your world—not just the tax forms.

1. **Do you specialize in working with physicians or high-income professionals?**
2. Look for someone who's familiar with W-2 and 1099 income, medical practice structures, and common physician deductions.
3. **How do you handle multi-state income or complex returns?**
4. Your return may not be "simple." A CPA with experience in complex tax situations can save you time, money, and stress.
5. **Will you proactively help with tax planning—not just tax preparation?**
6. You want more than a once-a-year meeting. Ask how they help reduce taxes throughout the year.
7. **Can you work alongside my financial advisor, attorney, or practice manager?**
8. Collaboration matters. Your CPA should be part of a team, not a solo act.
9. **How do you charge for your services?**
10. Be clear on fees: flat fee, hourly, or based on complexity. Make sure they provide value throughout the year—not just in March and April.

Tax Planning vs. Tax Preparation: Know the Difference

Many CPAs focus solely on tax **preparation**—historical reporting of what already happened.

But the greatest value comes from **tax planning**—strategies designed to minimize your tax burden *before* the end of the year. That might include:

- Adjusting retirement contributions
- Timing charitable donations
- Harvesting investment losses
- Deferring income
- Entity restructuring
- Managing your adjusted gross income (AGI) for student loans or tax credits

Planning gives you control. Preparation just reports the results.

Final Thoughts

You've spent your career treating complicated cases and working under pressure. Your taxes—and your financial well-being—deserve the same level of care and precision.

A great CPA will not only keep you compliant, but help you stay **strategic, protected, and proactive**.

Find someone who understands your profession, listens to your goals, and integrates with your financial team. Because in medicine and in money, **the right team makes all the difference**.

Chapter 18: Finding a Solid Estate Planning Attorney

Because Planning for the Unexpected Is the Most Responsible Thing You Can Do

Most physicians are used to planning ahead in medicine—but many delay estate planning in their personal lives. For busy professionals, it's easy to assume estate planning is something to tackle "later." The problem is, later isn't guaranteed.

Estate planning isn't about being morbid or assuming the worst. It's about **making sure your life's work—your income, your family, and your intentions—are protected** if something unexpected happens.

Whether you're just starting your career or preparing for retirement, having the right estate planning attorney can give you peace of mind and help you protect what matters most.

Why Every Doctor Needs a Will and Trust—Even Early in Their Career

You don't need millions of dollars or multiple properties to justify an estate plan. You just need a family, assets, or people who depend on you.

As a physician, your financial life often accelerates quickly—high income, student debt, real estate, investment accounts, and life insurance. These assets must be planned for, even early on.

Here's why estate planning matters, even for young doctors:

- If you're married, you need to ensure your spouse is legally protected.
- If you have children, guardianship and financial planning are critical.
- If you own property or have investments, you need to ensure they transfer according to your wishes.
- If you're incapacitated, someone needs legal authority to make decisions on your behalf.
- If you pass away without a plan, your assets are distributed by the **state's laws**—not yours.

Without proper planning, your family may face long probate delays, legal fees, disputes, and unnecessary stress.

How Estate Planning Intersects with Malpractice Risk

Physicians carry a unique kind of exposure—**malpractice liability**. Even with strong malpractice insurance, lawsuits (or threats of lawsuits) can jeopardize your assets.

While estate planning is not a substitute for asset protection, it works hand-in-hand with your overall risk management strategy.

- Trust structures (especially irrevocable trusts) can shield assets in some situations
- Separating personal and professional assets is crucial for high-income earners
- An experienced estate attorney can collaborate with asset protection attorneys and financial planners to protect your wealth from both taxation and litigation

Planning isn't just about **who gets what** when you pass. It's also about **what's protected** while you're alive.

What to Look For in an Estate Planning Attorney

Not all attorneys are created equal. Your estate planning needs to be handled by someone with both the **technical knowledge** and **real-world experience** to serve physicians and their families.

Look for:

1. State-Specific Experience

Estate laws vary widely by state. Choose an attorney licensed and experienced in your primary state of residence (and potentially other states if you own property elsewhere).

2. Familiarity with High-Income or High-Net-Worth Individuals

Doctors often face more complexity than the average household—multiple income streams, real estate holdings, insurance contracts, retirement plans, and family dynamics.

3. A Collaborative Approach

A good estate attorney will work alongside your financial advisor, CPA, and insurance agent to ensure your estate plan coordinates with your overall financial strategy.

4. Comfort with Complexity

Look for attorneys experienced in trusts for minor children, planning for blended families, and tax-efficient wealth transfers.

5. Transparent Fees and Ongoing Support

Estate planning isn't one-and-done. Choose an attorney who offers regular reviews, document updates, and clear fee structures.

Key Documents Every Physician Should Complete

Regardless of age or wealth, every doctor should have these estate documents in place:

1. Last Will and Testament

- Designates who will receive your assets
- Names guardians for your children
- Appoints an executor to carry out your wishes
- Without a will, your estate is subject to state intestacy laws

2. Revocable Living Trust

- Helps avoid probate
- Allows your trustee to manage your assets if you become incapacitated
- Offers privacy (unlike a will, which becomes public record)
- Allows you to control how and when assets are distributed to heirs

3. Durable Power of Attorney (POA)

- Appoints someone to make legal and financial decisions if you're unable to do so
- Ensures bills, taxes, and financial obligations are managed in an emergency

4. Advance Healthcare Directive (Living Will)

- Specifies your medical care preferences if you're unable to communicate
- Includes a healthcare proxy—someone to make medical decisions on your behalf

Special Considerations: Trust Planning for Families

Physician families often require thoughtful planning beyond the basics:

- **Minor Children:** Establish trusts to manage their inheritance, prevent early access to funds, and name a responsible trustee.

- **Disabled Dependents:** Consider a **special needs trust** to preserve government benefits while providing supplemental financial support.
- **Blended Families:** Use trusts and clear instructions to avoid unintended disinheritance or family conflict.
- **Charitable Goals:** Include donor-advised funds, charitable remainder trusts, or bequests in your planning if philanthropy is important to you.

Estate planning isn't just about "having a will." It's about **orchestrating your financial life for when you're no longer able to do it yourself**.

Final Thoughts

You wouldn't treat a patient without a diagnosis. Don't leave your loved ones without direction.

The right estate planning attorney will do more than draft documents. They'll guide you through some of life's most important decisions—with wisdom, sensitivity, and strategic insight.

This isn't just about what happens when you die. It's about protecting your life's work, your loved ones, and your peace of mind.

So plan like a professional. Because your family deserves nothing less.

Chapter 19: When You Need a Business Attorney

Because Smart Contracts and Strong Structures Start With the Right Legal Advice

As a physician, your role may start with clinical care—but for many, it quickly expands. You might join a private practice, start your own, get involved with a joint venture, invest in a startup, or begin speaking and consulting on the side.

Each of these opportunities carries potential—but also legal risk.

This is where a knowledgeable business attorney comes in. The right legal counsel can help you avoid costly mistakes, structure deals appropriately, protect your assets, and ensure your contracts actually reflect your best interests—not just your employer's.

Let's explore when and why doctors need a business attorney, what to look for, and how to ask the right questions.

Key Times to Hire a Business Attorney

You don't need to have a law firm on retainer. But at specific points in your career or business journey, a legal review is not optional—it's essential.

1. Employment Contract Review

Your first attending contract is likely your biggest financial decision to date. A business attorney can break down the fine print: salary, bonuses, benefits, malpractice coverage, non-competes, and termination clauses.

2. Practice Formation

If you're starting or joining a private practice, legal guidance is necessary for entity formation (LLC, PLLC, S-Corp, or C-Corp), operating agreements, and state-specific compliance.

3. Buy-In or Buy-Out Agreements

Joining an existing group or exiting a partnership requires careful analysis of valuation terms, ownership structure, payment timelines, and liability obligations.

4. Advisory Roles or Side Ventures

If you're joining a startup advisory board, investing in a healthcare business, or launching a consulting or speaking business, you'll need help with contracts, intellectual property clauses, and ownership terms.

5. Asset Protection Planning

A business attorney—especially one who works alongside estate planners—can help you structure ownership in a way that separates personal and professional risk.

What to Look For in a Business Attorney

Not every attorney understands the healthcare space. Choose someone with relevant experience who can speak both the language of law and the world of medicine.

Qualities to Prioritize:

- Experience representing **physicians and medical practices**
- Knowledge of **state-specific healthcare laws and corporate practice rules**
- Familiarity with **malpractice coverage**, **hospital systems**, and **non-compete laws**
- Ability to coordinate with your CPA, financial advisor, and insurance team
- Transparent billing and clear turnaround times

Look for someone who sees themselves as part of your **long-term professional team**, not just a one-off transaction.

Questions to Ask When Hiring a Business Attorney

Before engaging legal counsel, ask:

1. **Have you worked with physicians or medical practices before?**
2. You want someone who understands both clinical and business realities in healthcare.
3. **Can you review my employment contract, including non-compete and malpractice terms?**
4. These clauses can impact your career mobility, financial exposure, and insurance protection.
5. **What experience do you have with buy-in/buy-out deals or practice partnerships?**

6. Clarity on valuation, payout terms, and governance structure is critical.
7. **How do you structure asset protection strategies for high-income clients?**
8. Ask whether they collaborate with estate planners and understand liability concerns.
9. **Can you advise on the best business structure for my side ventures?**
10. Whether it's speaking, consulting, or investing, the right legal structure matters—for taxes, liability, and scalability.
11. **What are your fees, and how are they structured?**
12. Flat fee, hourly, or project-based—make sure the agreement is clear.

Incorporation Guidance: LLC, PLLC, S-Corp, C-Corp

Choosing the right business entity isn't just about taxes—it's about liability, licensing, and long-term scalability.

A business attorney can help you understand:

- Whether your state requires a **PLLC** (Professional LLC) for licensed medical work
- When a **Sole Proprietorship** is too risky
- If a **S-Corp** is the right structure to reduce self-employment tax
- How a **C-Corp** might be appropriate for larger ventures or those seeking investors
- What you need to legally separate your business and personal assets

Don't guess your way through this process—get the structure right from day one.

Legal Structure for Side Ventures

More physicians than ever are building income outside the hospital or clinic. Whether you're:

- Teaching or speaking
- Building an online course
- Consulting with health tech firms
- Creating medical content
- Investing in healthcare startups

You need a legal structure that protects your intellectual property, separates your liabilities, and supports tax efficiency.

An attorney can help you set up an LLC or S-Corp, review contracts, ensure you're complying with state licensing, and protect any branding or content you create.

Even side gigs can carry legal and financial exposure—don't overlook the fine print.

Final Thoughts

As a physician, your name, your license, and your reputation are among your most valuable assets. Don't put them at risk by signing documents you don't fully understand or entering business relationships without proper legal review.

A business attorney isn't just a formality. They're a strategic advisor who helps you:

- Structure your opportunities
- Limit your liabilities
- Negotiate smarter
- Protect your future

Think of them the way you think of a specialist: someone with deep expertise, a specific role, and critical value at key moments.

Because in medicine and in business, knowing when to consult the right expert is a sign of strength—not weakness.

Chapter 20: Asset Protection Strategies

Because Protecting What You've Built Is Just as Important as Building It

As a physician, your high income, professional status, and visibility can make you a target—not just for malpractice claims, but also for lawsuits stemming from everyday life. Whether it's a car accident, rental property issue, or a business dispute, the reality is this:

The more you earn, the more you have to protect.

Asset protection isn't about secrecy or dodging legitimate claims. It's about putting legal structures and risk management strategies in place **before** something happens—so you can shield your hard-earned assets from unnecessary exposure.

This chapter walks you through the fundamentals of protecting both your personal and professional wealth.

Why Physicians Are Common Lawsuit Targets

Even with malpractice insurance, doctors remain attractive legal targets for several reasons:

- **Perceived deep pockets:** Plaintiffs and attorneys often assume doctors have significant assets or income.
- **High-visibility roles:** Your name, credentials, and public presence raise your profile.
- **Multiple income streams:** Real estate, side businesses, or investment activity add complexity and potential liability.

- **Professional liability crossover:** Not all legal threats are clinical. You can also be sued for business disputes, employment issues, auto accidents, or tenant injuries on your property.

Asset protection is about creating **legal separation** and **layered defenses** that make it harder for a creditor, claimant, or opportunist to access your personal wealth.

Titling Property Properly: Tenants by the Entirety and Trusts

How you **own** assets matters just as much as what you own.

Tenants by the Entirety (TBE)

This is a special form of joint ownership available to married couples in many states. When property is titled this way:

- Both spouses own the property equally
- Creditors of only one spouse **cannot seize** the asset
- It's particularly useful for protecting a family home from personal liability

Check your state laws to see if TBE applies to real estate, bank accounts, or other property—and ensure titles are correctly recorded.

Revocable and Irrevocable Trusts

- A **revocable living trust** offers probate avoidance and privacy but does not protect assets from creditors during your lifetime.
- An **irrevocable trust** removes assets from your estate and can offer protection—but you lose control over the asset.
- For high-risk professionals, trusts can play a role in long-term protection, estate planning, and Medicaid eligibility—but require legal

guidance.

Using Umbrella Insurance and LLCs for Added Protection

Umbrella Insurance

This is one of the simplest and most cost-effective asset protection tools available.

- It provides **additional liability coverage** above and beyond your home and auto policies.
- A $1–5 million policy typically costs only a few hundred dollars a year.
- Covers legal claims like personal injury, property damage, slander, and some landlord liability.

Think of it as your financial firewall.

LLCs for Real Estate and Side Businesses

If you own rental property or earn income through a side venture (consulting, speaking, telemedicine), consider creating a **Limited Liability Company (LLC)** to hold the asset or operate the business.

Benefits include:

- **Legal separation** from your personal finances
- Protection from tenant or business-related lawsuits
- Ability to partner with others or bring in investors more cleanly
- Potential tax benefits (when paired with the right structure, such as an S-Corp election)

Proper formation, documentation, and separate accounting are essential—so don't DIY this without legal and tax guidance.

Homestead Exemptions and State-Specific Protections

Every state has its own set of **homestead laws** that can protect a portion—or in some states, all—of your primary residence's value from creditors.

For example:

- Florida and Texas offer **unlimited** homestead protection (with conditions)
- Other states protect only a fixed dollar amount (e.g., $125,000 or less)
- Homestead rules may not apply if the home is placed in a trust or LLC

Understanding your state's laws helps you decide how to title your property, whether to invest in home equity, and what risks still remain.

Other state-specific protections may include:

- Retirement account exemptions
- Life insurance and annuity protections
- Tenancy protections for jointly held assets

This is where working with a **state-licensed estate planning or asset protection attorney** becomes essential. Generic advice can backfire if it doesn't align with your local law.

Keeping Personal and Professional Finances Separate

Many physicians blur the lines between business and personal finances, especially when owning a small practice or multiple income streams. This can erode legal protection.

Basic but essential practices include:

- Never mix personal and business bank accounts
- Maintain formal accounting records for any LLC or business venture
- Avoid personal guarantees if possible when signing contracts

- Use proper insurance for each entity (malpractice, E&O, general liability, business property)
- Consult with your attorney before moving assets between personal and business accounts

The more you treat your finances like a professional enterprise, the more protection you gain.

Final Thoughts: Protect First, Don't React Later

You spent years becoming a doctor, building your career, and accumulating wealth. Don't lose it—or jeopardize it—because of preventable legal risks.

Asset protection isn't about hiding money. It's about **structuring your life so that your success is resilient**—no matter what happens.

The right time to put these protections in place is **before** you need them.

Because in medicine and money, proactive planning is always better than emergency treatment.

Chapter 21: Financial Considerations for Dual-Physician Households

When Two High-Income Careers Collide: The Power—and Pressure—of Planning Together

When both partners in a household are physicians, the opportunities for financial growth are substantial—but so are the complexities. Dual-physician couples often face a fast-paced lifestyle, high earning potential, and significant financial decisions that require careful coordination.

You're not just navigating two incomes. You're balancing **two careers, two sets of student loans, two retirement paths**, and often the needs of a growing family.

Done right, your financial potential is tremendous. But without a unified plan, high income can lead to high stress, inefficiency, and even unintentional tax penalties.

This chapter helps you plan as a team—with clarity, coordination, and confidence.

Coordinating Retirement Contributions

With two sets of workplace benefits, dual-physician couples have **double the opportunity** to build long-term wealth through retirement savings. The key is to **maximize contributions without overlap** and take advantage of all available options.

Strategies to Consider:

- Contribute to both 403(b) or 401(k) plans—each spouse can contribute up to the IRS limit ($23,000 in 2025, plus catch-up contributions if age 50+)
- If one or both of you have access to **457(b) plans**, that's an additional bucket of tax-deferred savings
- Don't neglect **Roth IRAs or backdoor Roth contributions**—these can add tax diversification
- Coordinate **Health Savings Account (HSA)** contributions if eligible through a high-deductible health plan
- For any moonlighting or side income, consider **Solo 401(k) or SEP IRA** plans

The goal is to **diversify both accounts and tax treatment**—so your future withdrawal strategy is flexible.

Tax Bracket Planning and Managing the "Marriage Penalty"

In a dual-physician household, both incomes combined can easily push you into the **highest federal tax brackets**. This triggers what's commonly referred to as the "**marriage penalty**"—when two high earners pay more together than they would separately.

Ways to Reduce Your Tax Burden:

- Maximize **pre-tax retirement contributions** to lower taxable income
- Consider **filing separately** in rare cases (if one spouse is pursuing Public Service Loan Forgiveness, for example), though this can limit deductions
- Invest in **tax-efficient vehicles**—such as municipal bonds, Roth accounts, or real estate with depreciation advantages
- Use **Donor-Advised Funds (DAFs)** or bunch charitable giving into

high-income years
- Consider income splitting strategies, like **real estate or business ownership**, where one spouse may take the lead operationally

Consulting with a CPA who specializes in high-income households is essential to develop a customized tax mitigation plan.

Insurance Duplication vs. Coordination

Dual-physician couples often duplicate coverage unintentionally—especially with employer benefits. This can lead to wasted premiums or gaps in protection.

Steps to Optimize Insurance Coverage:

- Review both **health insurance plans** annually. Choose the better plan or evaluate whether one is better for dependents and the other for the couple.
- Coordinate **life insurance**: If both partners are working, each should carry sufficient coverage to replace income. If you have children, don't overlook stay-at-home or part-time spouses.
- Evaluate **disability insurance** for both partners, making sure each policy has "own-occupation" definitions.
- Consider a shared **umbrella policy** for liability protection across personal and professional risks.
- Avoid overlapping premiums where coverage is redundant—focus on comprehensive, cost-effective coordination.

Student Loan Strategies for Two High-Income Earners

When both partners carry student loans, planning becomes more nuanced—especially if pursuing forgiveness or trying to minimize interest.

Key Considerations:

- If either spouse is pursuing **Public Service Loan Forgiveness (PSLF)**, filing taxes separately might reduce their income-based payments—but must be weighed against higher tax costs.
- If not pursuing forgiveness, consider refinancing both loans **individually** to secure the best rates and terms.
- Use **aggressive payoff strategies** based on your interest rates, savings goals, and timeline for children or home purchases.
- Some couples choose to **focus on one loan at a time** (debt snowball or avalanche approach), while others split payments evenly.
- Ensure both partners are on the **same repayment philosophy**—aggressive payoff vs. strategic minimums with investing.

Debt doesn't need to be emotional—just strategic. Tackle it as a team with a plan you both believe in.

Planning for Children's Education

With two strong incomes, dual-physician couples are well-positioned to **start early and fund generously** when it comes to their children's future education.

Tools to Use:

- **529 College Savings Plans:**
- Tax-free growth and withdrawals for qualified education expenses
- Many states offer tax deductions or credits for contributions
- One parent can own the plan, or both can contribute to multiple beneficiaries
- Consider front-loading contributions for compounding growth
- **Trusts for Education or Support:**
- Establish an **Irrevocable Trust** to earmark funds for education or

legacy purposes

- Useful for estate planning and creating financial guardrails for future generations
- **Custodial Accounts (UTMA/UGMA):**
- Allow gifts to minors but offer less control than 529s or trusts
- These count as the child's asset for financial aid purposes and may be best for smaller, flexible gifts

Educational planning isn't just about saving—it's about aligning **values, goals, and long-term family vision**.

Final Thoughts

A dual-physician household comes with immense financial opportunity—but also requires coordination, intentionality, and partnership.

Together, you can:

- Build long-term wealth faster
- Manage taxes more effectively
- Protect each other and your family from risk
- Align on goals for your children and legacy
- Make decisions that reflect your shared vision—not just your bank account

With the right strategy, dual-income doesn't mean double complexity—it means **double the power to build a secure, meaningful financial future.**

Plan together. Grow together. Win together.

Chapter 22: Navigating Practice Ownership or Partnership

From Employee to Equity: What Every Physician Should Know Before Taking a Seat at the Table

For many physicians, becoming a partner in a medical practice is a career milestone. It's a sign of professional recognition—and a path to building long-term wealth, influence, and autonomy in your work.

But practice ownership or partnership also comes with risks, responsibilities, and a steep learning curve. From understanding the true cost of a buy-in to planning your eventual exit, it's essential to enter this phase with your eyes wide open.

This chapter breaks down the key financial and legal considerations for physicians transitioning into ownership or partnership roles—so you can make informed decisions and maximize the opportunity.

Buy-In Costs, Timelines, and Contract Review

Joining a practice as a partner usually requires a **buy-in**—your financial contribution to "purchase" your share of the business. This amount can vary widely based on practice structure, valuation, and expected revenue.

What to Know:

- **Typical buy-in costs** range from $50,000 to $500,000+, depending on the size, location, and profitability of the practice.
- The **timeline** may include a probationary or associate period (e.g., 1–3 years) before partnership eligibility.
- Buy-in may be paid **upfront or financed** over time, with or without interest.
- Some practices offer **sweat equity**, where a portion of the buy-in is earned over time through performance or seniority.

What to Review in Your Partnership Agreement:

- How buy-in amounts are calculated
- Voting rights and decision-making powers
- Ownership percentage and how it can change
- Responsibilities and call coverage expectations
- What happens in the event of disability, retirement, or dispute

Work with a healthcare attorney to **review all contracts** before signing. This is not a DIY process—these documents will govern your income, responsibilities, and legal exposure for years.

Practice Valuation: What It's Worth and How It's Calculated

Before you buy in, you need to know what you're actually buying.

How Practices Are Valued:

1. **Asset-Based Approach:**
2. Calculates the value of tangible assets (equipment, furniture, supplies) minus liabilities.
3. **Income-Based Approach:**

4. Based on the practice's historical and projected cash flow, adjusted for risk.
5. **Market-Based Approach:**
6. Compares the practice to others recently sold in the same specialty and region.

Most buy-in agreements are based on a **blended valuation**, sometimes including goodwill (the intangible value of the patient base and reputation). Make sure the valuation:

- Is recent (within 12 months)
- Is performed by an independent third party
- Includes a breakdown of assets, liabilities, and methodology

Understanding the valuation helps ensure you don't **overpay** or **undervalue your own stake** if you're already in the group.

Profit-Sharing, Distributions, and Cash Flow

As a partner, your income may come from **multiple sources**:

- **Base salary or productivity-based compensation** (e.g., wRVUs)
- **Profit-sharing** based on ownership percentage
- **Distributions** of retained earnings
- **Bonuses** tied to performance or group revenue

Before buying in, understand:

- How and when profits are distributed
- Who makes financial decisions (and how often distributions occur)
- Whether cash flow is stable and predictable
- How overhead and shared expenses are allocated among partners

Ask to review **at least 3 years of financials**, including profit/loss statements, partner distributions, and accounts receivable.

If your compensation relies on group performance, make sure the **group is healthy and transparent** with its finances.

Exit Planning and Timelines for Leaving a Group

It may feel early to think about leaving—but a smart partner asks what happens at the **end** before entering at the beginning.

Questions to Clarify:

- What is the **buy-out** formula if I leave or retire?
- Is the value of my ownership protected if I become disabled?
- Are there **vesting requirements** (i.e., must I stay a certain number of years to receive full value)?
- Can I sell my share to another physician—or does the group buy it back?
- What happens if a partner is terminated or voluntarily exits?

A clear exit strategy protects your investment—and reduces the risk of costly disputes down the road.

Succession Planning and Retaining Top Associates

If you're already an owner, planning for the next generation of partners is just as important as managing current operations.

Key Steps for Succession:

- Identify talented associates early and be transparent about the path to partnership
- Offer mentorship, leadership training, and financial education to

groom future owners
- Regularly revisit the practice's valuation and buy-in terms to reflect market realities
- Balance fairness with affordability—buy-ins should be attainable, but not undervalued

Retaining High-Performing Physicians:

- Create incentives for long-term commitment, such as profit-sharing, performance bonuses, or deferred compensation
- Make sure your culture supports work-life balance, fairness, and shared decision-making
- Consider creative structures (e.g., phased buy-ins or part-time partnership models) to retain flexibility

A successful partnership is a **blend of financial equity and shared purpose**. When both are present, your practice can thrive for decades.

Final Thoughts

Owning part of a practice is a big leap—but for many physicians, it's one of the most rewarding and profitable decisions of their career.

Just make sure you do your due diligence:

- Understand what you're buying—and what it's really worth
- Negotiate with your head, not just your heart
- Protect your investment with clear contracts and professional guidance
- Build systems that serve both patients and partners
- Start planning for your exit, even as you enter

Because when done right, practice ownership isn't just a job—it's a legacy.

Chapter 23: Real Estate Decisions for Physicians

Balancing Lifestyle, Location, and Long-Term Wealth

For physicians, real estate is often one of the biggest financial decisions—personally and professionally. Whether it's buying your first home, relocating for a new position, or investing in rental properties, your choices can have long-term consequences for your cash flow, taxes, and lifestyle.

This chapter helps you think through the key real estate decisions you'll face at various stages of your career, and how to make those choices strategically—not emotionally.

Should I Buy a Home During Residency or Wait?

It's tempting. You're starting your career, interest rates might be low, and you want to "stop throwing money away on rent." But buying a home during residency often brings more risk than reward.

Considerations Before Buying:

- **Length of Training:** If your program is less than five years and you'll need to relocate, you may not have time to build equity before selling.
- **Market Volatility:** If the local market declines, you could lose money on a sale—or worse, be unable to sell at all.

- **Time and Bandwidth:** Homeownership comes with responsibilities—maintenance, repairs, property taxes—that can be stressful during intense training.
- **Financing:** Physician mortgage programs exist, but without significant savings or job security, they can stretch your finances.

Unless you're confident you'll stay in the area for several years **after** residency and the market is stable, renting is usually the safer choice.

Rent or Buy When Relocating for a New Position?

When you move for a new attending job, the question of renting vs. buying becomes more nuanced.

Rent First If:

- You're unsure how long you'll stay
- You want time to explore neighborhoods
- Your new job is probationary or your specialty has high burnout risk
- You have debt or financial goals that would be delayed by a down payment

Consider Buying If:

- You plan to stay for at least 5–7 years
- The local real estate market is stable or appreciating
- Your job is secure, and your income supports the mortgage
- You've saved for a down payment, closing costs, and an emergency fund

Buying a home can be a strong long-term wealth strategy—but only if it doesn't compromise your flexibility or strain your finances early in your career.

Vacation Properties and Investment Rentals

Once your income stabilizes, you may consider buying real estate beyond your primary residence. This could include:

Vacation Properties

- Pros: Enjoyment, potential appreciation, rental income when not in use
- Cons: High upfront costs, ongoing maintenance, difficulty managing from afar
- Tip: Don't buy a vacation home purely for investment. Make sure you'll use and enjoy it first.

Investment Rentals

- Pros: Cash flow, tax deductions, long-term equity, diversification
- Cons: Property management, tenant risk, liquidity issues
- Tip: Consider starting with a single-family home in a market you know. Hire a property manager if you're busy or out-of-state.

Remember that real estate is **not truly passive**—even with help, it requires attention and planning.

Risks of Being "House Poor" in a High-Cost-of-Living Area

Physicians living in major cities often face a painful trade-off: owning a home vs. maintaining financial flexibility.

You are "house poor" if:

- A large portion of your income goes to housing costs (mortgage, taxes, insurance, maintenance)
- You delay or underfund retirement savings or student loan repayment

- You feel financially stuck or unable to pursue other goals due to your mortgage

How to Avoid It:

- Keep total housing costs under 28–30% of gross monthly income
- Avoid buying at the top of your approved mortgage range
- Consider more affordable neighborhoods or renting to free up cash flow
- Don't sacrifice liquidity—keep a strong emergency fund even after closing

Owning a home should support your life—not strain it. Focus on long-term comfort, not short-term status.

Tax Deductions, Depreciation, and Passive Income from Rentals

Owning real estate offers several tax advantages, especially when used for business or investment purposes.

Key Tax Benefits:

- **Mortgage Interest Deduction:** For your primary home, up to certain limits
- **Depreciation:** For rental properties, this allows you to deduct a portion of the property's value each year (even if the property is appreciating)
- **Operating Expenses:** Property management, repairs, insurance, and travel to your rental property may be deductible
- **1031 Exchange:** Allows you to defer capital gains tax when selling one investment property and buying another
- **Qualified Business Income (QBI):** Certain rental activities may

qualify for a 20% deduction on net rental income under Section 199A

Work with a tax advisor who understands real estate investing to structure your holdings for **maximum efficiency and compliance**.

Final Thoughts

For physicians, real estate can be both a home and a financial tool—but only if approached with planning and perspective.

Ask yourself:

- Does this property support my lifestyle and financial goals?
- Am I buying for emotional reasons—or strategic ones?
- What's the opportunity cost of this down payment?
- Can I afford this *and* continue saving, investing, and enjoying life?

There's no one-size-fits-all answer to real estate. But the right decision is the one that balances security, flexibility, and long-term impact.

Buy when you're ready—not just when you're approved.

Chapter 24: Wealth Preservation and Charitable Planning

As your medical career matures and your financial capacity expands, your mindset begins to shift. What started as a focus on student loan repayment and building net worth evolves into a deeper desire for stewardship: to protect what you've built, to give back, and to ensure that your legacy reflects your values—not just your income. Physicians are often natural givers. You've spent your professional life improving the lives of others—patients, families, students, communities. Now, with intentionality and structure, you can direct your financial resources to extend that impact far beyond your working years.

This expanded chapter provides a comprehensive guide for physicians seeking to align their financial plans with their charitable goals, multigenerational legacy, and wealth preservation strategies. It covers giving structures, tax-efficient gifting to heirs, generational planning tools, and how to embed philanthropy into your overall financial strategy without compromising your own security.

Section I: Giving With Strategy – From Spontaneity to Structure

Why Structured Giving Matters

Unstructured charitable giving—sporadic donations, emotional giving, or holiday generosity—may feel fulfilling in the short term, but it lacks the strategic advantage that high-income earners like physicians need. When your giving is structured and aligned with your financial plan, it can:

- Maximize tax benefits
- Extend the impact of every dollar
- Reduce estate size for tax purposes
- Support your values and community more effectively

Think of structured giving as clinical care. Diagnosis comes first (your values, goals, capacity), followed by treatment (financial strategies and tools), and then monitoring and follow-up (ongoing planning and adjustments).

The Giving Spectrum

Here's a simplified framework to think about charitable strategies by stage:

Stage	Common Action	Strategic Opportunity
Early Career	Small, spontaneous donations	Open a donor-advised fund (DAF) to start long-term giving habits
Mid-Career	Giving appreciated stock or event support	Explore charitable remainder trusts (CRTs) or legacy planning
Peak Earning Years	Giving to alma maters, hospitals, missions	Maximize DAF contributions and estate tax planning
Late Career	Larger bequests, legacy building	Establish a foundation or GST trust for multi-gen impact

Section II: Charitable Giving Vehicles for 2025 and Beyond

1. Donor-Advised Funds (DAFs)

A DAF is a tax-advantaged charitable giving account that allows you to:

- Make a charitable contribution in a high-income year and receive an immediate tax deduction.
- Let the assets grow tax-free.
- Recommend grants to IRS-approved charities over time.

Why DAFs are great for physicians:

- You retain flexibility—you don't have to decide immediately where your money will go.
- They are simple to set up and maintain.
- They allow you to gift appreciated securities without triggering capital gains.

Example: In 2025, Dr. Chen sells her private practice and receives a large payout. She deposits $250,000 into a DAF, receives a full deduction for that year, and can then distribute grants to her chosen nonprofits over the next decade.

2025 Updates:

- The annual deduction limit remains 60% of AGI for cash gifts and 30% for appreciated securities.
- DAF sponsors are now required to file more detailed annual activity reports, which increases transparency.

2. Charitable Remainder Trusts (CRTs)

A CRT allows you to donate assets (especially highly appreciated ones like real estate or stock), defer capital gains, and generate income for yourself or a beneficiary before the remainder goes to charity.

Why CRTs work well for physicians:

- Convert low-yield or highly appreciated assets into lifetime income.
- Receive an immediate charitable deduction.
- Reduce estate size and associated estate taxes.

Types of CRTs:

- **CRAT (Annuity Trust):** Pays a fixed dollar amount each year.
- **CRUT (Unitrust):** Pays a fixed percentage of the trust's assets, revalued annually.

Example: Dr. Martinez donates $1 million in highly appreciated tech stock to a CRUT. She avoids $250,000 in capital gains tax, receives annual income, and eventually donates the remainder to a rural health clinic.

3. Private Foundations

Private foundations provide complete control over the structure, mission, and investment of your charitable dollars—but with increased complexity.

Best for:

- Physicians with estates over $10–20 million.
- Families looking to create a legacy of giving.
- Those who want to fund scholarships, clinics, or international missions.

Key Requirements:

- Must distribute at least 5% of assets annually.
- Must file IRS Form 990-PF annually.
- Subject to excise tax and self-dealing restrictions.

Example: Drs. Reed and Silva form a family foundation focused on pediatric oncology. They employ their children part-time, fund international care partnerships, and educate the next generation about philanthropy and accountability.

Section III: Gifting to Heirs – 2025 Tax Rules and Lifetime Planning

Annual Gift Tax Exclusion – 2025 Update

- In 2025, individuals can gift **$19,000 per recipient** annually without incurring gift tax or using any of their lifetime exemption.
- Married couples can **jointly gift $38,000** per recipient per year.

Eligible Gifts Include:

- Cash
- Stocks or mutual funds
- Real estate interests
- Paying tuition or medical expenses directly to the provider (exempt from limits)

Lifetime Gift and Estate Tax Exemption – 2025 Update

- The federal lifetime exemption for 2025 is **$13.61 million per individual** or **$27.22 million for married couples**.
- Gifts exceeding the annual exclusion reduce this lifetime limit.
- Unused exemptions pass tax-free to heirs at death (unless sunset provisions reduce limits after 2025).

Strategy Tip: Use annual gifting to gradually transfer wealth while reducing the size of your taxable estate. Consider funding Roth IRAs for children or gifting interests in real estate or business entities.

Reporting:

- File **IRS Form 709** for gifts exceeding the annual exclusion.

- Work with a CPA to track lifetime exemption usage across years and trust structures.

Section IV: Multi-Generational Wealth – Planning With the Next Generation in Mind

As your estate grows, so does your responsibility to consider how that wealth will serve—not burden—future generations. The goal is not just transfer, but thoughtful stewardship. Physicians who've worked hard to accumulate wealth often want to pass on not only assets but values, vision, and financial knowledge.

Generation-Skipping Trusts (GSTs)

A **Generation-Skipping Trust** allows you to transfer wealth to grandchildren or other beneficiaries at least two generations below you, bypassing your children's estate and avoiding double taxation.

Benefits:

- Skips a generation for estate tax purposes.
- Assets grow and are protected from creditors, divorce, or mismanagement.
- You can apply your GST exemption (equal to the lifetime exemption—$13.61M in 2025).

Example: Dr. Samuels creates a GST for each grandchild. The assets are invested and grow tax-deferred, with distributions restricted to education, first homes, or emergencies. The trust bypasses the children's estates and avoids estate tax twice.

Education Trusts

Set up a trust specifically for your descendants' education expenses:

- Helps prevent misuse of funds.
- Keeps control over timing and purpose of distributions.
- Can be combined with 529 plans for maximum tax benefit.

Strategy Tip: Pair an education trust with annual gifting or direct tuition payments for a multi-tiered approach to legacy planning.

Section V: Family Governance – Teaching Stewardship and Purpose

Wealth that lasts beyond one generation requires more than financial planning—it requires education, communication, and values. Family governance is the system by which families with wealth engage the next generation and align decisions with shared goals.

Establish a Family Giving Mission

Clarify your shared values:

- What issues or causes matter most?
- What role do you want your children or grandchildren to play in giving?
- Should giving be tied to family meetings, votes, or joint projects?

Create a mission statement and review it annually.

Hold Family Financial Education Meetings

Teach:

- The basics of investing
- How to read a financial statement
- The history and purpose of your family's wealth
- How to vet a charity or review a grant proposal

Bring in outside educators if needed—your CPA, estate planner, or financial advisor can be part of this team.

Use Philanthropy as a Teaching Tool

By involving your children in giving, you:

- Teach budgeting and values simultaneously

- Encourage a long-term mindset
- Reduce entitlement and increase purpose

Example: The Kapoor family hosts an annual "impact retreat" where each family member presents a grant recommendation. The selected charities receive funding through the family's DAF.

Section VI: Family Limited Partnerships (FLPs) and LLCs

For high-net-worth families, **Family Limited Partnerships (FLPs)** or **Family LLCs** offer a method for consolidating assets, reducing estate value, and teaching financial responsibility through ownership.

Key Benefits:

- Allow gifting of non-controlling interests at discounted valuations
- Consolidate management of real estate, investment portfolios, or business shares
- Provide asset protection from creditors or divorces
- Encourage financial literacy and accountability among family members

Example: Dr. Nguyen contributes $3M in rental properties to an LLC. Over time, she gifts 1% interests to her children and grandchildren, reducing her estate while introducing them to property management and cash flow planning.

Important: Work with legal counsel to ensure compliance with IRS valuation and operating agreement rules.

Section VII: Real Estate, Practice Equity, and Other Legacy Assets

Physicians often hold concentrated wealth in real estate or their medical practice. Proper planning ensures these assets are not just preserved, but passed on tax-efficiently and intentionally.

Transferring Real Estate

- Use LLCs to transfer interests gradually.
- Use stepped-up basis rules at death to minimize capital gains.
- Consider charitable strategies like retained life estates or partial interest gifts.

Practice Sale or Transition

If you're selling or passing on your practice:

- Structure the deal to minimize taxes (installment sale, CRT, or qualified opportunity zones).
- Build succession into your estate plan if gifting to children or partners.

Intellectual Property or Royalties

If you've authored books, invented devices, or hold patents:

- Assign rights to trusts or family LLCs
- Separate income from control
- Clarify inheritance terms in estate documents

Section VIII: Final Words on Purposeful Legacy Planning

Wealth, when built through years of patient care and sacrifice, should serve something greater than accumulation. As a physician, you understand better than most the value of a life well spent—of helping others, of showing up when it matters, of healing.

Your legacy isn't just the money you leave behind—it's the values, education, habits, and opportunities you set in motion.

By aligning your financial plan with your values and charitable intent, you build a legacy that endures through:

- Structure
- Intentionality
- Education
- Generational stewardship

Your tools are here: donor-advised funds, trusts, gifting strategies, governance systems, and purposeful planning.

Your impact is waiting.

Let your legacy heal, lift, educate, and empower—just as you've done throughout your career.

Part 3: The Doctor Life – Protecting and Growing Your Wealth

Part 3: The Doctor Life – Protecting and Growing Your Wealth

By now, you're established in your career.

You've gone from surviving on resident paychecks to earning real income. You've probably paid down some debt, built a bit of savings, and maybe even started investing. You're no longer "just getting started"—you're in the middle of your journey. And for many doctors, **this is the most financially powerful chapter of your life.**

You're in your peak earning years.

And that's exactly why **this is the time to get intentional about protecting and growing your wealth.**

Because here's the truth:

High income doesn't automatically lead to long-term wealth.

In fact, many physicians spend decades earning well—and still retire stressed, overworked, or unsure if they've done enough to secure their future.

Why?

Because they didn't take the steps to **protect what they built**, or didn't know how to **grow it intentionally.**

You've worked too hard to leave your future to chance.

This part of the book is about making sure the wealth you're earning **lasts**, and the lifestyle you're living **doesn't come at the cost** of the life you want later.

The Goal of Part 3:

To help you make smarter decisions in the years where your money has the most potential—to not only support your present, but fund your freedom, retirement, and legacy.

In This Section, You'll Learn:

- How to evaluate and optimize your investment strategy
- Why asset protection (insurance, trusts, legal planning) matters for high earners
- The role of disability, malpractice, life, and umbrella insurance
- How to prepare for career shifts, burnout, or a desire to slow down
- Why estate planning isn't just for the ultra-wealthy—and how to start
- How to keep your lifestyle aligned with your long-term goals
- How to identify opportunities for passive income or practice ownership
- How to work with a team of professionals (financial advisor, CPA, attorney) to keep your plan on track

This is where you shift from playing financial defense to running a strong offense.

You're not just protecting income—you're building wealth.

You're not just covering your bases—you're preparing for **choice, freedom, and options**.

Whether you want to retire early, start a business, leave a legacy, or just stop working weekends, **this is the chapter that helps you make it real.**

You've earned the income.

Now let's make sure it builds the future you've always imagined.

Chapter 25: Taking Care of Your Spouse and Family

Financial Literacy Is a Family Skill—Not Just a Personal One

You've worked hard to build a strong financial foundation. But financial security isn't truly complete unless your loved ones are protected and empowered—especially your spouse or life partner.

Whether you're the "money person" in the relationship or not, financial planning should be a **shared responsibility**. Because life is unpredictable. And when the unexpected happens—disability, death, job changes, or health issues—clarity and preparation can mean the difference between peace and panic.

This chapter walks through the essential steps every physician should take to **protect, educate, and equip their family**—both for today and for whatever the future holds.

Financial Literacy for Your Partner—Even If They're Not the 'Money Person'

In many households, one person handles most of the day-to-day finances. But if that person is suddenly unavailable—due to illness, incapacity, or worse—the spouse can be left in an unfamiliar and overwhelming situation.

The goal isn't for both partners to become financial experts. It's to ensure **both partners understand the basics**, can access critical accounts, and know where to turn for help.

Start With These Key Conversations:

- Where are our financial accounts located, and how do we access them?
- What are our monthly and annual expenses?
- What insurance do we have (life, disability, umbrella, etc.)?
- Who are our key financial professionals (advisor, CPA, attorney)?
- What's our general plan for retirement, debt, savings, and education funding?

Financial literacy is a form of **love and leadership**. Helping your spouse feel confident about your shared financial life is one of the most important gifts you can give.

Updating Beneficiaries on Accounts Regularly

Too many families discover too late that a retirement account, insurance policy, or investment account has **an outdated or missing beneficiary designation**.

Beneficiary forms often supersede what's written in your will—meaning they determine who gets what, and how quickly.

What to Check Annually:

- 401(k), 403(b), or 457(b) retirement plans
- Roth and Traditional IRAs
- Life insurance policies
- Health Savings Accounts (HSAs)
- Brokerage and investment accounts with transfer-on-death (TOD) instructions
- Pension or annuity plans

Make sure beneficiaries reflect your current wishes—especially after major life events like marriage, divorce, birth of a child, or death of a relative.

Coordinating Social Security Strategies

While it may seem far off, **how and when you and your spouse claim Social Security** can impact your long-term income—especially if one of you earns more, retires earlier, or expects a shorter lifespan.

Key Considerations:

- Delaying benefits until age 70 increases monthly payments significantly
- Spousal benefits allow a lower-earning spouse to receive up to 50% of the other's benefit
- Survivor benefits can provide income to a widow or widower for life
- Coordinating when and how each of you claims benefits is essential to **maximizing lifetime income**

A good financial planner can model multiple claiming strategies based on your career timeline, age difference, and health history.

Creating a "Financial Playbook" in Case of Death or Disability

Imagine your spouse or children having to figure out your finances during a crisis. That's why every family should have a **financial playbook**—a simple, written guide to your financial life.

Your Financial Playbook Should Include:

- A list of all bank, retirement, and investment accounts
- Contact information for your financial advisor, CPA, and estate attorney
- Copies or locations of insurance policies and estate planning documents
- Debt obligations and monthly payment responsibilities
- Login credentials or directions to secure storage of passwords

- Location of your will, trust documents, healthcare proxy, and power of attorney
- Emergency contact instructions for each financial provider

This document doesn't need to be complicated—but it should be **easy to find, easy to follow, and reviewed annually**.

Holding Annual Family Financial Meetings

One of the best ways to build long-term confidence and trust in your family is to **normalize talking about money**.

An annual family financial meeting gives you a chance to:

- Review goals, budgets, and big decisions
- Update on new accounts, changes in insurance, or professional contacts
- Clarify roles and expectations—who handles what, and who to call for help
- Involve children in age-appropriate financial conversations (budgeting, saving, generosity, etc.)

This doesn't need to be formal. It can be as simple as an annual dinner or weekend check-in. What matters most is the habit of **shared awareness and open dialogue**.

Final Thoughts

You've likely spent years protecting your patients. Now it's time to apply that same care and foresight to **the people you love most**.

Financial literacy for your family isn't about spreadsheets or investments—it's about **communication, security, and peace of mind**. When something goes wrong (and eventually, it will), your family deserves to have the tools and clarity to carry on.

Because at the end of the day, your greatest legacy won't be your income—

it will be your intentionality.

Take care of them. Teach them. Empower them.

They're your team. Make sure they're ready for every quarter—especially the unexpected ones.

Chapter 26: Physician Burnout and Its Financial Impact

When Your Well-Being Suffers, So Does Your Wealth

Burnout is no longer an occasional experience—it's a systemic issue across healthcare. Long hours, bureaucratic overload, moral injury, EMR fatigue, and the weight of caring for others under constant pressure take a cumulative toll.

For physicians, burnout isn't just emotional—it's financial.

Whether it's reducing clinical hours, switching careers, taking an unpaid leave, or stepping away altogether, the downstream impact of burnout often affects your income, your investments, your insurance, and your long-term goals.

This chapter isn't just about prevention. It's about **understanding the real cost of burnout—and designing a financial strategy that gives you options, dignity, and recovery when you need it most.**

The Hidden Financial Costs of Burnout

Burnout doesn't show up on your credit card statement. But its ripple effects are profound:

1. Lost Income

Physicians experiencing burnout often cut back hours, decline extra shifts, or take early retirement—sometimes abruptly. Even reducing clinical work by 25% could translate into a six-figure annual loss.

2. Therapy and Mental Health Support

While mental health care is essential (and worth every dollar), therapy, coaching, and self-care programs often come out of pocket—especially when providers are out of network.

3. Career Change or Exit

Some physicians pursue non-clinical roles, lower-paying jobs, or completely different careers to preserve their mental health. These transitions can result in temporary or long-term income reductions and require retraining or relocation.

4. Lost Investment Opportunities

When burnout leads to time off, reduced pay, or inconsistent income, it can derail savings goals, retirement contributions, and compounding returns.

5. Relationship Strain and Divorce

Burnout can strain marriages and family dynamics. In worst-case scenarios, divorce adds additional emotional and financial costs, including asset division and alimony.

Financial Strategies to Reduce Stress: Automation, Delegation, and Professional Support

The best way to address burnout is to **create space**—and that includes financial space.

1. Automate Everything You Can

- Automate savings, bill payments, and retirement contributions
- Set up budgeting tools like YNAB or Monarch Money to reduce decision fatigue
- Use recurring transfers to build emergency funds effortlessly

2. Delegate to Trusted Professionals

- Work with a **fee-only financial advisor** to manage your investments and big-picture planning
- Hire a **CPA** to reduce tax-time stress and optimize deductions
- Use a **bookkeeper** or family office (if needed) to manage day-to-day financial details

You're the expert in medicine. Let experts help manage your money—so you can preserve your energy.

3. Build a "Burnout Buffer"

- Set aside 3–6 months of living expenses not just for emergencies, but for **planned recovery**
- Think of it as a "mental health sabbatical fund"—available if and when you need to step back

Burnout isn't always preventable—but being financially prepared can make it less devastating.

Knowing When to Take a Break—and How to Afford It

Many physicians know they need a break—but feel trapped by financial obligations. That's where proactive planning changes everything.

Questions to Ask Yourself:

- Can I cover my essentials for 3–6 months if I stop working?
- Do I have short-term disability insurance to supplement my income?
- What would I need monthly to take a break and heal—without guilt or panic?

If You're Considering a Leave:

- Review your employment contract for **leave of absence, short-term disability, or FMLA options**
- Check your insurance policies: do you have coverage for mental health-related disability?
- Talk to your advisor about cash flow and funding your sabbatical without dipping into long-term assets

Taking a break might feel indulgent—but it could be the **most strategic decision** for your long-term wellness and career.

Income Protection If Stepping Away from Clinical Duties

1. Disability Insurance

If burnout progresses to depression, anxiety, or another health condition that limits your ability to work, disability insurance may help replace a portion of your income.

- **Own-occupation policies** are ideal for physicians

- Ensure your policy covers **mental health conditions**
- Know the **elimination period** and **monthly benefit limit**

Disability coverage isn't just for physical injuries. It's for any condition that prevents you from doing your job—including burnout-related illness.

2. Partial or Residual Disability Riders

These allow you to **reduce your hours** while still receiving a portion of your benefit, protecting income while you ease back into work or explore new roles.

3. Transitioning to Non-Clinical Roles

If you step into education, consulting, telemedicine, or administrative work, your income may shift. Budget conservatively during transitions, and speak with a career coach or financial planner to understand the long-term implications.

Final Thoughts

Burnout is not a personal failure—it's a systemic issue. But while you can't always control the system, you **can** control how well you prepare for it financially.

Give yourself permission to rest. Permission to say no. And permission to protect your time, energy, and peace.

Because a healthy financial life isn't just about saving more or investing better—it's about creating the **freedom to choose recovery when you need it most**.

You've spent your life taking care of others. Now it's time to design a financial plan that takes care of you.

Chapter 27: Doctors and Divorce – The Financial Fallout and How to Protect Yourself

Introduction: Love, Loss, and Ledger Sheets

Divorce is one of the most emotionally taxing and financially devastating events a person can go through. For doctors, who spend years training, accumulating debt, and building high-income careers, the stakes are even higher. The intersection of a physician's career trajectory, compensation complexity, long hours, and often delayed wealth building means that a poorly managed divorce can derail financial goals for decades. This chapter is not about judgment—it's about preparation, protection, and recovery.

Section 1: Why Divorce Hits Doctors Especially Hard

1.1 High Income, High Exposure

Doctors often earn significantly more than their spouses, which puts them at greater risk of paying large sums in alimony or spousal support. In many cases, the non-physician spouse may have made sacrifices during medical school and residency (e.g., relocating, pausing their own career, or raising children), which a court will weigh in dividing assets and awarding support.

1.2 Long Road to Financial Success

Doctors spend years training without income and accumulating student loan debt. When they finally reach attending status and begin earning a high income, it may coincide with marital stress, lifestyle inflation, and growing financial obligations—all of which are vulnerable during divorce.

1.3 Complex Compensation Packages

Physician income is often comprised of multiple streams:

- Base salary
- Productivity bonuses (RVUs)
- Call stipends
- Deferred compensation
- Partnership buy-ins or equity
- Moonlighting income

Courts and opposing attorneys may not understand these structures, and physicians must often provide detailed financial disclosures and testimony to explain them.

1.4 Practice Ownership and Valuation

If the doctor owns a practice, part of its value may be considered marital property. Even if the spouse never worked there, courts may grant the non-owner spouse a portion of the business value, requiring the doctor to buy out their interest or take on additional debt.

1.5 Licensing and Reputation Risks

Accusations of misconduct during divorce proceedings (whether true or exaggerated) can impact medical licensure and hospital privileges. Doctors must tread carefully and document everything.

Section 2: What Gets Divided in Divorce

Divorce divides more than just emotions—it divides everything:

2.1 Marital Property vs. Separate Property

Marital property includes assets acquired during the marriage, regardless of whose name is on the title. Separate property typically includes:

- Inheritances
- Pre-marital assets
- Gifts from third parties

However, if separate property is commingled (e.g., using an inheritance to pay for a jointly titled home), it can become marital.

2.2 Retirement Accounts

IRAs, 401(k)s, 403(b)s, and pensions earned during the marriage are subject to division. Division is done via a QDRO (Qualified Domestic Relations Order), which allows tax-free transfer to the non-employee spouse.

2.3 Real Estate

This includes:

- Primary residence
- Vacation homes
- Rental properties
- Land investments

Homes may be sold and proceeds divided, or one spouse may buy out the other's interest.

2.4 Student Loans

Debt acquired during marriage is often treated like marital property. A doctor's medical school loans may be considered joint debt depending on the state and circumstances.

2.5 Business Interests

Whether you're a solo practitioner or partner in a large group, the value of your business could be on the table. Courts may hire forensic accountants to appraise the business, including goodwill, equipment, receivables, and real estate.

2.6 Investments and Brokerage Accounts

Brokerage accounts, mutual funds, and stocks purchased during the marriage are divided. Tax basis must be considered. For example, one spouse may end up with high capital gains taxes if the division is not structured properly.

2.7 Bank Accounts and Emergency Funds

All cash accounts are reviewed. Joint accounts are usually split, and separate accounts may be scrutinized to see if they were funded with marital income.

2.8 Intellectual Property and Royalties

If you've authored a textbook, developed a patented tool, or licensed medical software, future royalties and usage fees could be deemed marital assets.

Section 3: Alimony and Child Support

3.1 Spousal Support (Alimony)

Factors include:

- Length of marriage
- Disparity in earning capacity
- Age and health of both spouses
- Contributions to the household or your career

Doctors often end up paying alimony because of higher earning power. Judges can award:

- Temporary support (during divorce proceedings)
- Rehabilitative support (to allow spouse to get education or training)
- Permanent support (less common now, but possible in long-term marriages)

3.2 Child Support

Each state uses a formula based on income, number of children, and parenting time. For high-income earners:

- Some states cap the income considered
- Others include all income (e.g., bonuses, call pay, moonlighting)

Child support often includes payments for:

- Health insurance
- Daycare
- Extracurriculars
- College savings

Section 4: Prenups and Postnups

4.1 Prenuptial Agreements

Doctors should consider prenups before marriage, especially if they:

- Own a practice
- Expect a large inheritance
- Have already built retirement savings
- Are marrying during residency or early practice

Prenups can specify:

- Separate vs. marital assets
- Division of business interests
- Spousal support limitations

4.2 Postnuptial Agreements

Similar to prenups but created after marriage. Useful when:

- One spouse receives inheritance
- A business is started during the marriage

- A couple reconciles after separation and wants clarity moving forward

Section 5: Protecting Your Assets Before, During, and After Divorce

5.1 Before Marriage

- Get a prenup with full disclosure
- Keep assets in separate accounts
- Avoid commingling inheritance or pre-marital property

5.2 During Marriage

- Track all joint vs. separate spending
- Keep business records up to date
- Consider life insurance to secure future alimony or child support

5.3 During Divorce

- Hire a family law attorney familiar with physician finances
- Work with a Certified Divorce Financial Analyst (CDFA)
- Avoid emotional decisions (e.g., keeping the house you can't afford)

5.4 After Divorce

- Update your estate plan (will, power of attorney, beneficiaries)
- Change account passwords and remove ex-spouse from joint accounts
- Create a post-divorce budget and financial plan

Section 6: Case Studies

Case Study A: Divorce During Residency

Dr. Smith married her college sweetheart during her second year of medical school. Her spouse supported her financially during that time.

They divorced in her final year of residency. Though she hadn't built significant assets, she was required to pay spousal support for five years after she began practicing.

Case Study B: Practice Partner Divorce

Dr. Jones owned a 30% stake in a cardiology practice. During divorce, his practice was valued at $3 million. His ex-spouse was awarded $450,000 of his share, which required him to take out a loan and restructure his ownership.

Case Study C: No Prenup, Big Fallout

Dr. Patel got married after fellowship and accumulated $1.2 million in net worth over 10 years. His spouse, who did not work, was awarded half of all assets. He also pays $5,000 per month in spousal support. A prenup would have changed this outcome.

Case Study D: Smart Planning

Dr. Chen had a prenup, separate accounts, and her own legal and financial team. When she divorced after 7 years of marriage, she kept her practice, paid a lump sum settlement, and walked away financially intact.

Section 7: Psychological and Emotional Impact

- Divorce is a leading cause of physician burnout.
- Depression and substance abuse rates rise during and after divorce.
- Mental health support is crucial.
- Financial counseling can help restore confidence and control.

Section 8: Rebuilding After Divorce

- Reestablish financial goals (retirement, college savings, debt reduction)
- Rebuild emergency fund
- Maximize workplace retirement contributions
- Consider downsizing or simplifying lifestyle temporarily
- Invest in therapy or life coaching if needed

Section 9: Takeaways and Best Practices

1. **Prenups matter.**
2. **Documentation matters.** Keep receipts, records, and contracts.
3. **Separate means separate.** Don't commingle if you want to protect assets.
4. **Hire the right professionals.** A regular CPA won't cut it.
5. **Think long-term.** Don't trade retirement security for a house you can't afford.
6. **Don't hide assets.** It's illegal and usually backfires.
7. **Plan for child support and alimony in your financial future.**

Conclusion: Divorce Doesn't Have to Derail Your Life

Divorce is painful. But it doesn't have to ruin you financially. With planning, professionalism, and purpose, you can emerge with clarity and control. Just as you plan for retirement or disability, plan for the potential of divorce—not because you expect it, but because you value peace of mind.

You've spent a lifetime building your career. Protect it—even in love, and especially in loss.

Chapter 28: Student Loan Management and Forgiveness Programs

For most physicians, student loans are not just a footnote — they're a defining element of their financial picture for at least the first decade (or more) of their career. It's not uncommon for doctors to finish medical school with $200,000 to $400,000 in student loan debt. When you add interest and the years of delayed repayment during residency and fellowship, that number can balloon quickly. Even high-earning physicians can feel trapped by these balances well into their 40s.

The good news is that doctors have more repayment and forgiveness options than most professions — but taking advantage of them requires strategic planning and awareness of how each path affects your long-term goals. This chapter unpacks the most important repayment and forgiveness programs available to physicians, including how and when to consider refinancing, and how these choices fit into your broader financial plan.

Understanding Your Loans: Federal vs. Private

Before diving into repayment strategies, you must understand what types of loans you carry. Most physicians graduate with a mix of federal and sometimes private loans.

- **Federal Loans** (e.g., Direct Subsidized, Direct Unsubsidized, Grad PLUS): These loans are eligible for income-driven repayment (IDR) plans, Public Service Loan Forgiveness (PSLF), and other federal protections.

- **Private Loans**: Issued by banks or private lenders, these loans often carry less flexible repayment terms and are not eligible for federal forgiveness programs.

Pro tip: Never refinance federal loans into private loans unless you're sure you won't qualify for PSLF or any IDR forgiveness. Once you refinance out of the federal system, you lose access to those options permanently.

The Residency Years: Smart Moves from the Start

Residency is one of the most critical windows for long-term loan strategy. Your income is low, your debt is high, and the interest on your loans is accruing. This is when you want to make your loans work for you — especially if you're considering PSLF.

1. **Consolidate Your Federal Loans (Strategically)**
2. If your federal loans are from multiple loan programs, consolidating them into a Direct Consolidation Loan can be necessary to qualify for PSLF. But timing matters — consolidating resets the PSLF clock. If you've already made qualifying payments during medical school, consolidating could wipe those out.
3. **Choose the Right Income-Driven Repayment Plan (IDR)**
4. Plans like **PAYE, REPAYE**, or **SAVE** (formerly known as REPAYE/SAVE overhaul) cap your monthly payments at a percentage of your discretionary income. For residents, this means extremely low monthly payments — often less than the interest accruing on the loans.

- **REPAYE/SAVE** can be a smart choice in residency due to its interest subsidy feature, where the government covers 50% to 100% of unpaid interest, preventing negative amortization.

- The new **SAVE** plan can result in $0 payments for many residents while still counting toward PSLF.

Public Service Loan Forgiveness (PSLF): The Golden Ticket

PSLF is arguably the most valuable forgiveness program for doctors who plan to work at nonprofit hospitals, universities, or qualifying public health organizations.

How It Works:

- Make **120 qualifying monthly payments** (10 years) under a qualifying IDR plan.
- Work full-time at a **501(c)(3) or government employer**.
- Have **Direct Loans** (or consolidate to make them Direct).
- Submit the **Employment Certification Form (ECF)** annually.

After 10 years of payments — which can include your residency and fellowship years — the remaining loan balance is **forgiven tax-free**.

Key Tips:

- Start tracking your PSLF payments from Day 1 of residency.
- Submit your ECF every year and whenever you switch employers.
- Be careful with forbearance or deferment — those months don't count.
- Keep proof of every payment and document correspondence with servicers.

Real-World Example: Dr. Martin, a family medicine doctor at a nonprofit hospital, made 4 years of qualifying payments during residency and fellowship, then 6 years as an attending. His remaining $150,000 loan balance was forgiven tax-free under PSLF — a huge win, made possible by early awareness and consistency.

Forgiveness Without PSLF: The 20-25 Year Option

If PSLF isn't a fit (e.g., you work in private practice or a for-profit hospital), you may still qualify for loan forgiveness under an income-driven repayment plan:

- **PAYE**: 20 years to forgiveness
- **SAVE/REPAYE**: 20 years for undergraduate loans, 25 years for graduate/professional loans
- **IBR**: 20 or 25 years depending on when you borrowed

The catch? This forgiveness is **taxable as income**. That means if you have $200,000 forgiven, you could owe taxes on that amount — a potential six-figure tax bill in your final forgiveness year. Many borrowers plan ahead by saving into a "tax bomb" fund.

When to Refinance

Refinancing is a hot topic in physician finance circles — and for good reason. Once you're certain you don't need federal protections (PSLF, IDR, forbearance options), refinancing can significantly reduce your interest rate and total repayment cost.

Best Time to Refinance:

- After training, when you have a stable attending income
- When you're working in the **private sector** and PSLF is off the table
- If you can secure a lower interest rate (ideally <5%)

Caution:

- Never refinance during residency unless you have outside financial support or a special resident refinancing program with flexible payments.

- Once you refinance, you permanently lose federal protections.

Pro tip: Some companies offer physician-specific refinance programs with perks like low minimum payments during training and career coaching. Shop around — and don't be afraid to negotiate.

Private Loans: Managing What You Can't Forgive

If you have private loans from undergrad or medical school, you won't qualify for PSLF or IDR. Your options are:

- **Aggressively pay them off** if they carry high interest rates
- **Refinance** to secure a better rate
- **Avoid deferment or forbearance**, which can lead to capitalized interest

Private loans are less flexible, so prioritize them if forgiveness is not an option. Consider refinancing them separately from your federal loans if it benefits your total repayment picture.

Tax Planning and Loan Repayment

Loan repayment and tax planning go hand-in-hand. For example:

- If you're using **IDR**, your adjusted gross income (AGI) affects your monthly payment.
- Use pre-tax retirement contributions, HSA deposits, and FSA contributions to lower your AGI.
- If you expect forgiveness under PSLF, **keep payments low** and avoid accelerating repayment.
- If you're planning taxable forgiveness after 20–25 years, prepare for the "**tax bomb**" with a long-term savings strategy.

Collaborating with a CPA or financial advisor who understands physician loan strategy can save you thousands and reduce stress.

Marriage and Student Loans

Marriage adds a layer of complexity. If your spouse earns a high income, it can affect your IDR payments — unless you file **taxes separately** (which can have its own trade-offs).

Key Considerations:

- **PAYE** and **IBR** let you exclude your spouse's income by filing separately.
- **REPAYE/SAVE** always includes spousal income, regardless of tax filing status.
- Consider whether PSLF is more valuable than the tax benefits of filing jointly.

Make these decisions in partnership with your spouse and your tax professional.

Strategic Loan Planning Across Career Phases

Let's break it down by where you might be in your journey:

In Training (Med School / Residency / Fellowship):

- Use SAVE or PAYE
- Make qualifying PSLF payments
- Don't refinance federal loans
- Submit ECFs annually
- Explore hardship deferment cautiously

Early Attending:

- Decide: PSLF path or private sector?
- Reevaluate IDR vs. refinance
- Adjust repayment strategy based on goals
- Increase retirement contributions to reduce IDR payments

Mid-Career and Beyond:

- Consider lump-sum paydowns if you're not pursuing forgiveness
- Refinance again if rates drop
- Ensure estate planning covers any remaining loans (especially private)
- Evaluate whether to shift from aggressive paydown to investment prioritization

Final Thoughts: Your Debt Doesn't Define You

It's easy to feel overwhelmed by six-figure student loans, even as your income climbs. But with the right plan, discipline, and ongoing evaluation, your loans can become a manageable — and even strategic — part of your financial life.

Start early, know your options, and align your loan strategy with your career and personal goals. Whether forgiveness or full repayment is the path you choose, what matters most is that you're in control — not your debt.

Chapter 29: Tax Strategies for High-Income Physicians

As a physician, your income is among the highest in the workforce—but so is your tax liability. With earnings that often push you into the top federal tax brackets, smart tax planning becomes essential. The difference between paying 35% or 37% in taxes, and finding legal strategies to reduce your taxable income, can equate to tens or even hundreds of thousands of dollars in savings over your career.

This chapter explores tax planning techniques that can help you reduce your tax exposure while maximizing wealth accumulation. From optimizing retirement accounts and charitable giving to utilizing health savings accounts and backdoor Roth IRAs, each of these strategies can play a key role in building a more tax-efficient financial life.

Understanding the Tax Landscape

Before diving into specific strategies, it's important to understand how your income is taxed. The United States has a progressive tax system, meaning the more you earn, the higher the marginal rate on each additional dollar. Most attending physicians find themselves in the 35% or 37% federal tax brackets, not including additional state or local income taxes.

The key to tax planning isn't just minimizing income, but structuring your income and deductions in a way that keeps more of your money working for you. High-income professionals like physicians need to plan proactively rather than reactively.

Maximize Retirement Account Contributions

One of the most effective ways to reduce your taxable income is through tax-advantaged retirement accounts.

Traditional 401(k), 403(b), and governmental 457(b) plans allow you to defer income and lower your current taxable earnings. For 2025, you can contribute up to $23,000, or $30,500 if you are age 50 or older with catch-up contributions.

If your employer offers matching contributions, be sure to contribute enough to get the full match. Total contributions, including both employee and employer portions, can reach up to $69,000 or $76,500 with catch-up contributions.

If you're employed by a nonprofit or academic hospital, you may also have access to a 457(b) plan in addition to a 403(b). This dual eligibility can double your tax-deferred savings.

Backdoor Roth IRA Strategy

Due to income limits, high-earning physicians are often ineligible to contribute directly to a Roth IRA. However, you can use a strategy called the backdoor Roth IRA to get around these restrictions.

This involves making a non-deductible contribution to a Traditional IRA and then converting it to a Roth IRA. While this seems simple in theory, complications can arise if you have other pre-tax IRA balances due to the IRS pro-rata rule. This rule requires you to consider all of your IRAs when calculating the taxable portion of the conversion.

For physicians without other IRA balances, the backdoor Roth strategy can allow for thousands of dollars each year in tax-free Roth growth—a powerful benefit over the long term.

Health Savings Accounts (HSAs)

For those with high-deductible health plans, the Health Savings Account (HSA) offers a rare triple tax advantage. Contributions are tax-deductible, growth is tax-free, and withdrawals for qualified medical expenses are also tax-free.

In 2025, individuals can contribute up to $4,150, and families can contribute $8,300. Those age 55 or older can add an additional $1,000 as a catch-up contribution.

While many people use HSAs to cover current medical expenses, the most strategic use is to let the money grow for years. If you can pay for current medical expenses out of pocket, allowing your HSA to accumulate investment growth can create a tax-free healthcare nest egg for retirement.

Defined Benefit and Cash Balance Plans

If you're a practice owner or a high-income partner in a group, adding a defined benefit or cash balance plan to your retirement strategy can allow you to defer even more income. These plans are structured like traditional pensions, with contributions determined by actuarial calculations based on age and income.

In some cases, annual contributions to a defined benefit plan can exceed $100,000 or more. Contributions are tax-deductible to the practice and grow tax-deferred for the individual.

These plans are especially beneficial for older physicians in their peak earning years who are looking to rapidly accelerate retirement savings and reduce tax liability. They do require long-term funding commitments and annual filings, so work with a qualified administrator and CPA to ensure compliance.

Tax-Loss Harvesting in Taxable Accounts

For physicians who invest outside of retirement accounts, taxable brokerage accounts provide flexibility but also come with tax exposure. One powerful strategy to manage taxes in these accounts is tax-loss harvesting.

This involves selling investments that have declined in value to realize a capital loss. These losses can offset capital gains, and if losses exceed gains, they can reduce up to $3,000 of ordinary income per year. Any remaining losses can be carried forward indefinitely to future years.

Tax-loss harvesting requires attention to detail to avoid wash sale rules, which disallow a deduction if you repurchase the same or a substantially identical security within 30 days. Many financial advisors and digital investment platforms offer automated tax-loss harvesting to optimize this process.

Charitable Giving Strategies

Charitable giving is both a personal and financial decision. If philanthropy is part of your values, there are several tax-efficient ways to give.

One of the most versatile tools is a donor-advised fund (DAF). You can contribute appreciated securities or cash to a DAF and receive an immediate tax deduction. The assets then grow tax-free within the fund, and you can distribute grants to charities over time. This is particularly helpful in high-income years or when experiencing a financial windfall.

If you're over age 70½ and have IRA assets, you can make Qualified Charitable Distributions (QCDs) directly from your IRA to a qualified charity, up to $100,000 per year. This satisfies required minimum distributions (RMDs) and excludes the amount from taxable income.

More complex strategies, such as charitable remainder trusts or charitable lead trusts, can be used for legacy planning and tax minimization when working with advanced estate planning advisors.

Filing Status and Income Planning for Couples

For married physicians or dual-physician households, filing status can affect overall tax exposure. While filing jointly is generally more favorable, in some scenarios—especially where student loans are involved—filing separately can reduce the monthly payment under certain income-driven repayment plans.

It's important to model both scenarios with your CPA or financial advisor to understand the trade-offs. Filing separately may lead to loss of deductions or credits but could also be beneficial in managing cash flow in the short term.

In dual-income households, coordination is key. Make sure both spouses are maximizing workplace retirement benefits, flexible spending accounts, and health savings accounts. Synchronizing your tax strategies can reduce overall liability and increase household net worth.

Structuring Bonuses and Compensation

Physicians often receive variable compensation, including signing bonuses, annual productivity bonuses, and incentive-based pay. These payments can cause income spikes that push you into higher tax brackets or trigger phaseouts for deductions and credits.

When possible, work with your employer to spread out or defer bonus payments into the next calendar year. For self-employed physicians or practice owners, consider accelerating deductible business expenses into the current year or deferring income if you expect a lower income next year.

Also, be mindful of timing charitable gifts or large contributions to retirement accounts to offset bonus income in high-earning years.

Professional Guidance for Advanced Tax Planning

At this income level, tax planning should be an ongoing process—not a once-a-year event. Physicians benefit tremendously from having a financial team that includes a proactive CPA and a financial advisor who understands physician-specific tax issues.

Make sure your advisors are collaborating on your behalf. Topics they should coordinate on include estimated tax payments, business structure optimization, asset location strategies, charitable giving plans, and retirement contribution timing.

Tax strategies can and should be tailored to your life stage. Early-career physicians may focus on reducing student loan payments and maximizing Roth growth, while mid-career and late-career physicians may benefit more from defined benefit contributions, advanced charitable strategies, and estate planning.

Conduct an Annual Tax Review

Each year, set aside time to review your tax strategy in the fall. This ensures you have time to make contributions, execute transactions, or adjust your withholdings before year-end.

Ask yourself the following:

- Am I maximizing all available retirement accounts?
- Are there opportunities to reduce taxable income through charitable giving?
- Have I taken advantage of HSA contributions or tax-loss harvesting?
- Do I need to adjust my estimated taxes due to variable income?
- Are my financial advisors and tax professionals aligned on my goals?

With consistent review and intentional planning, your tax strategy will evolve as your career and financial situation grow.

Final Thoughts

The goal of tax planning isn't just to save money—it's to align your income, lifestyle, and values in a way that supports your long-term goals. As a high-income physician, taxes will always be a reality. But with the right strategies and support team in place, you can legally and effectively reduce your liability while investing more into your future.

By being proactive and strategic, your high income becomes not a burden, but a tool. When your financial decisions are intentional, your tax bill becomes just another part of your wealth-building journey—not a roadblock to it.

Chapter 30: Teaching, Mentoring, and Leaving a Legacy in Medicine

When physicians think about their legacy, it's often tied to the patients they've helped or the financial wealth they hope to leave their family. But there's another kind of legacy that doesn't show up in account balances or estate plans — the legacy of teaching, mentoring, and guiding the next generation of doctors.

Giving back doesn't always mean writing a check. It can mean taking the time to help a medical student navigate a difficult rotation, mentoring a resident on how to negotiate a contract, or speaking at a local high school to inspire future healthcare leaders. These moments, though intangible, can ripple for decades and shape the culture of medicine in meaningful ways.

As you move through your career, opportunities to contribute beyond the exam room become more frequent — and more impactful. This chapter explores how to use your time, knowledge, and experience to build a non-financial legacy that complements the wealth you're working so hard to build.

Why Legacy Matters — Especially in Medicine

Medicine is a field that's passed down person to person. Every physician can look back and name a few people — a mentor, professor, attending, or colleague — who made a difference in their journey. These relationships often influence not just clinical skill, but confidence, ethics, decision-making, and resilience.

The reality is that medicine is tough. Burnout, isolation, moral injury, and bureaucratic strain are at all-time highs. Now more than ever, younger physicians need support. Your legacy can be about helping others find joy, balance, and meaning in their work.

Leaving a legacy isn't about ego — it's about impact. It's about using the platform you've built to elevate others.

Mentorship: The Multiplier Effect

Mentorship is one of the most powerful and scalable ways to make a difference. A good mentor can guide decisions, open doors, and offer perspective that textbooks can't.

Who Needs Mentors?

- **Medical students** navigating specialty choices
- **Residents** facing long hours and high stakes
- **Fellows** learning to balance clinical expertise with life planning
- **Young attendings** adjusting to new income, leadership, and independence

Mentorship doesn't require formal programs. A simple coffee meeting, phone call, or open-door policy can provide more value than any lecture.

How to Be an Effective Mentor:

- **Listen more than you speak.** Ask what they're struggling with.
- **Share your failures**, not just your successes.
- **Be honest.** Sugar-coating reality helps no one.
- **Respect boundaries.** Everyone's journey is different.
- **Follow up.** A quick check-in months later can mean the world.

The best mentors are not always the most accomplished — they're the most accessible, empathetic, and real.

Contributing to Academia

For physicians who enjoy teaching, research, or thought leadership, academia offers structured paths to leave an intellectual legacy.

Here are ways to contribute:

Teaching Roles

- **Adjunct clinical faculty** positions at medical schools
- **Preceptorships** for students or residents
- **Lecturing** at grand rounds or CME conferences
- **Simulation-based teaching** and skills workshops

These roles often offer modest compensation or CME credits, but their real value lies in shaping minds and expanding your professional influence.

Research and Publication

- Publish in peer-reviewed journals
- Contribute to case studies or guideline development
- Participate in clinical trials or institutional research

Your real-world insights can help steer academic medicine toward more practical, patient-centered outcomes.

Curriculum Development

- Help design or update training modules
- Develop wellness or financial literacy content for trainees
- Advocate for diversity, equity, and inclusion in education

By helping shape what and how the next generation learns, you influence medicine's future long after you retire.

Speaking, Writing, and Advocacy

You don't have to be in a classroom to teach. You can leave a legacy through speaking, writing, and advocacy on issues you care about.

Public Speaking

Speaking at local schools, churches, community groups, or professional events builds public trust and inspires future clinicians. Topics could include:

- Pathways to becoming a doctor
- Navigating the emotional toll of the profession
- Health disparities and equity in care
- Financial literacy for medical professionals

You don't need a polished TED Talk — you need passion and authenticity.

Writing

Consider contributing articles to:

- Medical association newsletters
- Op-eds in local newspapers
- Online platforms like KevinMD or Doximity
- A personal blog or LinkedIn series

Writing not only amplifies your message, but also clarifies your thinking. It turns your experience into something others can revisit again and again.

Advocacy

Use your experience and voice to advocate for:

- Better healthcare policy
- Improved working conditions
- Increased diversity in medicine
- Access to care for underserved populations

Many physicians underestimate their influence in public or policy spaces. You've earned credibility. Use it.

Role Modeling Outside of Work

Your legacy isn't confined to the walls of a hospital. How you show up in your family, community, and social circles matters too.

- Support pre-med students in your neighborhood
- Sponsor scholarships or mentorship programs
- Volunteer at health fairs or free clinics
- Participate in school career days
- Coach youth sports or lead wellness initiatives

Being a visible, grounded role model as a physician — especially for underrepresented groups — can change lives.

Building Programs, Not Just Moments

If you're inclined to create something lasting, consider formalizing your legacy through:

Mentorship Programs

Start or support structured mentorship programs in your institution, alma mater, or specialty society.

Scholarship Funds

Establish a named scholarship for students from underrepresented or underserved backgrounds. You can do this through your university or a community foundation.

Foundations or Nonprofits

Create a nonprofit that addresses a specific cause — mental health, physician burnout, medical education, or access to care.

Endowed Lectureships or Fellowships

If you have significant philanthropic capacity, fund an annual lectureship or research fellowship at your training institution.

Big legacies often start with small efforts. Begin with one mentee or one volunteer role. Scale later if the vision expands.

Time as a Legacy Asset

As you gain seniority, the most valuable thing you can give may be your time. Time to teach. Time to listen. Time to support.

In early career, you may not have time to give much — and that's okay. But mid-career and pre-retirement years often bring flexibility. Consider allocating dedicated hours for mentoring, teaching, or volunteering.

Block off one afternoon a month to speak at a local school. Commit to quarterly mentorship check-ins. Schedule time to write, reflect, or advocate. These are intentional acts that compound over time.

The Personal Benefits of Giving Back

Contributing beyond your clinical work isn't just good for others — it's good for you.

- **Reignites purpose.** Mentoring reminds you why you chose medicine in the first place.
- **Reduces burnout.** Teaching and guiding others can be energizing and fulfilling.
- **Expands your network.** Mentors often become mentees' allies, partners, and collaborators.
- **Enhances your reputation.** You become known as more than a clinician — as a leader and contributor.

Many physicians report that their most meaningful career moments were not tied to financial gains or titles — but to relationships they built along the way.

Legacy Is a Daily Decision

You don't have to be a department chair, program director, or medical influencer to leave a legacy. Legacy isn't one big act. It's a series of small, consistent decisions to lift others as you climb.

When you:

- Take time to explain a concept to a student
- Offer encouragement after a tough shift
- Recommend someone for an opportunity
- Share your own mistakes so others can learn

You're building your legacy, moment by moment.

Whether you realize it or not, someone is watching you. Someone looks up to you. And someone will carry part of you into their own career.

Final Thoughts

In a profession so often defined by outcomes, numbers, and systems, legacy reminds us of the human side of medicine. Long after your last patient encounter, your teachings, influence, and mentorship will live on.

The financial wealth you accumulate can take care of your family. But the professional and personal legacy you build can uplift an entire generation of healers.

Legacy in medicine is not about ego — it's about stewardship. Stewardship of wisdom, of compassion, and of community.

Give what you know. Give what you've learned. And in doing so, you'll leave behind something that no tax return or balance sheet can measure — a meaningful, lasting impact.

Chapter 31: Lifestyle Design - Living Well Without Overspending

The phrase "live like a doctor" carries a certain expectation — a big house, luxury car, designer wardrobe, and lavish vacations. After years of intense training, delayed gratification, and personal sacrifice, many physicians feel entitled to a lifestyle that reflects their years of hard work. And rightfully so. You've earned the right to enjoy life.

But lifestyle inflation — the gradual increase in spending as income rises — can quietly sabotage long-term financial security. Without a plan, the gap between what you earn and what you keep can shrink faster than you expect. That's why intentional lifestyle design is a crucial part of financial literacy for doctors.

This chapter explores how to enjoy your income without jeopardizing your future. It's about aligning your spending with your values, creating room for meaningful indulgences, and designing a life that brings joy — not just status.

The Trap of Lifestyle Inflation

Lifestyle inflation is when your expenses increase as your income increases. It usually happens slowly and subtly. You finish residency, land your first attending job, and finally have a six-figure paycheck. You upgrade your car, sign for a mortgage that's 4-5 times your salary, start dining out more often, and begin to outsource everything that used to be DIY.

Suddenly, you're making $300,000 a year but feel just as stretched as you did when you were making $60,000 in residency.

Why? Because your **fixed costs** have expanded to meet your new income. And when those fixed costs include a high mortgage, multiple car payments, private school tuition, and vacation club memberships, your financial freedom narrows quickly.

Worse, many doctors feel pressure to match the lifestyles of peers, colleagues, or even patients. This "invisible competition" fuels decisions that have little to do with personal satisfaction and everything to do with image.

Redefining Wealth and Success

One of the first steps toward intentional living is redefining what wealth means to you.

For some, it's time. For others, it's travel, security, autonomy, or giving back. The key is to avoid letting society or your profession define it for you.

Start by asking:

- What do I value most?
- What experiences bring me the greatest joy?
- What purchases feel worthwhile — and which feel hollow?
- What would financial peace look like in five, ten, or twenty years?

By answering these questions, you begin to design your lifestyle around your **values**, not just your income.

The First Attending Paycheck: A Critical Juncture

The biggest jump in income during a physician's career is often the transition from residency or fellowship to attending status. This is where many doctors set their long-term trajectory — for better or worse.

While it's tempting to immediately "reward" yourself for years of delayed gratification, this period is also your greatest opportunity to build wealth. The habits and decisions made in the first three to five years can determine how long you'll need to work and how much flexibility you'll have later in life.

Here's a strategy many financially successful physicians follow:

Live like a resident for the first 2–3 years.

Instead of maxing out lifestyle expenses, use the income bump to:

- Pay off student loans
- Max out retirement accounts
- Build a six-month emergency fund
- Save for a home down payment
- Invest in your future freedom

This doesn't mean total deprivation. It just means giving your financial foundation a head start.

Value-Based Spending: The Joy-Per-Dollar Metric

Not all spending is bad. In fact, some spending enhances quality of life and well-being. The key is to focus on **value-based spending** — using your money in ways that align with what matters most to you.

Ask yourself:

- Does this purchase reflect my values?
- Will it still bring joy or utility six months from now?
- Am I buying this for myself — or to impress someone else?

Examples of high-value spending:

- A family vacation that creates lasting memories
- Home upgrades that enhance daily living

- Time-saving services (like meal delivery or house cleaning) if they free you to do more meaningful things
- Learning experiences or hobbies that improve well-being

Low-value spending often includes:

- Keeping up with other physicians' lifestyles
- Impulse purchases driven by stress or boredom
- Upgrades for the sake of upgrades (e.g., replacing a working car with a newer one because of appearances)

Train yourself to ask: *Is this purchase improving my life — or just draining my wallet?*

Smart Splurging: Guilt-Free Indulgence

Not all financial discipline means austerity. In fact, building room into your budget for *intentional splurging* can reduce burnout and prevent larger, emotionally-driven spending later.

Smart splurging means:

- Planning indulgences rather than reacting to stress
- Paying cash rather than using debt
- Avoiding lifestyle creep by keeping splurges occasional and deliberate
- Being selective rather than saying yes to everything

Examples:

- Celebrate milestones with a luxury purchase or trip
- Dine at a Michelin-star restaurant once or twice a year
- Invest in high-quality gear or equipment for hobbies you love

When these indulgences are planned and appreciated, they can be both enjoyable and financially sustainable.

The House, the Car, and the Trap

Two of the biggest contributors to lifestyle inflation are housing and vehicles. While there's nothing inherently wrong with buying a nice home or driving a high-end car, problems arise when those purchases crowd out other priorities.

The house: Many physicians overbuy, leading to large mortgages, high maintenance costs, and reduced flexibility. Just because a bank will lend you $1 million doesn't mean you should spend it.

Guideline: Aim for a home that costs no more than 2–2.5 times your annual gross income, especially early in your career. This leaves room for savings, investing, and other life goals.

The car: Cars are depreciating assets. Buying a $100,000 car that loses half its value in five years is not a wealth-building move — even if you're making $400,000 a year.

Guideline: If you can't buy the car outright, aim to keep your auto loan under 10% of your gross annual income, and avoid long loan terms that hide the real cost.

Designing a Life You Don't Need a Vacation From

The best lifestyle is one that doesn't leave you constantly needing escape. Lifestyle design is about creating a rhythm and environment where you enjoy your work, relationships, health, and free time.

Key elements of intentional lifestyle design:

- Work-life boundaries that protect your time and energy
- A schedule that allows for regular rest, hobbies, and family time
- Living in a community that supports your well-being
- Avoiding over commitment to material things that require ongoing stress to maintain

It's not about frugality for the sake of frugality — it's about *freedom.* A modest home in the right city can bring more joy than a mansion with a brutal commute. A used car can provide the same utility without the stress of a giant monthly payment.

Freedom often looks like saying **no** to more stuff so you can say **yes** to more life.

The Balance: Delayed Gratification vs. Present Joy

Physicians are taught to delay gratification — study now, relax later. But taken too far, this mindset can lead to under-living. Some doctors become so focused on saving and investing that they forget to enjoy their lives.

The answer isn't extremes — it's balance.

Ask:

- Am I saving and investing consistently each year?
- Am I spending time and money on things that truly matter to me now?
- Am I sacrificing joy today for a future that may never come?

Build a system that supports both. Automate savings, contribute to retirement, and then spend the rest *without guilt.* This balance is the key to financial health and emotional well-being.

A Note on Social Media and Comparison Culture

Social media can make it seem like everyone is living a more glamorous, exciting life. In medicine, this often shows up as Instagram posts of lavish homes, cars, exotic travel, or even surgical tools and case stats meant to signal status.

It's important to remember:

- What people post is not the whole picture.
- Many high-spending professionals are also highly leveraged.

- True wealth is quiet. It doesn't need to be advertised.

Focus on your values and your plan. Build a life that feels good on the inside, not one that just looks good on the outside.

Final Thoughts

You don't need to wait until retirement to enjoy your life. And you don't need to live in financial stress to enjoy your success. With thoughtful lifestyle design, you can create a life that feels rich — not just looks rich.

Spend in alignment with your values. Make room for smart splurges. Avoid tying your self-worth to material things. And most importantly, build a lifestyle that supports your long-term goals, your well-being, and your peace of mind.

In the end, it's not about denying yourself joy. It's about creating a version of joy that doesn't come with regret.

Chapter 32: Understanding Disability Insurance – Protecting Your Earning Power

As a physician, your greatest financial asset isn't your house, your car, or even your investment portfolio—it's your ability to earn an income. Over a 30-year career, a doctor earning $300,000 a year will generate $9 million in income, not including raises, bonuses, or investment growth. That's your engine—the source of everything else you'll build.

Now imagine that engine shuts down due to an injury, illness, or medical condition. It happens more often than we like to think. In fact, according to the Social Security Administration, one in four 20-year-olds will experience a disabling event before retirement.

This chapter is about protecting that engine—your income—through disability insurance. Specifically, we'll focus on "own-occupation" disability insurance, the type best suited to physicians, and walk through the essential features, riders, and planning considerations that every doctor should understand.

Why Disability Insurance Is Non-Negotiable for Physicians

You've likely spent over a decade training for your career. You've taken on six-figure student loan debt. You've invested thousands of hours into acquiring your skills. And you've entered a field where, if your health fails, your ability to continue in your specialty—or even in medicine at all—could vanish.

Disability insurance exists to replace your income if you can no longer work due to illness or injury. For physicians, this is especially critical because:

- You often have **delayed earnings** and **high opportunity cost** of education.
- Many specialties involve **fine motor skills**, **physical endurance**, or **visual acuity**—traits that disability can affect.
- Your debts and obligations don't disappear if your income does.

In short, if you're a working physician without long-term disability coverage, you're gambling with your future.

The Importance of "Own-Occupation" Coverage

There are several definitions of disability in insurance policies, and the most favorable for physicians is the **own-occupation** definition.

Own-occupation means you're considered disabled if you can't perform the specific duties of your own medical specialty—even if you could work in another capacity.

Let's say you're an orthopedic surgeon who develops tremors and can no longer operate. Under an **own-occupation** policy, you would receive disability benefits **even if you start working as a general physician, medical director, or in a non-clinical job**.

Compare that to other definitions:

- **Any-occupation**: Only pays benefits if you can't work in *any* job based on your training and experience. Much harder to qualify for.
- **Modified own-occupation**: Pays if you're not working in any other occupation; if you take another job, you lose benefits.
- **Transitional own-occupation**: Pays partial benefits if your new

income is lower than your previous income, but caps the benefit.

Recommendation: Physicians should prioritize **true own-occupation** disability coverage, especially early in their careers or in procedural specialties.

Key Features to Look For in a Disability Policy

A quality disability policy is more than just the premium and benefit amount. Here are the components you need to understand and evaluate:

1. **Benefit Amount**

- Aim to replace 60–70% of your gross income.
- Benefits are typically **tax-free** if you pay the premium with after-tax dollars.
- There's usually a cap ($15,000–$20,000/month), but high earners can stack policies or get supplemental coverage.

2. **Elimination Period**

- The waiting period before benefits begin—usually 90 days.
- A shorter elimination period costs more; most doctors choose 90 days as a good balance of cost and protection.

3. **Benefit Period**

- How long the policy will pay once you're disabled.
- Options include 2 years, 5 years, to age 65, to age 67, or lifetime.
- The most common (and recommended) is **to age 65 or 67**, which protects you until traditional retirement age.

4. **Non-Cancelable & Guaranteed Renewable**

- These two features protect you from future changes.
- **Non-cancelable** means the insurer can't cancel your policy or raise premiums as long as you pay.
- **Guaranteed renewable** means the policy will be renewed each year as long as premiums are paid, though premiums can rise for a class of policyholders.

Riders That Matter

Riders are optional additions to your policy that enhance protection. While they increase the premium, some are essential for physicians.

1. **Residual or Partial Disability Rider**

- Provides benefits if you're partially disabled and experiencing a loss of income.
- Crucial for conditions where you can still work part-time or in a reduced capacity.
- Prevents "all-or-nothing" benefit scenarios.

2. **Future Increase Option (FIO)**

- Allows you to increase your benefit later without medical underwriting.
- Important early in your career when income is lower, and health is good.
- Guarantees the ability to scale your policy as you earn more.

3. **Cost-of-Living Adjustment (COLA) Rider**

- Increases your monthly benefit annually while you're on claim to keep up with inflation.
- Especially important for younger physicians who could be on claim for decades.

4. **Catastrophic Disability Rider**

- Adds an additional benefit if you suffer a severe disability that affects daily living activities.
- Acts as an extra layer of financial support for worst-case scenarios.

Employer Coverage vs. Private Policies

Many physicians have group disability coverage through their employer. While this can be a helpful baseline, it's rarely enough—and often misunderstood.

Here's what to consider:

- **Taxable benefits**: If your employer pays the premium, benefits are **taxable**.
- **Limited benefit caps**: Group plans often cap benefits at $10,000–$15,000/month, which may not replace 60–70% of your income.
- **No portability**: You lose the coverage when you leave or change employers.
- **Weaker definitions**: Group policies often use **any-occupation** or **modified own-occupation** definitions.

Recommendation: Supplement employer-provided disability insurance with an **individual own-occupation policy** that is portable and tailored to your income.

The Cost of Coverage

Disability insurance for physicians is not cheap—expect to pay **1% to 3% of your annual income** for quality own-occupation coverage.

Premiums vary based on:

- Age

- Gender (policies are often more expensive for women)
- Specialty (procedural or surgical specialties cost more)
- Health history
- Smoking status
- State of residence

Applying early, while healthy, locks in lower premiums and broader eligibility for riders and options.

When and How to Apply

The best time to apply is in medical school, residency, or fellowship, especially through a training program that offers simplified underwriting and discounts.

Even if your current income is low, policies can be structured with a **Future Increase Option**, allowing your coverage to grow with your income—without more medical exams.

If you're already an attending, it's not too late. Apply as soon as possible, and be honest during underwriting. Full disclosure helps avoid claim denials later.

Work with an independent insurance broker who understands physician-specific policies from multiple carriers, not just one company.

Reviewing Your Policy Over Time

Disability insurance isn't a one-time decision. Your policy should evolve as your career does.

Revisit your policy when:

- Your income increases significantly
- You change employers or go into private practice
- You experience major life events (marriage, children, home purchase)
- You approach financial independence and consider reducing coverage

Schedule a disability review every 2–3 years with your advisor or insurance specialist.

Common Mistakes Physicians Make

1. **Relying solely on employer coverage**
2. **Choosing a cheaper policy with weaker definitions**
3. **Delaying purchase until income increases—then facing health issues**
4. **Not adding the right riders, especially Residual Disability and FIO**
5. **Letting a policy lapse during a career transition**

Avoid these missteps by staying proactive and informed. Disability insurance is one of those things you can't buy *after* you need it.

Final Thoughts

Disability insurance isn't flashy. It won't get you likes on social media or turn heads at a medical conference. But it's one of the most foundational pieces of your financial security.

You insure your car, your home, your phone—why wouldn't you insure your **income**, the very thing that makes all those things possible?

In medicine, your ability to earn isn't just a paycheck—it's your most powerful asset. Protect it fiercely. The right disability insurance policy won't just safeguard your finances—it will protect your future, your family, and your peace of mind.

Part 4: The Mid-Career & Leadership Years

E*arning More, Leading More—But Also Preparing for What's Next*

At this stage in your medical journey, you're no longer "figuring it out." You've arrived.

You've established your clinical reputation. You've gained experience, maybe earned a few titles, and built credibility among peers, staff, and even administrators. Whether you're a lead surgeon, a department chair, a medical director, or simply someone others turn to for guidance, you're no longer just practicing medicine—**you're helping shape the system.**

But here's what's important to recognize:

The decisions you make in these years will define the rest of your career—and the quality of your retirement.

Mid-career physicians often find themselves caught in a strange in-between zone:

- You're earning more than ever... but so are your expenses.
- You're mentoring others... but may still feel like you're figuring out your own financial plan.
- You're managing departments or programs... but unsure if your retirement portfolio is truly "on track."
- You're leading teams... but not always clear on how to lead your family or legacy financially.

This is the stage where burnout becomes real.

Where golden handcuffs start to tighten.

Where your lifestyle grows—but your **freedom** may not.

The Purpose of Part 4:

To help you step into the next level of leadership—with your finances just as aligned and intentional as your clinical expertise.

Because if you're not planning now—**not just for the next job, but for the next phase of life**—you may wake up one day with a high income, a prestigious title... and very little true financial flexibility.

In This Section, You'll Learn:

- How to reevaluate your financial goals mid-career
- Strategies for managing rising lifestyle costs and shifting priorities
- Retirement planning: Are you saving enough, and in the right places?
- How to maximize hospital or group-sponsored retirement benefits (401a, 403b, 457 plans)
- What to know about deferred compensation and executive benefits
- How to think about wealth transfer, charitable giving, and legacy-building
- How to protect your time and mental energy from financial distractions
- Leadership-level financial decisions: when to buy into a practice, invest in real estate, or step into a side business
- Why mid-career is the best time to **get brutally honest** about what you want your next chapter to look like—and how to fund it

You may not be at the finish line yet, but you're far enough along to **course-correct, optimize, or accelerate.**

This section isn't about financial perfection. It's about **alignment**—making sure your wealth, your work, and your values are working in the same direction.

Because leadership isn't just about the patients you serve or the teams you manage. It's about how you steward everything you've worked so hard to build.

This is your chance to lead with clarity, finish strong, and create margin—for your family, your future, and your freedom.

Let's keep building.

Chapter 33: The Business of Medicine – From Employed to Entrepreneur

Most physicians begin their careers working for someone else—whether it's a hospital system, academic medical center, or group practice. For many, this employed model offers security, benefits, and a predictable schedule. But as your career evolves, you might feel the itch to take more control—of your income, your schedule, your practice philosophy, or your impact.

That's where the entrepreneurial path begins.

Whether you dream of starting a private practice, launching a telehealth service, opening a med-spa, or offering consulting services, this chapter is your blueprint for navigating the transition from clinician to business owner. We'll explore the pros and cons, common legal structures, financial considerations, and what it really takes to thrive in the business side of medicine.

Why Physicians Consider Entrepreneurship

Medicine today is more corporatized than ever. Many physicians feel increasingly restricted by productivity quotas, insurance red tape, and loss of autonomy. Entrepreneurship offers a way to reclaim that freedom.

Common motivations include:

- Desire for **autonomy** and control

- Passion for a **niche or underserved market**
- Opportunity to **diversify income streams**
- Vision for a **new or better model of care**
- Burnout or dissatisfaction in traditional roles

While entrepreneurship isn't for everyone, it can be deeply fulfilling—and financially rewarding—when done strategically.

Pros and Cons of Leaving Employment

Before making the leap, it's important to weigh the trade-offs.

Pros:

- Greater control over schedule, operations, and patient care
- Higher income potential, especially over the long term
- Ability to build equity in your own brand or practice
- Creative freedom to offer new services or business models
- Opportunity to hire and mentor your own team

Cons:

- Loss of a steady paycheck and employer benefits
- Responsibility for business operations, compliance, and HR
- Financial risk, including personal liability if not structured properly
- Long hours, especially in the early stages
- Need to manage marketing, billing, and logistics

Entrepreneurship is not a cure for burnout if you're simply swapping one form of stress for another. It's a different kind of challenge—one that requires resilience, vision, and a tolerance for uncertainty.

Choosing the Right Business Structure

Your choice of business entity affects your taxes, liability, and growth potential. Consult with an attorney or CPA, but here's a general breakdown:

Sole Proprietorship

- Easiest to set up
- No legal separation between you and the business
- Personal liability for all debts and lawsuits
- Rarely recommended for physicians due to liability risk

Partnership

- Shared ownership with another person or group
- Profits and losses flow through to partners' personal taxes
- Requires a solid partnership agreement
- Each partner may be personally liable for the actions of others

Limited Liability Company (LLC)

- Popular for solo physicians or small groups
- Limits personal liability
- Flexible taxation (can be taxed as sole prop, partnership, or S Corp)
- Simpler paperwork than corporations

S Corporation

- Offers liability protection and potential tax savings on self-employment taxes
- Owners must pay themselves a "reasonable salary"
- Profits pass through to personal income
- Requires more compliance and formal structure

C Corporation

- Suitable for practices seeking outside investors
- Double taxation (corporation pays taxes, and shareholders do too)
- Complex reporting and corporate formalities

For most solo or small group physician practices, an **LLC taxed as an S Corporation** offers a good balance of flexibility, protection, and tax efficiency.

Startup Considerations: What You Need Before You Launch

Starting your own medical business requires more than clinical expertise. You need a business plan, licenses, insurance, and a solid understanding of your market.

Key steps include:

1. **Define Your Business Model** What are you offering? A traditional clinic? Concierge medicine? Telehealth? A niche like weight loss, dermatology, or hormone therapy? Be specific about your services and ideal patient population.
2. **Build a Business Plan** Include:

- Executive summary
- Market analysis
- Target patient demographics
- Revenue model (insurance, cash pay, memberships)
- Operational plan (hours, staffing, location)
- Marketing strategy
- Financial projections

3. Secure Licensing and Credentialing

- State medical license(s)
- DEA registration
- Business license
- Malpractice insurance
- NPI number
- Medicare/Medicaid enrollment and/or private payer credentialing

4. Choose Your Location and Platform Will you have a physical clinic, work from a co-working medical space, or offer services virtually? The location and setup impact cost, branding, and patient experience.

5. Establish Systems and Technology

- Electronic Medical Record (EMR)
- Billing and coding software
- Patient scheduling and communication tools
- HIPAA-compliant telehealth platforms (if applicable)
- Website and domain name

6. Develop a Marketing Plan Even if you're the best physician in your field, patients won't show up unless they know you exist.

Use:

- Website and SEO optimization
- Social media
- Local outreach and networking
- Google business profile and reviews
- Physician and community referrals

Financial Planning for the Transition

Going from employee to entrepreneur has major financial implications. You'll need to plan for income disruption, startup costs, and ongoing cash flow management.

Estimate Startup Costs Common expenses include:

- Legal and accounting fees
- Licensing and credentialing
- Malpractice insurance
- EMR and billing software
- Office space and equipment
- Marketing and branding

Startup costs can range from $10,000 to over $250,000 depending on your model. Create a conservative estimate and build in a buffer.

Build a Financial Runway Set aside at least 6–12 months of living expenses before launching. Business revenue may be slow to start, and it takes time to build a patient base.

Open a Business Bank Account Separate your personal and business finances from day one. This simplifies accounting, improves professionalism, and protects you legally.

Track Cash Flow Diligently Use accounting software or a bookkeeper to monitor revenue, expenses, payroll, and taxes. Know your numbers every month.

Consider a Business Line of Credit You may not need it right away, but having access to credit can help with cash flow fluctuations or expansion needs.

Insurance and Liability Protection

Business ownership exposes you to additional risks, so it's essential to have proper coverage in place.

Consider:

- **Malpractice Insurance** (Tail coverage if leaving a previous employer)
- **General Liability Insurance**
- **Business Owner's Policy (BOP)**

- **Cyber Liability Insurance** (for practices storing sensitive data)
- **Workers' Compensation Insurance** (if hiring employees)
- **Disability Insurance** (to protect your personal income)

Consult a commercial insurance broker who works with healthcare professionals to ensure you're adequately protected.

Transitioning Gracefully from Employment

If you're currently employed, be sure to review your employment contract. Look for:

- **Non-compete clauses**: These may limit where you can practice or for how long after leaving.
- **Non-solicitation clauses**: These may prevent you from recruiting staff or patients.
- **Tail coverage obligations**: Ensure your malpractice coverage extends after you leave.

Always provide ample notice, exit respectfully, and maintain professional relationships. Your reputation will follow you into your business.

Building a Team

Even if you start solo, you'll eventually need help—whether clinical or administrative. Build slowly, hire carefully, and invest in team culture from the beginning.

Early hires might include:

- Medical assistant or nurse
- Office manager or receptionist
- Billing/coding specialist or service
- Marketing support (freelancer or agency)

- Bookkeeper or accountant

Delegate tasks that are outside your zone of genius. Your time is best spent in high-impact areas: patient care, business strategy, and leadership.

Measuring Success Beyond Profit

Entrepreneurship offers more than financial upside—it offers fulfillment, autonomy, and impact. Define your own success metrics:

- Patient satisfaction and retention
- Work-life balance
- Practice growth and innovation
- Team engagement and development
- Personal well-being and joy

Make time to periodically reflect on what's working, what's draining, and how to evolve your business into something sustainable and meaningful.

Final Thoughts

The business of medicine isn't just for MBAs or corporate executives. As a physician, you're already running a complex human-centered system every day. With the right tools, guidance, and mindset, you can transition from employed to entrepreneur and build something that reflects your values, fuels your passion, and delivers care the way you believe it should be delivered.

Entrepreneurship won't be easy—but it can be deeply rewarding. Start with a clear vision, build the right foundation, and surround yourself with trusted advisors. The future of medicine is being shaped not just in boardrooms, but in the minds of entrepreneurial physicians like you.

Chapter 34: Kids and Money – Teaching the Next Generation Financial Literacy

As physicians, we spend years mastering the art and science of medicine. We read, train, sacrifice, and dedicate ourselves to the care of others. But when it comes to our own homes, especially our children, it's easy to unintentionally neglect one of the most powerful forms of care we can provide: financial education.

Financial literacy isn't just about dollars and cents — it's about values, responsibility, and preparation. And for high-income families like those of physicians, it's about avoiding entitlement, building character, and raising grounded, confident kids who understand the value of money.

This chapter explores how to teach your children about money at every stage of their development. We'll walk through age-appropriate lessons, practical strategies, the use of tools like custodial accounts and 529 plans, and how to model the kind of financial behavior you want to see reflected in your children's lives.

Why Financial Education at Home Matters

In most schools, kids learn algebra, chemistry, and literature — but they rarely learn how to open a bank account, budget, invest, or manage debt. That gap becomes a problem, especially for children growing up in financially secure households.

Physician households often provide a lifestyle that can mask the effort it took to get there. If we're not careful, our children may only see the outcome of our work — not the sacrifice, discipline, and years of planning behind it. Financial education helps them understand:

- Where money comes from
- How to earn, spend, save, and give responsibly
- The difference between needs and wants
- That their lifestyle is a result of choices and trade-offs

Without this foundation, it's easy for children to grow up with unrealistic expectations, poor financial habits, or a sense of entitlement.

Start Early: Financial Lessons for Young Children (Ages 4–10)

Even young children can grasp basic financial concepts. In these early years, it's all about exposure, conversation, and setting habits.

Key lessons:

- Money is earned by working
- Things cost money — and you must choose how to spend it
- Delayed gratification is powerful

Tactics:

- Use a clear jar or piggy bank so they can see money grow
- Give small allowances tied to chores or good behavior
- Take them to the store and let them use their money to buy something (and feel the trade-off)
- Read children's books about money and choices
- Play simple board games like Monopoly Junior or The Game of Life

Conversation starters:

- "What's something you want to save up for?"
- "If you had $10, what would you do with it?"
- "Why do you think we work?"

Middle Years: Developing Habits and Values (Ages 11–14)

This is a key period for reinforcing habits and exposing kids to real-life financial decision-making. Their cognitive abilities are expanding, and they're beginning to notice differences in lifestyle among peers.

Key lessons:

- Budgeting: You can't spend more than you have
- Saving for goals is rewarding
- Comparison is a trap — make decisions based on values

Tactics:

- Introduce a basic allowance split into spend/save/give categories
- Open a savings account with them at a local bank or credit union
- Show them the family budget (in age-appropriate ways)
- Give them financial responsibilities like paying for their own gifts or extras
- Watch finance-related movies or YouTube videos together and discuss

Start talking about:

- What things cost
- How your own money is earned and managed
- Charitable giving and generosity

Teen Years: Practice, Exposure, and Independence (Ages 15–18)

Now is the time to move from theory to practice. Teenagers can—and should—start earning money, managing expenses, and understanding investing basics.

Key lessons:

- Earning money takes time and effort
- Compound interest and investing create long-term wealth
- Credit can be helpful or harmful
- Every financial decision has a trade-off

Tactics:

- Encourage a part-time job or side hustle (babysitting, tutoring, etc.)
- Set up a **custodial Roth IRA** if they have earned income
- Open a **custodial brokerage account** to introduce them to investing
- Teach them how to use a debit card responsibly
- Show them how to track expenses using budgeting apps or spreadsheets

Prepare them for adulthood by teaching:

- How to file a simple tax return
- How credit scores work
- The basics of student loans and debt
- What insurance is and why it matters

Let them make mistakes — it's better to overdraft a $10 purchase at 17 than a $10,000 decision at 27.

College Years: Adult-Level Financial Planning (Ages 18–22)

If your child is in college or transitioning to independence, it's time to reinforce what you've taught and give them more financial responsibility.

Key lessons:

- You are 100% responsible for your financial decisions
- Living within your means is freedom
- Investing early builds lifelong wealth
- Avoid lifestyle inflation — just like physicians must

Tactics:

- Give them a monthly budget and let them manage it
- Introduce them to compound interest calculators and Roth IRAs
- Talk about credit card debt, student loans, and how to avoid financial traps
- Encourage internships or summer jobs to grow experience and financial maturity

If you're financially supporting them, be transparent about how much and for how long. Teach them to appreciate—not expect—support.

Tools to Set Kids Up for Success

Here are several tools that can help instill financial literacy while giving your children a head start.

529 College Savings Plans

- Tax-advantaged way to save for college expenses
- Grows tax-free and withdrawals are tax-free if used for qualified education expenses
- Set one up early and contribute monthly or annually

Custodial Brokerage Accounts (UTMA/UGMA)

- Allows you to invest on behalf of your child
- Assets become theirs at the age of majority (usually 18 or 21)
- Great for teaching long-term investing

Custodial Roth IRA

- Your child must have earned income (W-2 or 1099)
- You can contribute up to their earned income or $7,000 for 2025 (whichever is less)
- Tax-free growth and tax-free withdrawals in retirement
- Powerful way to teach investing and build generational wealth

Prepaid Debit Cards for Teens

- Apps like Greenlight, GoHenry, or Step let you manage spending while teaching budgeting
- You can automate allowance, set spending limits, and track purchases

Trusts or Inheritance Planning

- If you expect to pass on significant wealth, work with an estate attorney to structure inheritances responsibly
- Consider distribution triggers tied to education, age milestones, or financial literacy achievements

Avoiding Entitlement and Building Financial Character

High-income households are particularly vulnerable to raising children with an entitlement mindset. This doesn't happen because parents spoil kids—it often happens because parents *protect* them too much from financial reality.

Here are ways to build humility, gratitude, and financial awareness:

Model the Behavior You Want to See

- Live below your means
- Talk openly about financial decisions
- Avoid excessive consumerism

Don't Say Yes to Everything

- Make kids save for things they want
- Set boundaries on spending—even if you can afford more

Expose Them to a Broader World

- Volunteer together
- Travel to less affluent areas
- Discuss inequality, privilege, and responsibility

Make Giving Part of Their Routine

- Help them choose a charity to support
- Talk about why giving is important in your own life

Making Financial Conversations a Normal Part of Life

Normalize money talk in your home. Don't make it a secret or a source of stress. Treat it like you would nutrition, school, or health.

Start conversations like:

- "How do you think people decide what to spend money on?"
- "What would you do if you got a $500 check right now?"
- "Do you think being rich makes people happier?"
- "What's something smart we could do with our money as a family?"

By creating a safe, open environment, your kids will learn to think critically about money — and they'll feel comfortable coming to you with questions down the line.

Final Thoughts

As a physician, you've worked hard to build a financially stable life. One of the most meaningful ways to multiply that success is by teaching your children how to manage money wisely.

Financial literacy is not a one-time lesson. It's a lifelong conversation — one that evolves as your child grows. Start early, be consistent, and lead by example. When you empower your children with financial knowledge and strong values, you're not just securing their future — you're building a legacy that lasts beyond your career, your wealth, and your name.

Chapter 35: Branding, Side Hustles, and Expert Witness Work – Monetizing Your Expertise Outside the Clinic

For decades, physicians primarily earned income through clinical practice — seeing patients, performing procedures, and billing insurance or cash. But today, the game is changing. More and more doctors are finding new ways to leverage their expertise outside of traditional medicine. From testifying in courtrooms as expert witnesses to building educational platforms on YouTube or writing articles for national media outlets, physicians are expanding their reach, income, and influence.

Whether it's consulting for a tech startup, offering second opinions through a telehealth platform, writing a book, reviewing cases for attorneys, or becoming an expert voice on social media, there are more opportunities than ever to diversify your income and build a meaningful brand around your knowledge.

This chapter explores how physicians can develop side hustles and secondary income streams while staying compliant with licensing boards, managing legal and tax implications, and preserving their reputation and integrity in the process.

Why Physicians Are Diversifying Their Income

The reasons are many — and often personal. Some doctors want to escape burnout. Others want more flexibility or financial independence. Many want to explore interests outside of clinical practice or prepare for life after medicine.

Common motivators include:

- Reducing reliance on clinical income
- Exploring creative or entrepreneurial interests
- Building a personal brand or professional identity
- Using existing skills in new, lucrative ways
- Creating scalable or passive income streams

In an era where job security in medicine isn't what it once was, having multiple income sources isn't just smart — it's essential.

Common Physician Side Hustles and Consulting Roles

Here are several paths physicians are taking outside traditional clinical work:

1. **Expert Witness Work**

Doctors can be hired by attorneys to review medical records, prepare case summaries, and testify in court. This work is well-paid and intellectually stimulating.

Pros:

- High hourly compensation ($300–$1,000+ per hour)
- Flexible hours
- Opportunity to use medical expertise in legal settings

Cons:

- Requires attention to detail, strong communication, and willingness to be cross-examined
- Potential for criticism from opposing counsel or public opinion

Tips:

- Build a CV specifically for legal consulting
- Understand the rules of evidence and deposition protocols
- Be objective — your credibility depends on it

2. **Independent Medical Examinations (IMEs)**

Physicians are often hired by law firms or insurance companies to perform objective medical exams for injury, disability, or workers' comp claims.

Requirements:

- Must be licensed and current in your field
- May involve travel or virtual assessments
- Detailed reports and strong documentation skills are essential

3. **Medical-Legal Consulting**

This can include chart reviews, standard-of-care opinions, or advising attorneys without testifying. Some physicians also help legal teams prepare cross-examinations of opposing experts.

4. **Speaking and Medical Writing**

From CME events and grand rounds to keynotes and conferences, doctors are in demand as public speakers. Writing can range from journal articles and books to content for major media outlets.

5. **Telehealth, Second Opinions, and Concierge Advice**

You can offer second opinions or consultations through cash-pay telehealth platforms — without running a full practice. Be mindful of licensure laws across state lines.

6. **Startups, Health Tech, and Advisory Boards**

Physicians are valuable advisors to digital health startups, medical device firms, and biotech companies. Equity, consulting fees, and networking opportunities can be part of these relationships.

7. **Social Media and Content Creation**

Doctors are growing audiences on Instagram, TikTok, YouTube, LinkedIn, and blogs. With the right strategy, these platforms can become sources of:

- Sponsored content
- Ad revenue
- Product sales
- Book or course launches
- Brand partnerships

If you have a voice and a message — and you're willing to show up consistently — content creation can build influence and income.

Branding with Integrity

Building a brand means crafting a professional identity beyond your job title. This isn't about self-promotion for the sake of ego — it's about creating a platform to share knowledge, serve others, and open doors to new opportunities.

Key brand elements to consider:

- **Your niche or expertise** (e.g., sports medicine, physician wellness, pediatric nutrition)
- **Your message** — What do you believe in? What problems do you solve?
- **Your audience** — Who are you speaking to? Patients? Other doctors? The public?
- **Your platform** — Are you on social media? Hosting a podcast? Writing articles?

Consistency and authenticity are critical. Don't try to be everything to everyone. Lean into what makes your perspective valuable.

Legal and Licensing Considerations

Before launching any side hustle, ensure you stay within the boundaries of your license and maintain your professional integrity.

Check with your state medical board:

- Are there rules about advertising your credentials?
- Can you use the title "doctor" in non-clinical settings?
- Are there restrictions on medical advice through social media?

If testifying or consulting:

- Maintain objectivity at all times — this isn't advocacy, it's analysis
- Disclose any conflicts of interest
- Stay updated on legal expectations of expert witnesses

Protect patient privacy:

- Never share patient info without consent — even in anonymized stories
- Be careful about what you post online — screenshots live forever

Get it in writing:

- For consulting and legal work, always use contracts that outline scope, fees, and expectations
- If building an online course or content, read platform terms carefully

Tax and Financial Planning for Side Income

All side income is taxable. Whether it's $500 from a speaking gig or $50,000 from a consulting retainer, you'll need to plan accordingly.

Here's what to do:

1. Set Up a Business Entity

- Many physicians operate under a sole proprietorship or LLC
- Consider an S Corporation for tax efficiency once income exceeds ~$50,000
- Talk to a CPA who understands physician side businesses

2. Open a Separate Business Bank Account

- Keep business income and expenses separate from personal funds
- Makes tax filing, expense tracking, and audits much easier

3. Pay Estimated Quarterly Taxes

- The IRS expects taxes to be paid throughout the year, not just in April
- Avoid penalties by sending in estimated payments every quarter

4. Deduct Legitimate Business Expenses

- Travel, internet, marketing, subscriptions, home office, education, software — all may be deductible
- Keep receipts and good records

5. Contribute to a Solo 401(k) or SEP IRA

- You can shelter side income through a retirement plan, reducing taxable income
- These plans are especially powerful if you already max your employer

401(k)

Managing Time and Avoiding Burnout

The goal of a side hustle isn't to add stress — it's to create opportunity, passion, or additional freedom.

Be realistic about your bandwidth. Set boundaries. Time block your week. And ensure your side pursuits align with your energy, not just your ambition.

Ask yourself:

- Does this energize me?
- Is this aligned with my long-term goals?
- Am I sacrificing family, health, or rest for short-term gain?

If the answers are out of alignment, pause and reassess. Your side hustle should *add* to your life, not subtract from it.

Final Thoughts

You are more than your clinical role. You are a leader, a thinker, a creator, and a communicator. The same skills that make you a great physician — discipline, problem-solving, empathy, and resilience — can also make you a great consultant, educator, content creator, or expert witness.

Explore opportunities beyond the clinic. Monetize your knowledge with integrity. And design a professional life that reflects your talents, passions, and long-term vision.

The business of medicine is evolving — and so can you.

Chapter 36: How Doctors Get Paid – Salaries, Specialties, and Career Trajectories

The title "Doctor" carries weight. It conjures respect, years of education, and often—whether fairly or not—the assumption of financial prosperity. But while medicine can be a high-income profession, not all white coats earn the same. From the first day of medical school to retirement, a physician's income journey varies significantly based on specialty, setting, location, experience, and individual choices.

In this chapter, we'll break down how doctors are compensated, how their pay evolves over time, and what financial expectations to realistically prepare for throughout the career lifecycle—from investment-heavy training years to high-income peaks and the transition into retirement.

1. Medical School – The Investment Phase

At this stage, there's no income—only cost.

Medical students are investors, not yet earners. The cost of this investment? On average, **over $200,000** in student loan debt. For those attending private institutions or out-of-state programs, the figure can exceed $300,000. Factor in four years of tuition, fees, and living expenses, and most students graduate owing more than the down payment on a house.

Other Healthcare Professions:

- **Dental** and **veterinary** students often take on similar debt loads, though they may complete their education sooner or transition to income faster.
- **Pharmacy** and **optometry** students may face total tuition and costs of $150,000 to $250,000.
- The debt burden is real across all advanced clinical professions.

Key takeaway: You're not earning yet, but your financial behavior starts now. How you borrow, budget, and plan during medical school can set the tone for your financial mindset for the rest of your career.

2. Residency – The Low Pay, High Workload Phase

After graduation, medical school is followed by **residency**, where newly minted physicians earn a salary—albeit a modest one—while working long hours in training.

Typical **resident salaries** range from **$60,000 to $75,000** per year, depending on the program and geographic region. Most residents work **60 to 80 hours a week**, and despite the high workload, income remains limited. Many residents live paycheck to paycheck.

Dental and pharmacy residencies are sometimes optional and may pay even less—or be unpaid altogether.

Financial themes of residency:

- Learning how to **budget under pressure**
- Avoiding **lifestyle inflation**, even when friends in other professions are already earning more
- Starting to understand **loan repayment programs** like PSLF, IDR, or private refinancing
- Laying the foundation for healthy money habits

This is a critical phase for **financial literacy**. Residents have little room for error, but a huge opportunity to learn.

3. The Attending Years – Entry-Level Physician Pay

When residency ends, a physician finally begins earning real income. This is where the financial landscape begins to vary widely by **specialty** and **practice setting**.

Here's a general breakdown of **starting annual salaries**:

Specialty Typical Salary Range

Family Medicine, Pediatrics, IM

$200,000 – $280,000

OB-GYN, Psychiatry, Emergency, Hospitalist

$300,000 – $400,000

Specialties (Derm, Cardiology, Radiology, Anesthesiology)

$400,000 – $700,000

Surgical Specialties (Ortho, Neuro, Plastics, ENT)

$500,000 – $1,000,000+

General Dentist

$150,000 – $250,000

Orthodontist, Oral Surgeon

$300,000 – $600,000

Pharmacist

$120,000 – $150,000

Optometrist

$100,000 – $140,000

Chiropractor

$90,000 – $130,000

Factors that influence early attending income:

- Geographic location (urban areas may pay less due to competition)
- Academic vs. private setting
- Demand for your specialty
- Business savvy and negotiation

Even within specialties, there can be large ranges based on how compensation is structured. For instance, a cardiologist in private practice in a rural area may earn significantly more than one working at an academic center in a coastal city.

4. Practice Ownership vs. Employment

One of the biggest financial decisions a physician will make is whether to **remain employed** or **own their practice**.

Employed Physicians

Most doctors today begin (and often remain) as employees of hospitals, health systems, or large medical groups.

Pros:

- Steady income
- Employee benefits (health, retirement, malpractice)
- Less administrative burden

Cons:

- Less control over schedule and practice style
- Salary ceilings
- Vulnerability to hospital mergers or contract renegotiations

Practice Owners

Starting or buying into a private practice offers higher upside but more complexity.

Pros:

- Business ownership and potential equity
- More autonomy and decision-making power
- Ability to scale income over time

Cons:

- Administrative, legal, and financial responsibility
- Higher stress
- Must manage overhead, payroll, marketing, and operations

Some physicians transition from employment to ownership after a few years, while others start in ownership models immediately—especially in dentistry, optometry, and chiropractic fields.

Other Models:

- **Locum Tenens:** Short-term contract work. High hourly pay, flexibility, no long-term commitment.
- **Hospitalists:** Employed doctors focusing exclusively on inpatient care. Often salaried with bonus structures.
- **Telemedicine:** A growing field with flexible hours and scalable income potential.

5. Bonuses, Incentives, and Alternative Income

Beyond salary, many physicians earn income through a variety of **bonuses and incentives**.

RVU-Based Compensation

Used in hospital systems, RVUs (Relative Value Units) tie pay to productivity. The more you see, do, or bill, the more you earn. This rewards efficiency but can lead to burnout if mismanaged.

Profit Sharing & Partnership Models

In private or group practices, physicians may become partners and share in profits. This can significantly boost earnings beyond salary.

Call Pay

Some specialties offer extra pay for being on call nights, weekends, or holidays. Rates vary by specialty and institution.

Non-Clinical Revenue Streams

Many doctors are exploring **non-clinical income sources**, such as:

- Expert witness or medical-legal consulting
- Speaking, writing, or course creation
- Real estate investing
- Financial coaching or consulting
- YouTube, social media monetization
- Telehealth side gigs

Multiple income streams reduce financial vulnerability and create long-term wealth.

6. Retirement – Slowing Down and Transitioning Out

For many physicians, retirement isn't an abrupt stop — it's a **gradual transition**. Some reduce their hours, take on teaching roles, or continue consulting.

Common income sources in retirement:

- Pensions or defined benefit plans
- Withdrawals from 401(k), 403(b), IRAs, and brokerage accounts
- Real estate income
- Buyouts from selling a practice
- Social Security

Physicians who've lived below their means and invested consistently can retire comfortably—and even early. Others choose to work into their 70s, not out of necessity, but fulfillment.

Retirement planning should begin early. It's easier to scale back at 60 when you've been contributing to retirement plans since age 30.

7. What Determines a Doctor's Income?

Several variables impact how much a physician earns:

Specialty Choice:

Surgeons and specialists tend to earn more than primary care doctors, largely due to reimbursement models.

Geographic Location:

Rural areas often pay more to attract talent. Urban areas may offer more stability but lower compensation.

Practice Setting:

Academic medicine typically pays less than private practice but may offer other benefits like prestige or work-life balance.

Years of Experience:

Physician income generally grows with experience, peaking around mid-to-late career.

Ownership Status:

Partners and business owners have higher upside potential than employees.

Negotiation Skill:

Many physicians underestimate the importance of negotiating starting salaries, bonuses, and raises.

Demand:

Some specialties—such as psychiatry, endocrinology, or dermatology—are in high demand and command higher rates due to supply shortages.

8. U.S. Physician Income Rankings (Approximate Averages)

Here's a snapshot of average physician salaries in the U.S. across specialties:

SpecialtyAverage Salary

Neurosurgeon

$800,000+

Orthopedic Surgeon

$600,000 – $750,000

Cardiologist
$500,000 – $600,000
Anesthesiologist
$450,000 – $550,000
Radiologist
$450,000 – $500,000
Dermatologist
$400,000 – $500,000
OB-GYN
$350,000 – $400,000
Psychiatrist
$300,000 – $350,000
Family Medicine
$250,000 – $300,000
Pediatrician
$220,000 – $280,000
Dentist (General)
$150,000 – $250,000
Orthodontist
$300,000 – $500,000
Pharmacist
$120,000 – $150,000
Optometrist
$100,000 – $140,000
Chiropractor
$90,000 – $130,000

These numbers fluctuate yearly and by region, but the disparities reflect both training demands and reimbursement models.

Final Thoughts: It's Not Just About the Money

Becoming a doctor is one of the most demanding and expensive paths a person can choose. It often comes with years of delayed gratification, mounting debt, and physical and emotional exhaustion. But it also offers profound rewards — including financial ones.

Still, **money alone doesn't define success** in medicine. The happiest physicians are not always the highest earners. They're the ones who align their career path with their values, understand how they're compensated, and make intentional decisions with their income.

Knowing how you get paid is about more than tracking paychecks. It's about understanding **how your effort converts into income**, how to **protect that income**, and how to **maximize the years you have** to turn that income into long-term wealth and well-being.

Whether you're a medical student, resident, seasoned attending, or preparing to retire, now is the time to be strategic. Know your worth. Negotiate with confidence. Spend with purpose. Invest with vision.

Because in medicine—as in money—clarity is power.The title "Doctor" carries weight. It conjures respect, years of education, and often—whether fairly or not—the assumption of financial prosperity. But while medicine can be a high-income profession, not all white coats earn the same. From the first day of medical school to retirement, a physician's income journey varies significantly based on specialty, setting, location, experience, and individual choices.

In this chapter, we'll break down how doctors are compensated, how their pay evolves over time, and what financial expectations to realistically prepare for throughout the career lifecycle—from investment-heavy training years to high-income peaks and the transition into retirement.

1. Medical School – The Investment Phase

At this stage, there's no income—only cost.

Medical students are investors, not yet earners. The cost of this investment? On average, **over $200,000** in student loan debt. For those attending private institutions or out-of-state programs, the figure can exceed $300,000. Factor in four years of tuition, fees, and living expenses, and most students graduate owing more than the down payment on a house.

Other Healthcare Professions:

- **Dental** and **veterinary** students often take on similar debt loads, though they may complete their education sooner or transition to income faster.
- **Pharmacy** and **optometry** students may face total tuition and costs of $150,000 to $250,000.
- The debt burden is real across all advanced clinical professions.

Key takeaway: You're not earning yet, but your financial behavior starts now. How you borrow, budget, and plan during medical school can set the tone for your financial mindset for the rest of your career.

2. Residency – The Low Pay, High Workload Phase

After graduation, medical school is followed by **residency**, where newly minted physicians earn a salary—albeit a modest one—while working long hours in training.

Typical **resident salaries** range from **$60,000 to $75,000** per year, depending on the program and geographic region. Most residents work **60 to 80 hours a week**, and despite the high workload, income remains limited. Many residents live paycheck to paycheck.

Dental and pharmacy residencies are sometimes optional and may pay even less—or be unpaid altogether.

Financial themes of residency:

- Learning how to **budget under pressure**
- Avoiding **lifestyle inflation**, even when friends in other professions are already earning more
- Starting to understand **loan repayment programs** like PSLF, IDR, or private refinancing
- Laying the foundation for healthy money habits

This is a critical phase for **financial literacy**. Residents have little room for error, but a huge opportunity to learn.

3. The Attending Years – Entry-Level Physician Pay

When residency ends, a physician finally begins earning real income. This is where the financial landscape begins to vary widely by **specialty** and **practice setting**.

Here's a general breakdown of **starting annual salaries**:

Specialty/Typical Salary Range

Family Medicine, Pediatrics, IM

$200,000 – $280,000

OB-GYN, Psychiatry, Emergency, Hospitalist

$300,000 – $400,000

Specialties (Derm, Cardiology, Radiology, Anesthesiology)

$400,000 – $700,000

Surgical Specialties (Ortho, Neuro, Plastics, ENT)

$500,000 – $1,000,000+

General Dentist

$150,000 – $250,000

Orthodontist, Oral Surgeon

$300,000 – $600,000

Pharmacist

$120,000 – $150,000

Optometrist
$100,000 – $140,000
Chiropractor
$90,000 – $130,000
Factors that influence early attending income:

- Geographic location (urban areas may pay less due to competition)
- Academic vs. private setting
- Demand for your specialty
- Business savvy and negotiation

Even within specialties, there can be large ranges based on how compensation is structured. For instance, a cardiologist in private practice in a rural area may earn significantly more than one working at an academic center in a coastal city.

4. Practice Ownership vs. Employment

One of the biggest financial decisions a physician will make is whether to **remain employed** or **own their practice**.

Employed Physicians

Most doctors today begin (and often remain) as employees of hospitals, health systems, or large medical groups.

Pros:

- Steady income
- Employee benefits (health, retirement, malpractice)
- Less administrative burden

Cons:

- Less control over schedule and practice style
- Salary ceilings

- Vulnerability to hospital mergers or contract renegotiations

Practice Owners

Starting or buying into a private practice offers higher upside but more complexity.

Pros:

- Business ownership and potential equity
- More autonomy and decision-making power
- Ability to scale income over time

Cons:

- Administrative, legal, and financial responsibility
- Higher stress
- Must manage overhead, payroll, marketing, and operations

Some physicians transition from employment to ownership after a few years, while others start in ownership models immediately—especially in dentistry, optometry, and chiropractic fields.

Other Models:

- **Locum Tenens:** Short-term contract work. High hourly pay, flexibility, no long-term commitment.
- **Hospitalists:** Employed doctors focusing exclusively on inpatient care. Often salaried with bonus structures.
- **Telemedicine:** A growing field with flexible hours and scalable income potential.

5. Bonuses, Incentives, and Alternative Income

Beyond salary, many physicians earn income through a variety of **bonuses and incentives**.

RVU-Based Compensation

Used in hospital systems, RVUs (Relative Value Units) tie pay to productivity. The more you see, do, or bill, the more you earn. This rewards efficiency but can lead to burnout if mismanaged.

Profit Sharing & Partnership Models

In private or group practices, physicians may become partners and share in profits. This can significantly boost earnings beyond salary.

Call Pay

Some specialties offer extra pay for being on call nights, weekends, or holidays. Rates vary by specialty and institution.

Non-Clinical Revenue Streams

Many doctors are exploring **non-clinical income sources**, such as:

- Expert witness or medical-legal consulting
- Speaking, writing, or course creation
- Real estate investing
- Financial coaching or consulting
- YouTube, social media monetization
- Telehealth side gigs

Multiple income streams reduce financial vulnerability and create long-term wealth.

6. Retirement – Slowing Down and Transitioning Out

For many physicians, retirement isn't an abrupt stop — it's a **gradual transition**. Some reduce their hours, take on teaching roles, or continue consulting.

Common income sources in retirement:

- Pensions or defined benefit plans
- Withdrawals from 401(k), 403(b), IRAs, and brokerage accounts
- Real estate income
- Buyouts from selling a practice
- Social Security

Physicians who've lived below their means and invested consistently can retire comfortably—and even early. Others choose to work into their 70s, not out of necessity, but fulfillment.

Retirement planning should begin early. It's easier to scale back at 60 when you've been contributing to retirement plans since age 30.

7. What Determines a Doctor's Income?

Several variables impact how much a physician earns:

Specialty Choice:

Surgeons and specialists tend to earn more than primary care doctors, largely due to reimbursement models.

Geographic Location:

Rural areas often pay more to attract talent. Urban areas may offer more stability but lower compensation.

Practice Setting:

Academic medicine typically pays less than private practice but may offer other benefits like prestige or work-life balance.

Years of Experience:

Physician income generally grows with experience, peaking around mid-to-late career.

Ownership Status:

Partners and business owners have higher upside potential than employees.

Negotiation Skill:

Many physicians underestimate the importance of negotiating starting salaries, bonuses, and raises.

Demand:

Some specialties—such as psychiatry, endocrinology, or dermatology—are in high demand and command higher rates due to supply shortages.

8. U.S. Physician Income Rankings (Approximate Averages)

Here's a snapshot of average physician salaries in the U.S. across specialties:

Specialty Average Salary

Neurosurgeon

$800,000+

Orthopedic Surgeon

$600,000 – $750,000

Cardiologist

$500,000 – $600,000

Anesthesiologist

$450,000 – $550,000

Radiologist

$450,000 – $500,000

Dermatologist

$400,000 – $500,000

OB-GYN

$350,000 – $400,000

Psychiatrist

$300,000 – $350,000

Family Medicine

$250,000 – $300,000

Pediatrician

$220,000 – $280,000

Dentist (General)

$150,000 – $250,000

Orthodontist

$300,000 – $500,000

Pharmacist

$120,000 – $150,000
Optometrist
$100,000 – $140,000
Chiropractor
$90,000 – $130,000

These numbers fluctuate yearly and by region, but the disparities reflect both training demands and reimbursement models.

Final Thoughts: It's Not Just About the Money

Becoming a doctor is one of the most demanding and expensive paths a person can choose. It often comes with years of delayed gratification, mounting debt, and physical and emotional exhaustion. But it also offers profound rewards — including financial ones.

Still, **money alone doesn't define success** in medicine. The happiest physicians are not always the highest earners. They're the ones who align their career path with their values, understand how they're compensated, and make intentional decisions with their income.

Knowing how you get paid is about more than tracking paychecks. It's about understanding **how your effort converts into income**, how to **protect that income**, and how to **maximize the years you have** to turn that income into long-term wealth and well-being.

Whether you're a medical student, resident, seasoned attending, or preparing to retire, now is the time to be strategic. Know your worth. Negotiate with confidence. Spend with purpose. Invest with vision.

Because in medicine—as in money—clarity is power.

Chapter 37: Culture and Cash – How Your Background Shapes Your Money Mindset (Even If You're a Doctor)

Introduction: You Wear a White Coat, But Your Culture Wears the Stethoscope

You've made it through medical school. Survived residency. You're earning six figures, and society assumes you have it all figured out. But the truth is, many doctors — despite their education, title, and income — struggle with money.

Not because they don't make enough. Not because they don't work hard. But because they haven't addressed the hidden force that quietly shapes every financial decision they make: their culture.

Your upbringing, values, family dynamics, religion, race, gender norms, and even geographic location all contribute to how you view money, how you spend it, save it, give it, and talk (or don't talk) about it.

A white coat may standardize your profession, but it doesn't erase your past. Culture matters — and if you don't understand the impact it has on your financial mindset, you'll find yourself repeating patterns that don't serve your future.

This chapter explores how doctors from diverse backgrounds can acknowledge their cultural money stories, break free from limiting beliefs, and begin creating a new financial narrative that honors both their heritage and their goals.

Section 1: What Is Culture, Really?

Culture is more than language or cuisine — it's how your people think, act, and relate to the world. It's the lens through which we view success, work ethic, responsibility, and yes — money.

Culture includes:

- Family traditions and expectations
- Religious beliefs and spiritual values
- Views on gender roles and financial authority
- Unspoken rules about giving, saving, and investing
- Community pressures and obligations
- Socioeconomic status during childhood
- Immigrant or first-generation experiences

You may not even realize your money mindset is cultural — because for most of us, it just feels like "how things are done." But doctors from different backgrounds often come into their careers with vastly different financial starting lines and playbooks.

Section 2: Scarcity vs. Abundance – The Core Money Narrative

Some doctors grow up in homes where the dominant message around money is scarcity:

- "We can't afford that."
- "Money doesn't grow on trees."
- "Don't talk about what you earn — people will expect things from you."

Others grow up with a mindset of abundance:

- "We're blessed to be a blessing."
- "We'll find a way."
- "Let's make our money work for us."

These early lessons stick — and often determine your relationship with risk, investing, and even generosity.

A doctor who grew up with scarcity may:

- Keep excessive cash in checking accounts due to fear of investing.
- Say yes to every financial request from family, even to their own detriment.
- Feel guilt around spending money on themselves.

A doctor who grew up with abundance may:

- Be more open to entrepreneurship or real estate.
- Take smart financial risks earlier in their career.
- Seek out financial education as empowerment.

Neither approach is right or wrong — but one leads to growth, the other to stagnation.

Section 3: The First-Gen Physician Experience

If you're a first-generation doctor, you carry more than a stethoscope — you carry the hopes, dreams, and expectations of your entire family lineage.

Your parents may have worked multiple jobs to get you through school. Your siblings may be waiting for you to "make it" so they can catch a break. You may be the first in your family to speak fluent English, own a home, or have access to a financial advisor.

This unique experience creates powerful (and sometimes heavy) emotions:

- Gratitude: You don't want to complain — you've "made it," after all.
- Guilt: You're thriving while others back home are struggling.
- Fear: You're one misstep away from losing it all.
- Pressure: Everyone's counting on you — financially and emotionally.

This can lead to overworking, under-saving, and poor boundaries. You may say yes to loans you shouldn't co-sign, give more than you can afford, or live paycheck-to-paycheck despite earning six figures.

The key is to acknowledge the weight — and then learn how to carry it without breaking.

Section 4: Race, Culture, and the Wealth Gap

For many physicians of color, financial literacy isn't just about spreadsheets — it's about history.

African American Doctors

African American physicians often navigate a complex legacy of redlining, wage disparities, under representation in medicine, and cultural mistrust of financial institutions. Many grew up without examples of wealth-building — not because their families weren't smart or hardworking, but because systemic barriers made wealth accumulation difficult.

Stereotypes around Black wealth may include:

- "If you have money, you're obligated to share it."
- "Talking about wealth is showy or arrogant."
- "Buying luxury means you've made it."

These beliefs can lead to:

- Overgiving to family or church
- Underinvesting in retirement
- Delaying estate planning

Hispanic/Latino Doctors

Latino doctors often grow up in collectivist cultures that prioritize family and community over individual financial success. There may be pressure to send money to relatives in the U.S. and abroad, co-sign loans, or support aging parents.

Stereotypes may include:

- "Family comes first, always."
- "Investing is for the wealthy."
- "If you're doing well, others must benefit."

Common patterns include:

- Limited emergency savings
- Delayed homeownership due to helping family
- Avoidance of financial advisors due to language/cultural gaps

Chinese Doctors

In many Chinese families, education is paramount, and frugality is a virtue. There may be a high savings rate, but also reluctance to take investment risks or discuss money openly.

Stereotypes include:

- "Wealth is private."
- "Debt is shameful."
- "Buy property; it's the safest investment."

Impacts may include:

- High cash reserves
- Limited diversification
- Infrequent financial collaboration with professionals

Indian Doctors

Indian American doctors are often raised in families that emphasize education, status, and intergenerational responsibility. Many grow up seeing their parents invest in real estate or family business ventures.

Stereotypes:

- "Doctors are the pinnacle of success."
- "Parents will live with us later."
- "Invest in what you know."

Behaviors may include:

- Early investing in property
- Financial support of extended family
- Pressure to match peers in lifestyle and prestige

Section 5: Religion and Financial Ethics

Your faith doesn't just shape how you worship — it influences how you save, spend, give, and invest.

Christianity

- Tithing 10% of income
- Stewardship over ownership
- Wealth with humility

Islam

- Zakat: Giving 2.5% of wealth annually
- Halal investing: No interest, no gambling
- Community upliftment through finance

Judaism

- Tzedakah: Charitable giving
- Wealth as a tool for justice
- Structured legacy planning

Eastern Religions

- Simplicity and detachment from materialism
- Generational harmony and financial balance
- Planning as spiritual discipline

Faith-based financial planning brings peace when aligned with values. The key is integration, not avoidance.

Section 6: Gender Roles and Financial Control

In many cultures, gender expectations continue to shape money dynamics in physician households.

- In some families, men are expected to be the financial leader, regardless of their partner's earning power.
- Female physicians may feel tension balancing income with caregiving roles.
- LGBTQ+ doctors may challenge gendered assumptions around income, spending, and support roles.

Breaking these cycles requires:

- Open dialogue
- Shared financial responsibilities
- Rejection of outdated cultural expectations

Money is not just math — it's emotional. And in partnerships, financial clarity is emotional safety.

Section 7: Community Expectations and Financial Boundaries

In tight-knit cultures, success comes with strings attached.

You may be expected to:

- Pay for extended family's education
- Co-sign loans or mortgages
- Fund religious or community events
- Employ relatives in your practice
- Never say no to financial requests

While generosity is a beautiful value, giving without boundaries becomes enabling. It also prevents you from building long-term wealth that could support future generations more sustainably.

Consider these boundary-building strategies:

- Create a "giving budget" annually
- Offer non-financial support (mentorship, networking)
- Set firm limits around co-signing or business partnerships
- Use financial advisors as a buffer ("Let me run this by my advisor")

The most successful doctors give back — but they do so with a plan.

Section 8: The Culture of Medicine

Beyond ethnicity or religion, there's a powerful force that affects every doctor's money mindset: the culture of medicine itself.

In medical training, you're taught:

- Work comes first — always.
- Talking about money is "not why we're here."
- Burnout is a badge of honor.
- Financial planning is for business people, not healers.

This mindset is dangerous — and costly.

Because here's the truth: You are a business. You produce revenue. You manage risk. You pay taxes. You hire or work for others. You retire someday.

The most financially free doctors are those who reject the old-school idea that medicine and money can't mix — and instead embrace their full identity as both healers and wealth builders.

Section 9: Rewriting the Script – Building a New Financial Culture

Once you acknowledge the cultural forces that shaped your money story, you gain the power to rewrite the script.

Ask yourself:

- What beliefs about money did I inherit?
- What are those beliefs costing me?
- What do I want to teach my children or mentees about money?
- How do I want to feel about money in 10 years?

From there, begin building your own financial culture:

- Talk openly with your partner and family about financial goals
- Work with professionals who respect your cultural background
- Create systems that support your values (automated giving, investing, saving)
- Pass down financial literacy as part of your legacy

Section 10: Cultural Fluency in Financial Planning

If you work with a financial advisor, make sure they understand that money isn't just numbers — it's nuance.

Ask them:

- How do you approach clients from diverse backgrounds?
- Are you familiar with cultural or religious considerations in estate planning or investing?
- Can you help me create a giving plan that aligns with my values?

And don't be afraid to speak up. Your voice, your story, and your values matter. Cultural fluency isn't a checkbox — it's the foundation of trust.

Final Thoughts: Honor Your Roots, Build Your Future

You don't have to choose between honoring your culture and building wealth.

You can do both.

You can send money home and max out your 401(k). You can support your community and protect your peace. You can give generously and invest wisely. You can be the first in your family to earn this much and make sure you're not the last.

Being a doctor is a privilege. But financial freedom is a responsibility. And the moment you stop letting your past dictate your present — and start designing your future with intention — is the moment you become truly wealthy.

Chapter 38: Can You Manage Your Own Investments?

Yes, You Can — But Should You?

Physicians are smart. We're used to making high-stakes decisions, managing complex systems, and continuously learning new information. So, it's no surprise that many doctors ask: *Do I really need a financial advisor? Can't I just manage my own investments?*

The short answer: **Yes, you absolutely can.**

The better question: **Do you have the time, temperament, and tools to do it well?**

This chapter explores what it really takes to manage your own investments, the common mistakes doctors make when going solo, and how to determine whether you're better off with professional help or running your own financial playbook — just like a doctor weighing whether to treat a condition or refer to a specialist.

The DIY Mindset: Why Some Doctors Want to Go It Alone

There's a good reason more physicians are leaning toward do-it-yourself investing:

- **We've been burned before.** Many doctors have had negative experiences with advisors who charged too much, underperformed, or pushed high-commission products.

- **We're lifelong learners.** We enjoy researching and understanding complex topics.
- **We're high achievers.** We're used to taking responsibility for big outcomes.
- **We want control.** Letting someone else manage our hard-earned money can feel unsettling.

If you're motivated, disciplined, and curious, you *can* learn to invest wisely on your own — just like you can learn to cook, change your oil, or fix a leaky faucet. But that doesn't mean it's always the most efficient or effective use of your time.

Ask Yourself: Would You Be Your Own Doctor?

Before deciding to go fully DIY, ask the physician's version of the golden question:

Would you be your own doctor?

Would you skip annual checkups or self-diagnose a complex condition with just WebMD?

Sure, you could learn how to remove your appendix by watching YouTube videos. But should you?

You're an expert in medicine because of your **training, repetition, judgment, and experience** — not just your intelligence. The same is true for financial planners. The tools are accessible, but mastery takes time.

That said, plenty of doctors manage their investments well on their own. The key is knowing what's involved — and whether you're willing to commit.

What You Need to Know to Manage Your Own Investments

If you're serious about going DIY, here's what you need to understand to succeed:

1. **Your Financial Goals**

- Retirement target age and lifestyle
- Short-term and long-term savings needs
- Risk tolerance and investment horizon
- Whether you're investing for income, growth, or legacy

2. **How the Market Works**

- Stocks, bonds, ETFs, index funds, mutual funds
- The importance of asset allocation and diversification
- Understanding market volatility and investor behavior
- The difference between **investing** and **speculating**

3. **Accounts and Tax Shelters**

- 401(k), 403(b), 457(b)
- Roth IRA and Backdoor Roth IRA
- HSA (Health Savings Account)
- Taxable brokerage accounts
- Solo 401(k), SEP IRA for side gigs or private practice income

4. **Investment Strategies**

- Buy and hold vs. active trading
- Dollar-cost averaging
- Rebalancing your portfolio
- Risk management strategies (including bond allocation or hedging)

5. **Behavioral Discipline**

- Not panicking in market downturns
- Not chasing trends or stock tips
- Avoiding emotional decision-making (greed and fear)
- Staying consistent with your plan over decades

6. **Fees and Fund Expenses**

- Knowing the difference between an index fund with a 0.05% expense ratio and an actively managed fund with a 1% fee
- Recognizing hidden costs like transaction fees or advisory fees embedded in products

7. **Tax Efficiency**

- Understanding capital gains taxes
- Using tax-loss harvesting in taxable accounts
- Asset location: placing the right types of investments in the right accounts to minimize taxes
- Planning for RMDs (Required Minimum Distributions)

If all of that sounds overwhelming — that's okay. Most of it isn't taught in medical school or residency. But it can be learned.

The Pros of Managing Your Own Investments

1. Lower Costs

By avoiding advisor fees (typically 0.5%–1% of assets annually), you can keep more of your returns — especially if your portfolio grows into the seven figures.

2. Full Control

You choose your strategy, your risk exposure, your allocation, and your timeline.

3. No Conflicts of Interest

You're not being sold products or paying commissions.

4. Personal Growth

Learning about investing can improve your confidence and financial literacy across the board.

The Cons (and Risks) of Going Solo

1. Time Commitment

Keeping up with markets, tax laws, asset allocation, and your financial plan can feel like a part-time job. Most physicians already have two full-time jobs: practicing medicine and being human.

2. Analysis Paralysis

There's a fine line between researching and procrastinating. Too many options can lead to inaction or constant second-guessing.

3. Emotional Mistakes

Even smart investors panic during downturns or get greedy during booms. Doctors are not immune. One bad decision in a volatile market can erase years of returns.

4. Lack of Accountability

A good advisor acts like a personal trainer — keeping you on track when motivation fades. Without external accountability, it's easy to drift.

5. Overconfidence

Many high-earning professionals believe they'll beat the market or "time the dip." Very few actually do.

A Hybrid Approach: The Best of Both Worlds?

You don't have to choose between full DIY and full delegation. Many physicians use a **hybrid approach**:

- Do most of the planning and investing yourself, but consult a fee-only planner once a year.
- Manage your portfolio but use a tax advisor or estate planning attorney for specialized areas.
- Handle your 401(k) and IRAs but outsource your business financials or side gig planning.

Some doctors use **robo-advisors** like Betterment or Wealthfront for low-cost, automated investing with simple asset allocation.

Others use platforms like Vanguard or Fidelity to manage portfolios with low-cost index funds while occasionally hiring a fiduciary advisor for second opinions.

Questions to Ask Yourself Before Going DIY

1. **Do I enjoy learning about personal finance and investing?**
2. **Am I willing to dedicate a few hours a month to managing my portfolio?**
3. **Do I have the emotional discipline to stay the course when markets get rough?**
4. **Do I understand the tax implications of my investment decisions?**
5. **Will managing my investments distract me from my clinical work or personal life?**

If your answer is "yes" to most of these, you're probably a good candidate to go DIY. If not, there's no shame in hiring help — just like patients come to you for expertise they don't have.

What to Watch Out for If You Do Hire an Advisor

Not all advisors are created equal. If you decide to work with a professional, make sure they are:

- **Fee-only** (not commission-based)
- **Fiduciary** (legally obligated to act in your best interest)
- **Experienced with physicians** (ideally, someone who understands RVUs, call pay, PSLF, etc.)

Avoid:

- Advisors who sell insurance as investment products without clearly disclosing commissions
- Anyone pushing annuities or actively managed funds with high fees without fully explaining alternatives
- Confusing titles like "financial consultant" or "wealth coach" with no credentialing

Look for certifications like **CFP® (Certified Financial Planner)** or **CFA® (Chartered Financial Analyst)**.

Final Thoughts: Know Thyself

Managing your own investments is 100% doable. But just like medicine, success depends on preparation, discipline, and recognizing your limits.

If you enjoy it, have the time, and stay focused on the long game, DIY investing can be highly rewarding — both financially and intellectually.

But if it stresses you out, takes too much time, or tempts you to time the market or make emotional decisions, then it's not a sign of weakness to hire help. It's a sign of wisdom.

Ultimately, your financial life should support your real life — not consume it. Whether you manage your own investments or hire someone to help, the goal is the same: **security, peace of mind, and freedom to live life on your terms.**

Chapter 39: How to Open an Investment Account

As a doctor, you're no stranger to long hours and hard work, but when it comes to investing, you deserve to make your money work just as hard for you. Opening an investment account is one of the first steps toward building wealth and securing your financial future. This chapter will guide you through the process of opening an investment account, what's needed, and why it's an essential part of your financial planning.

Why Open an Investment Account?

Opening an investment account is critical to growing wealth over time. Investment accounts allow you to take advantage of compound interest, capital appreciation, and other financial instruments such as stocks, bonds, and mutual funds. Whether you're saving for retirement, building wealth for future goals, or seeking to diversify your income sources, an investment account is a necessary tool in achieving those financial goals.

Types of Investment Accounts

Before diving into the steps of opening an investment account, it's important to understand the different types of investment accounts available. Each one serves different purposes and offers various tax benefits:

1. **Individual Brokerage Accounts**
2. This is the most common type of investment account. It allows you to invest in stocks, bonds, ETFs, and other securities. While there are

no tax advantages to this account type, it offers flexibility, as you can withdraw your funds at any time without penalties.

3. **Retirement Accounts (IRAs, 401(k))**
4. These accounts offer tax benefits, either up-front (Traditional IRA, 401(k)) or in the form of tax-free withdrawals (Roth IRA). These accounts are designed for long-term retirement savings, but they come with contribution limits and withdrawal restrictions.
5. **Health Savings Accounts (HSAs)**
6. If you have a high-deductible health plan, you may be eligible for an HSA. While primarily used for medical expenses, an HSA also allows you to invest funds in stocks, bonds, or mutual funds. Contributions are tax-deductible, and withdrawals for qualifying medical expenses are tax-free.

Steps to Open an Investment Account

Now that you understand the types of accounts available, let's walk through the steps to open an investment account:

1. Determine Your Investment Goals

Before you start, take time to evaluate your goals. Are you saving for retirement? Do you have a specific target, such as buying a house or funding your children's education? Understanding your goals will help you choose the right type of account and investment strategy.

2. Choose an Investment Account Provider

There are numerous online brokers, banks, and financial institutions where you can open an investment account. When choosing an account provider, consider the following:

- **Fees:** Look for an account that offers low fees or commissions, especially if you plan to make regular trades.
- **Ease of Use:** Choose a provider with a user-friendly platform, whether you prefer online tools or mobile apps.
- **Investment Options:** Make sure the platform offers a variety of investment options like stocks, bonds, ETFs, mutual funds, etc.

- **Customer Service:** Choose a provider with solid customer support in case you have questions or run into issues.

Popular brokers include Vanguard, Fidelity, Charles Schwab, and TD Ameritrade, but there are many other options to choose from.

3. Gather Required Documents

To open an investment account, you will need to provide the following information:

- **Personal Identification:** A government-issued ID (driver's license, passport, etc.)
- **Social Security Number (SSN) or Taxpayer Identification Number (TIN):** This is required for tax reporting purposes.
- **Address and Contact Information:** Most platforms will ask for your current address, email, and phone number.
- **Employment and Financial Information:** Some institutions may require details about your employment and annual income, especially if you are opening a retirement account.

4. Complete the Application

Once you've chosen a provider and gathered your information, you can fill out the application online. The process is typically straightforward and takes just a few minutes. The application will ask about your investment experience, risk tolerance, and goals. Some platforms will even help you set up a personalized portfolio based on your answers.

5. Fund Your Account

After your application is approved, the next step is to fund your account. There are several ways to do this:

- **Transfer from a bank account:** Most brokers allow you to transfer money directly from your checking or savings account.
- **Transfer from another investment account:** If you have existing investments, you can transfer them to your new account.

- **Deposit by check or wire transfer:** Some providers allow you to fund your account by sending a check or wire transfer.

Be sure to check for any minimum deposit requirements, as some accounts may require an initial investment of a few hundred to a few thousand dollars.

6. Choose Your Investments

Once your account is funded, it's time to choose your investments. As a doctor, you may not have a lot of time to actively manage your portfolio, so consider options such as:

- **Target-Date Funds:** These are automatically managed funds that adjust their asset allocation based on your target retirement date.
- **ETFs and Index Funds:** These are great for diversification. You can invest in a wide range of stocks or bonds through one fund.
- **Robo-Advisors:** If you're not sure where to start, robo-advisors like Betterment and Wealthfront can automatically build and manage a diversified portfolio for you based on your goals and risk tolerance.

7. Monitor and Adjust Your Portfolio

Once your account is up and running, you'll want to keep track of your investments over time. Set a schedule to review your portfolio quarterly or annually. Rebalance your portfolio as needed to maintain your desired asset allocation and adjust for any changes in your financial goals.

What's Next?

Opening an investment account is just the beginning of your financial journey as a doctor. Now that you have a solid foundation for growing your wealth, it's important to continue educating yourself about investment strategies, tax implications, and financial planning to ensure long-term success.

Consider speaking with a financial advisor or utilizing tools like financial planning software to help you stay on track. Investing can be complex, but with the right knowledge and resources, you can build a secure financial future that supports your goals both personally and professionally.

Chapter 40: Complex Investment Strategies for Doctors: Understanding the Risks and Why Sophisticated is Not Always Best

Investment strategies vary in complexity, and while some advanced strategies can potentially offer significant returns, they are not without their risks. For doctors—who often juggle demanding careers and long hours—understanding complex investment strategies is essential to making informed financial decisions. In this chapter, we'll explore some of the more sophisticated investment strategies, how they work, and why, in many cases, simplicity might be the better choice for medical professionals looking to grow their wealth.

Understanding Sophisticated Investment Strategies

Before diving into the pros and cons of various investment strategies, it's important to understand what we mean by "sophisticated" investments. Sophisticated strategies are those that require a high level of understanding, active monitoring, and sometimes, even a high risk tolerance. These strategies might be appealing to investors looking for high returns, but they also come with increased complexity, fees, and the possibility of significant losses.

Some common examples of sophisticated strategies include:

1. **Leveraged and Inverse ETFs**

2. **Options Trading**
3. **Hedge Funds and Private Equity**
4. **Real Estate Syndications**
5. **Tax-Advantaged Strategies like Tax Loss Harvesting**
6. **Global and Emerging Market Investments**

Let's take a closer look at each of these strategies to see what makes them "sophisticated" and why they might not always be the right fit for doctors.

1. Leveraged and Inverse ETFs: High Risk, High Reward

Leveraged ETFs use financial derivatives and debt to amplify the returns of a specific index or asset class. For example, a 2x leveraged ETF aims to return twice the performance of its underlying index. **Inverse ETFs**, on the other hand, aim to provide the opposite return to an underlying index, often used by investors betting that the market will decline.

How It Works:

- A leveraged ETF is designed to replicate an index's returns by using borrowed money, options, or futures contracts. If the index moves up by 1%, a 2x leveraged ETF might return 2%. Conversely, if the market falls by 1%, the leveraged ETF would lose 2%.
- An inverse ETF is used by investors who believe the market will decline. If the market drops by 1%, the inverse ETF might rise by 1%.

Why It's Sophisticated:

- **Leverage Increases Risk:** Using leverage amplifies both potential gains and losses, which can make these strategies highly volatile. For doctors, whose time is limited and who may lack the expertise to constantly monitor the market, this increased volatility can be difficult to manage.
- **Daily Reset:** Leveraged and inverse ETFs are often designed for short-

term trades, typically over a day. For long-term investors, like most doctors, these ETFs can lose value over time due to their daily reset mechanism, even if the underlying market trend is favorable.

What Doctors Should Be Aware Of:

- **Not Suitable for Long-Term Holding:** While these instruments may seem appealing for short-term market timing, they are generally not suitable for long-term investors. Doctors who are looking to build wealth over time should stick to simpler, more stable investments.
- **Constant Monitoring Required:** Leveraged ETFs require active monitoring and a deep understanding of market movements. Without the time to dedicate to daily trading, doctors may expose themselves to greater risk.
- **High Fees:** The costs of trading these products can quickly add up, eroding returns over time. These fees can be particularly high in hedge funds and leveraged ETFs, making it more difficult for investors to achieve their financial goals.

2. Options Trading: The Power of Betting on Price Movements

Options trading allows an investor to buy or sell the right to buy or sell an asset at a specified price within a specified time. This can be done in two ways—through **call options** (which give the buyer the right to buy) or **put options** (which give the buyer the right to sell).

How It Works:

- In options trading, you are speculating on the direction of a stock's price. If you believe the price of a stock will go up, you might buy a **call option**, which gives you the right to buy the stock at a specific price before the option expires.
- If you believe a stock will go down, you might buy a **put option**, which allows you to sell a stock at a certain price within a specific time frame.

Why It's Sophisticated:

- **Risk of Total Loss:** With options, the buyer can lose the entire investment if the stock doesn't move in the expected direction by the expiration date. This makes it inherently risky, especially for those without the time to closely monitor their positions.
- **Complexity in Execution:** Options strategies can become quite complex, involving various combinations of buying and selling options at different strike prices and expiration dates. For someone unfamiliar with options, it's easy to make costly mistakes.

What Doctors Should Be Aware Of:

- **Time Sensitivity:** Options have expiration dates, meaning that you have a limited window to make a profit. This makes them more suitable for short-term traders, but doctors often don't have the time to monitor markets constantly.
- **High Risk:** The potential for significant loss makes options unsuitable for most doctors looking for steady, long-term growth. Options are best left to experienced traders who understand the intricacies of options pricing, implied volatility, and market movements.
- **Complex to Understand:** The learning curve for options trading is steep. While it can offer substantial returns, it also carries the risk of losing your entire investment in a very short period.

3. Hedge Funds and Private Equity: High Fees and Limited Access

Hedge funds and **private equity funds** pool money from accredited investors to invest in a wide variety of assets, including stocks, bonds, real estate, and even private companies. These funds often use leverage, short-selling, and other complex strategies to try and beat the market.

How It Works:

- **Hedge Funds:** These funds aim to produce high returns by using various strategies such as arbitrage, long and short positions, and derivatives. They often invest in less-liquid assets and use leverage to maximize returns.
- **Private Equity Funds:** These funds invest directly in private companies, either through buyouts or early-stage investments. The goal is to eventually sell the company at a profit or take it public.

Why It's Sophisticated:

- **High Minimum Investment Requirements:** Hedge funds and private equity funds often require substantial minimum investments, sometimes in the range of $1 million or more. This limits their accessibility.
- **High Fees:** These funds typically charge high management fees and performance-based fees, meaning you pay a percentage of your profits to the fund manager. This can significantly eat into returns.
- **Illiquidity:** Hedge funds and private equity investments often lock up your money for years, making it difficult to access funds without incurring penalties.

What Doctors Should Be Aware Of:

- **High Fees Can Erode Returns:** Hedge funds and private equity often charge both management fees and a share of the profits. While they may offer higher returns, the costs can make it difficult to come out ahead, particularly when compounding over time.
- **Lack of Liquidity:** If you need access to your money, you might be unable to sell your investment quickly. Doctors with a busy lifestyle may not be comfortable with the lack of liquidity.
- **Complex Due Diligence:** To evaluate a hedge fund or private equity investment, a significant amount of due diligence is required. Without the time and expertise to thoroughly vet these investments, doctors

could be exposing themselves to unnecessary risks.

4. Real Estate Syndications: Pooling Resources for Large-Scale Investments

A **real estate syndication** is when multiple investors pool their resources together to invest in larger real estate projects, such as apartment complexes or commercial properties. This allows individual investors to take part in deals that they might not otherwise have access to.

How It Works:

- Investors contribute capital to a syndicate, which is managed by a sponsor who is responsible for acquiring and managing the real estate.
- The sponsor earns a management fee and a portion of the profits, while investors receive returns based on the performance of the property.

Why It's Sophisticated:

- **Complexity in Management:** Real estate syndications involve multiple parties, contracts, and property management issues. There's significant paperwork, due diligence, and management oversight involved.
- **High Minimum Investments:** Many real estate syndications require high minimum investments (often $50,000 or more), which can be difficult for doctors who are just starting to build wealth outside of their practice.

What Doctors Should Be Aware Of:

- **Illiquidity and Long-Term Commitment:** Like private equity, real estate syndications often lock up investments for years. This may not be ideal for doctors who want access to their money in the short term.
- **Management Fees:** While syndications can provide passive income,

they also come with management fees that can eat into your profits. Be sure to understand the fee structure before committing.

- **Market Risks:** Real estate markets can be volatile, especially in the face of rising interest rates or economic downturns. Even a well-managed property may experience challenges.

Why Sophisticated is Not Always the Best Option for Doctors

While these sophisticated strategies can be profitable, they often come with high fees, complex management, and risks that may not align with a doctor's investment goals or time commitments. Doctors, who typically have demanding careers, may not have the time or expertise to actively manage these types of investments.

Simplicity is Key

For many doctors, a simpler approach to investing—such as investing in low-cost index funds or using a robo-advisor—can be far more effective in the long run. These strategies provide:

- **Diversification:** Low-cost index funds and ETFs allow you to invest in a broad range of assets, reducing the risk associated with any single investment.
- **Passive Management:** Index funds and robo-advisors are typically set-it-and-forget-it strategies, which require minimal active management, freeing up time for doctors to focus on their practices.
- **Lower Costs:** Simple investments typically have lower fees, allowing more of your money to work for you.
- **Long-Term Growth:** A long-term, patient investment strategy is more likely to deliver steady, reliable returns without the high risk associated with complex strategies.

Conclusion

While sophisticated investment strategies may sound enticing, they are often more suitable for those who have the time, expertise, and risk tolerance to actively manage them. For most doctors, a more straightforward approach to investing, focusing on long-term growth through diversified, low-cost assets, will likely be a more effective way to build wealth. Keep it simple, stay patient, and allow your investments to grow steadily over time.

Chapter 41: The Backdoor Roth IRA: What It Is, How to Structure It, and Whether You Should Get One

A Roth IRA is one of the most popular retirement accounts due to its tax advantages: contributions are made with after-tax dollars, and qualified withdrawals are tax-free. However, there are income limits that restrict high earners from directly contributing to a Roth IRA. Enter the **Backdoor Roth IRA**, a legal strategy that allows high-income individuals to circumvent the income limits and still enjoy the benefits of a Roth IRA.

In this chapter, we will explore what a Backdoor Roth IRA is, how to structure it, and whether it's a good choice for you, especially if you're a high-income earner such as a doctor. We'll also discuss the pros and cons of this strategy to help you decide if it aligns with your retirement goals.

What is a Backdoor Roth IRA?

A **Backdoor Roth IRA** is a method for high-income individuals to contribute to a Roth IRA by first contributing to a Traditional IRA and then converting those funds to a Roth IRA. This strategy works because there are no income limits on who can contribute to a Traditional IRA (although tax deductibility may be limited based on income) and there are no income limits on conversions from a Traditional IRA to a Roth IRA.

Here's how it works in basic steps:

1. **Contribute to a Traditional IRA:** Even if your income exceeds the Roth IRA income limits, you can contribute to a Traditional IRA. However, if you are covered by an employer's retirement plan (like a 401(k)), your contributions to the Traditional IRA may not be deductible based on your income level.
2. **Convert to a Roth IRA:** Once the money is in your Traditional IRA, you can convert it to a Roth IRA. Since there are no income limits on Roth IRA conversions, you can effectively "backdoor" your way into a Roth IRA.
3. **Pay Taxes on Earnings (if applicable):** If you made non-deductible contributions to your Traditional IRA (i.e., after-tax money), you will not owe taxes on those contributions when converting. However, any pre-tax contributions and earnings in the account will be taxed at your ordinary income tax rate upon conversion.

Should You Get a Backdoor Roth IRA?

A Backdoor Roth IRA can be a powerful tool, but it's not suitable for everyone. The decision to use this strategy depends on your financial goals, income level, and overall retirement planning strategy. Here are some factors to consider:

1. High Income Limits for Roth IRAs

If your income exceeds the limits for direct Roth IRA contributions, the Backdoor Roth IRA can be an attractive alternative. For 2025, the Roth IRA income limits are as follows:

- **Single filer:** Phase-out begins at $138,000 and ends at $153,000.
- **Married filing jointly:** Phase-out begins at $218,000 and ends at $228,000.

If your income is above these limits, you cannot directly contribute to a Roth IRA, but you can still use the Backdoor method.

2. Desire for Tax-Free Growth

One of the main advantages of a Roth IRA is that it grows tax-free. For doctors, whose income typically peaks in their 40s or 50s, the ability to have tax-free growth and withdrawals in retirement can be an extremely valuable strategy, especially if you expect to be in a higher tax bracket when you retire.

3. Current and Future Tax Considerations

If you are in a high tax bracket now, contributing to a Roth IRA through the Backdoor method can be beneficial because you are locking in the current tax rate on your contributions. However, if you're planning to retire in a lower tax bracket, it might be more advantageous to invest in tax-deferred accounts like a Traditional IRA or 401(k) since you'd be paying less tax when you withdraw in the future.

4. Estate Planning Benefits

Roth IRAs offer excellent estate planning advantages. Since qualified Roth IRA withdrawals are tax-free, your heirs will not have to pay taxes on the distributions they inherit from your Roth IRA. This makes a Backdoor Roth IRA a powerful tool if you are considering passing wealth onto your heirs.

How to Structure a Backdoor Roth IRA

The process of opening and funding a Backdoor Roth IRA involves a few key steps. Here is a step-by-step guide to structuring a Backdoor Roth IRA:

Step 1: Open a Traditional IRA

First, you need to open a Traditional IRA. Most financial institutions offer a low-cost way to open a Traditional IRA, and many even allow you to do this online. There is no income limit for contributing to a Traditional IRA, but if you're above a certain income level and are covered by an employer's retirement plan (such as a 401(k)), your contributions may be non-deductible.

Step 2: Make a Non-Deductible Contribution

If you are a high-income earner, your contributions to the Traditional IRA will be non-deductible, meaning you will not get an immediate tax benefit. However, it is still beneficial because it allows you to contribute to a retirement account despite being ineligible for a direct Roth IRA contribution.

For 2025, the maximum contribution limit to an IRA (whether Traditional or Roth) is **$6,500** if you are under 50, or **$7,500** if you are 50 or older. You can contribute this full amount to your Traditional IRA, but keep in mind that this money is after-tax because it is non-deductible.

Step 3: Convert the Funds to a Roth IRA

Once your contribution has been made to the Traditional IRA, you can then convert those funds to a Roth IRA. The process is relatively simple and can usually be done online through your brokerage's website.

There are two main tax implications to consider:

- If you have made **non-deductible contributions** (i.e., after-tax money), you won't owe any taxes on the contribution portion of the conversion.
- However, if you have any **pre-tax funds** in the Traditional IRA (such as from previous years), those funds will be subject to taxes when converted.

It's a good idea to complete the conversion soon after making the contribution, so there is minimal time for earnings to accumulate, which would then be taxed when you convert.

Step 4: Report the Conversion

When you convert funds from a Traditional IRA to a Roth IRA, the IRS requires you to report the conversion on your tax return. You will receive **Form 1099-R** from the institution handling the conversion, and you will need to report this on your tax return, along with any income generated by the conversion.

You'll also file **Form 8606**, which keeps track of your non-deductible contributions to your Traditional IRA, ensuring you don't pay taxes twice on the same contributions.

Pros and Cons of the Backdoor Roth IRA

Like any financial strategy, the Backdoor Roth IRA has its advantages and disadvantages. Let's break them down:

Pros:

1. **Tax-Free Growth:** The biggest advantage of a Roth IRA is the tax-free growth and tax-free withdrawals in retirement. This is especially powerful for high earners like doctors, who may expect to be in a higher tax bracket in retirement.
2. **No Required Minimum Distributions (RMDs):** Unlike Traditional IRAs, Roth IRAs do not require you to take RMDs during your lifetime. This gives you greater control over your retirement funds and allows them to continue growing.
3. **Estate Planning Benefits:** Roth IRAs can be passed on to heirs without triggering income taxes. This makes it an attractive option for doctors who want to leave a tax-free legacy to their children or grandchildren.
4. **Access to a Roth IRA Despite Income Limits:** For high earners who exceed Roth IRA contribution limits, the Backdoor Roth IRA provides a legal means to access this valuable retirement account.

Cons:

1. **Complexity and Paperwork:** The Backdoor Roth IRA strategy involves several steps and requires careful tracking. You'll need to make sure you're following the correct procedure and file the necessary forms with your tax return.
2. **Pro-Rata Rule:** If you have other pre-tax IRA balances (such as in a Traditional IRA), the IRS requires that your conversion be done on a pro-rata basis. This means that if you have both pre-tax and after-tax money in your Traditional IRA, a portion of your conversion will be taxed at ordinary income tax rates, which could result in a

higher-than-expected tax bill.

3. **Taxes on Earnings:** If you don't convert your funds soon after contributing, any earnings in the Traditional IRA will be taxed when converted, which could reduce the benefit of the strategy.
4. **Limited to High-Income Earners:** While a Backdoor Roth IRA is a great option for high-income earners, it's not available to everyone. You must have income above the Roth IRA limits to consider this strategy.

Conclusion: Is a Backdoor Roth IRA Right for You?

A Backdoor Roth IRA is a powerful strategy for high-income earners who want to take advantage of the benefits of a Roth IRA but exceed the income limits. It allows you to enjoy tax-free growth and retirement withdrawals while avoiding the required minimum distributions (RMDs) that come with a Traditional IRA.

However, it is not without its complexities. The process involves contributing to a Traditional IRA, converting it to a Roth IRA, and potentially dealing with the pro-rata rule if you have other pre-tax IRA funds. The strategy also requires careful tracking and filing, so it's important to consult with a tax advisor or financial planner to ensure you're executing the strategy correctly.

For many doctors, a Backdoor Roth IRA can be a great way to maximize their retirement savings. But, as with any investment decision, it's important to carefully weigh the pros and cons and consider how it fits into your broader financial plan.

Part 5: The Transition Years – Preparing for Retirement

Shifting from Practicing Medicine to Living Life on Your Terms

Retirement. For years, it's felt like a distant concept—something other people talk about while you were still building your career, managing your practice, raising a family, or handling the daily demands of medicine.

But now, it's starting to feel real.

Whether you're five, ten, or even fifteen years out, this phase of your career—the transition years—is where preparation becomes purpose.

You've worked hard. You've earned well. You've impacted countless lives.

But here's the question every physician eventually faces:

Will the life I've built sustain me when the scrubs come off for good?

Retirement isn't just about stopping work. It's about **starting the next chapter of your life**—with clarity, security, and freedom. And how well you make that transition depends largely on how well you plan in these final working years.

This is where many doctors realize:

- They don't know if they've saved enough—or in the right way
- They've spent years deferring financial decisions
- They're unsure how to turn assets into sustainable income
- They're not clear on taxes, healthcare, or estate plans

- And they haven't talked to their spouse or family about what retirement actually looks like

That's where this part of the book comes in.

The Purpose of Part 5:

To give you the tools, frameworks, and foresight to prepare for retirement in a way that's aligned with your goals, values, and lifestyle.

Because retirement isn't the end of the story. It's the start of a new chapter—and you get to write it.

Chapter 42: Should a Doctor Invest in Real Estate or Restaurants? Understanding the Pros, Cons, and the Reality

As a doctor, you're already accustomed to managing complex tasks, making important decisions, and handling high-pressure situations. However, when it comes to building wealth outside of your medical practice, two popular investment options frequently come up: **real estate** and **restaurants**. These sectors are appealing because they offer the potential for income, tax advantages, and long-term appreciation. But, like any investment, they come with their own set of risks and challenges.

In this chapter, we will explore the realities of investing in **real estate** and **restaurants**—discussing the pros, cons, and considerations that doctors should take into account before deciding whether to venture into these investment spaces. We'll also provide a guide on how each investment option aligns with your lifestyle as a busy medical professional and how it may impact your financial future.

Investing in Real Estate: Building Wealth Through Property

Real estate has long been a favored investment choice for individuals looking to build long-term wealth. The basic appeal lies in its potential to appreciate in value over time, its ability to generate passive income through rental properties, and the various tax advantages it offers. However, real estate investment is not a "hands-off" business, especially if you're a beginner.

Pros of Real Estate Investment

1. **Steady Income Stream (Passive Income)**
2. One of the main attractions of real estate investment is the ability to generate consistent cash flow through rental income. For doctors, who often work long hours, rental properties can provide an income stream that requires minimal active management if the right systems are in place (such as property management companies).
3. **Appreciation Over Time**
4. Real estate typically appreciates in value over the long term. As the property market increases in value, your property could be worth significantly more than the initial investment, allowing you to sell for a profit later.
5. **Tax Benefits**
6. Real estate offers several tax advantages, including deductions for mortgage interest, property taxes, repairs, and depreciation. For doctors who are already in a high tax bracket, these tax breaks can provide significant savings and improve your overall investment returns.
7. **Leverage**
8. Real estate allows you to leverage borrowed money (via a mortgage) to increase the size of your investment. For example, with a down payment of 20%, you can control a property worth five times that amount. This is a powerful tool for maximizing returns, though it also increases risk.
9. **Hedge Against Inflation**
10. Real estate is often viewed as a hedge against inflation. As inflation rises, so do property values and rents, helping real estate investors preserve their wealth.

Cons of Real Estate Investment

1. **Illiquidity**
2. Real estate is an illiquid investment, meaning that it's not easy to sell quickly if you need cash. Doctors who may need to access funds in emergencies could face challenges when trying to sell a property in a short amount of time.
3. **Time and Effort for Property Management**
4. Managing real estate can be time-consuming. While you can hire property management companies, they come with a fee—typically around 10% of rental income. If you opt to manage the property yourself, you'll have to handle tenant issues, repairs, and vacancies, all of which can eat into your valuable time. Doctors already have demanding careers, and adding the responsibility of managing rental properties can be overwhelming without the right systems in place.
5. **Market Risk and Volatility**
6. Like any investment, real estate is subject to market risk. Property values can fluctuate depending on the local economy, interest rates, and housing demand. An economic downturn or an oversupply of rental properties could lead to vacancies and reduced income, leaving you with higher costs than anticipated.
7. **High Initial Capital Investment**
8. Real estate requires a significant upfront capital investment, including the down payment, closing costs, and potential renovations. Doctors, especially early in their careers, may find it challenging to allocate such a large portion of their savings to real estate without affecting their other financial goals.
9. **Property Maintenance Costs**
10. Even with property management services, maintenance costs are a fact of life when owning real estate. Roof repairs, plumbing issues, and appliance replacements can eat into profits, especially if you own multiple properties.

Is Real Estate Right for Doctors?

Given the relatively high initial investment and the potential time commitment, real estate may not be suitable for every doctor. However, for those with the capital to invest and a desire for long-term wealth-building, real estate can be a viable and profitable choice. Doctors should consider passive options, such as Real Estate Investment Trusts (REITs) or hiring a property management firm, to minimize the time and effort involved in managing properties.

Investing in Restaurants: A Business with High Risk and Potential Rewards

Restaurant investment is an entirely different animal. While it offers the possibility of high returns, it also presents one of the most challenging and volatile industries in which to invest. Doctors who are considering investing in restaurants should fully understand the operational risks and the commitment required.

Pros of Restaurant Investment

1. **Potential for High Returns**
2. A successful restaurant can yield significant returns, especially in high-demand areas. With the right concept, location, and management, restaurants can generate substantial income and offer potential for growth through expansion.
3. **Tangible Business Asset**
4. Restaurants are tangible assets that can be sold, franchised, or expanded. For doctors who want to be more actively involved in their investments, owning a restaurant could provide the opportunity to run a business and build a brand.
5. **Tax Deductions for Business Expenses**
6. As a restaurant owner, you can deduct business expenses, such as food, wages, utilities, and marketing, from your taxable income. These deductions can significantly reduce the overall tax burden, though

this will depend on the structure of your business and whether you decide to operate independently or through a franchise.

7. **Opportunities for Diversification**
8. Owning a restaurant can provide diversification in your investment portfolio. It allows you to tap into the food and hospitality sector, which moves differently than traditional stock market investments.

Cons of Restaurant Investment

1. **High Failure Rate**
2. Restaurants are notoriously risky investments. According to statistics, approximately **60% of restaurants fail within the first year**, and only about **20% make it past five years**. The restaurant industry is highly competitive, with changing consumer preferences, economic conditions, and rising costs contributing to high failure rates. Doctors who are used to stability may find the volatility of the restaurant business unsettling.
3. **Time-Consuming and Labor-Intensive**
4. Running a restaurant is extremely labor-intensive. From managing employees to handling food orders and customer service, it requires continuous oversight. While doctors may choose to be passive investors, restaurant owners often need to be involved daily, especially in the initial years.
5. **High Initial Investment and Ongoing Costs**
6. Starting or buying a restaurant requires significant capital. Costs include purchasing or leasing a location, kitchen equipment, décor, licenses, and initial staff wages. Furthermore, the restaurant industry is capital-intensive with high ongoing costs for ingredients, utilities, and employee salaries.
7. **Thin Profit Margins**
8. Even in a successful restaurant, profit margins are typically slim. According to industry reports, profit margins for restaurants tend to hover around **3-5%**. While the potential for growth is high, the costs

of operating a restaurant—staff, food, and overhead—can quickly eat away at profits.

9. **Operational Challenges**
10. Managing a restaurant involves a wide range of challenges, from dealing with health regulations and food safety standards to managing customer complaints and employee turnover. For a doctor who already has a busy schedule, taking on the responsibility of overseeing such a business could lead to burnout.

Is Investing in Restaurants Right for Doctors?

Restaurant investment can be appealing for doctors who want to build something tangible and have the entrepreneurial drive to actively participate in a business. However, for most doctors, especially those early in their careers or with significant time constraints, investing in restaurants presents too many risks and challenges. The time commitment, high failure rate, and operational hurdles may make restaurants better suited for someone who can dedicate significant time and effort to the business.

Conclusion: Real Estate or Restaurants?

Both **real estate** and **restaurants** offer opportunities for growth and wealth-building, but they come with their own sets of challenges. For most doctors, **real estate** is likely the more viable option, especially if they are looking for a relatively passive investment that offers long-term growth and tax advantages. However, it's important to recognize that real estate also requires substantial capital, and property management can be time-consuming.

On the other hand, **restaurant investments** offer high potential rewards but are fraught with risks, high failure rates, and operational demands. Restaurants require a hands-on approach and an entrepreneurial spirit, which may not align with the lifestyle of a busy doctor.

Ultimately, the decision should be based on your financial goals, available time, and risk tolerance. If you're looking for a stable, long-term investment that allows for passive income and capital appreciation, real estate is likely the better option. If you have the passion, time, and risk tolerance for managing a business, investing in a restaurant could be a rewarding—but high-risk—venture. As always, it's essential to consult with a financial advisor and do thorough research before diving into any investment.

Chapter 43: Should a Doctor Invest in Land? Understanding the Pros, Cons, and Realities of Land Investment

Land investment is often touted as a great long-term strategy for wealth creation. It provides the potential for high returns, the ability to diversify one's investment portfolio, and the opportunity to own a tangible asset. However, like any investment, it comes with its own set of challenges and risks. For doctors, who typically lead busy professional lives, it's essential to weigh the benefits and drawbacks of land investment carefully before diving in.

In this chapter, we will explore the advantages and disadvantages of investing in land, how it compares to other forms of real estate investment, and whether it makes sense for doctors to consider this option as part of their financial strategy.

What is Land Investment?

Land investment refers to purchasing parcels of land with the intention of holding, developing, or selling them for profit. Unlike residential or commercial real estate, land investment typically involves buying undeveloped plots, such as agricultural land, residential lots, or vacant plots for future development. The key appeal of land investment lies in the fact that land is a finite resource—there's only so much land available, and demand typically grows as populations increase or new developments are needed.

There are several types of land investment opportunities, including:

- **Raw Land:** Unimproved land with no utilities or infrastructure, typically in rural or undeveloped areas.
- **Agricultural Land:** Land used for farming, ranching, or other agricultural purposes.
- **Development Land:** Vacant land in areas that are likely to see development in the future, such as urban expansion zones or residential subdivisions.
- **Timberland:** Land used for growing timber, which can be harvested and sold for profit.
- **Recreational Land:** Land bought for recreational purposes, such as hunting or camping, which could appreciate in value over time.

Pros of Investing in Land

Land investment offers several advantages that can appeal to doctors looking to diversify their portfolios or explore more passive investment options.

1. Tangible Asset with Limited Depreciation

Unlike stocks, bonds, or even certain types of real estate, land is a **tangible asset** that doesn't degrade over time. While buildings and structures can deteriorate, land itself does not depreciate. In fact, land often appreciates in value as demand increases, especially in growing urban areas or desirable locations.

For doctors who may prefer more traditional, low-risk investments, land is an attractive option because it offers long-term stability and the potential for value growth without the concern of physical depreciation.

2. Long-Term Capital Appreciation

Land generally appreciates in value over time, especially in high-demand areas. This makes it an excellent option for long-term wealth building. While the short-term growth rate may not be as rapid as with stocks or real estate, over the course of several years or decades, the value of land can increase significantly, especially in areas poised for development or those near expanding urban centers.

This type of investment fits well with the financial goals of many doctors, who may be looking for a steady, long-term investment vehicle that aligns with their retirement planning or legacy goals.

3. Low Maintenance

One of the most appealing aspects of land investment is that it requires **minimal maintenance** compared to real estate investments that involve buildings. There are no tenants to manage, no plumbing to fix, and no roof to repair. The land owner's responsibility is typically limited to ensuring property taxes are paid and maintaining any legal requirements related to zoning, land use, and ownership.

For busy doctors who may not have the time or desire to manage a more hands-on investment, land provides a **low-maintenance** option to grow wealth passively. While you may occasionally need to maintain the land (e.g., cutting the grass, controlling weeds), the day-to-day requirements are relatively minimal compared to owning rental properties or running a business.

4. Diversification of Investment Portfolio

Land is an excellent tool for **portfolio diversification**. It is largely independent of the stock market, and its value is influenced by different factors, such as demand for real estate, zoning changes, or changes in local infrastructure development. By diversifying with land, doctors can protect their wealth against stock market volatility, economic downturns, or other risks that could affect traditional investments.

Additionally, land can be used to generate income in several ways, such as through agricultural leases or selling the land when it appreciates. This flexibility allows for customization based on the investor's financial needs and goals.

5. Potential for Development

Land provides the unique opportunity for development, whether it's residential, commercial, or agricultural. As a doctor, you may be able to buy land in an area that is expected to see significant development and hold it until the area becomes more desirable, at which point you can sell for a substantial profit. Alternatively, you can hold the land and lease it for farming, ranching, or timber harvesting.

In areas where land development is likely or urban sprawl is expected, buying land early can result in substantial gains once the property is re-zoned or developed.

Cons of Investing in Land

While land investment offers several advantages, it also has its drawbacks. Doctors, particularly those with limited time and investment experience, should carefully consider these factors before deciding to invest in land.

1. Illiquidity and Long Holding Period

Land is generally a **long-term investment**, and it can take years—if not decades—for it to appreciate significantly in value. Additionally, land is **illiquid**, meaning that it's not as easy to sell quickly as stocks or even rental properties. If you need to access cash in an emergency, selling land may not be the most practical option, as it could take time to find a buyer and negotiate the sale.

For doctors who are looking for more liquid investments that can be easily sold or accessed, land may not be the best option. It requires a longer horizon for value realization and may not align with your immediate financial needs.

2. Ongoing Costs

Although land doesn't require the same level of maintenance as buildings, it does come with **ongoing costs** such as property taxes, insurance, and potential management fees if you decide to lease the land or have someone oversee it. Property taxes can be especially burdensome in areas where land values have increased, and depending on the land's zoning, you may need to make additional investments in utilities or infrastructure to make it more marketable for development.

For doctors who are new to land investment, it's essential to account for these recurring costs and ensure they are prepared for them, especially during periods when the land is not generating income.

3. Potential for Limited Immediate Returns

Unlike stocks, which can produce dividends, or real estate, which can generate rental income, land typically **does not produce immediate cash flow**. While you may appreciate the land's value over time, you will not see ongoing income unless you lease the property for farming, recreational purposes, or other uses.

As a doctor, you may be accustomed to the active income from your practice, and land investment may seem passive to the point of feeling disconnected from your financial goals if you're looking for more immediate returns. It's important to understand that land should be viewed as a long-term, growth-oriented asset rather than an immediate source of income.

4. Zoning and Land Use Restrictions

Land is often subject to **zoning laws** and **land-use restrictions**, which can limit how you can develop or utilize the property. For example, if you purchase agricultural land, zoning laws might restrict its use for commercial development or residential housing. Furthermore, local governments may change zoning regulations, potentially decreasing the value of your land if the area transitions to less desirable land uses.

It's crucial to thoroughly research the zoning laws and potential development plans for the area in which you're considering purchasing land. Doctors who are unfamiliar with local regulations may face challenges when it comes to evaluating the land's potential or navigating the permitting process.

5. Market Volatility

While land is generally considered a stable investment, it is still subject to **market volatility**. Economic downturns, changes in interest rates, and shifts in demand for land (due to technological advances or population migration) can influence land values. As with any investment, land may not always appreciate in the way you expect.

Is Land Investment Right for Doctors?

For doctors, investing in land can be an attractive opportunity to diversify a portfolio and accumulate wealth over time. However, land investment is not without its challenges. It requires a long-term mindset, an understanding of zoning laws, and a willingness to hold the property through periods of illiquidity and fluctuating market conditions.

If you're considering land investment, it may be a good idea to start small, perhaps by purchasing rural or agricultural land in an area poised for growth. Alternatively, if you prefer a more hands-off approach, you might want to explore land investment through a **Real Estate Investment Trust (REIT)** that specializes in land development.

For those doctors with the capital to invest and a long-term financial horizon, land investment can provide significant rewards in terms of appreciation, tax advantages, and diversification. However, it's important to approach this investment carefully, and with the help of a financial advisor, to ensure it aligns with your overall goals and risk tolerance.

Conclusion:

Land investment offers doctors the potential for long-term capital appreciation, diversification, and tax benefits. However, it is not without risks, including illiquidity, ongoing costs, and zoning restrictions. Doctors interested in investing in land should weigh the benefits and challenges carefully, taking into account their long-term financial goals, risk tolerance, and available time. If done strategically, land can be a valuable addition to a doctor's investment portfolio, but it's important to approach it with caution and thorough research.

Chapter 44: Taking Investment Advice from Other Doctors: The Pros, Cons, and Rules of Thumb

As a doctor, you're surrounded by highly educated peers who are often skilled at problem-solving, making critical decisions under pressure, and managing complex tasks. It's natural to seek advice from fellow doctors when it comes to managing your finances, particularly when it comes to investing. After all, they understand the unique challenges and income levels that come with being in the medical profession.

However, while your colleagues may have valuable insights into their own investment experiences, relying solely on advice from other doctors—especially those who do not use a financial advisor—can be a double-edged sword. In this chapter, we'll explore the **pros and cons** of taking investment advice from fellow doctors who don't use financial advisors, and provide **rules of thumb** to guide you in making informed decisions.

The Appeal of Taking Investment Advice from Other Doctors

Doctors often have high incomes and significant disposable income, which gives them a level of financial sophistication that makes their opinions appealing. Many doctors also believe that their peers understand their unique financial circumstances, such as long hours, medical school debt, and high earning potential. The idea of receiving investment advice from a trusted colleague who's "been there" may feel comforting and relatable.

But is it the best route for your financial health?

Pros of Taking Investment Advice from Fellow Doctors

1. **Shared Understanding of Financial Challenges**

Doctors understand the unique financial challenges that come with the profession. They often deal with similar issues, such as:

- High student loan debt from medical school
- Limited time to dedicate to personal finance management due to their demanding careers
- The need to balance short-term income with long-term financial goals, such as retirement planning
- Potentially volatile or irregular income early in their career

Because of these shared challenges, advice from a peer can feel more relatable and tailored to your specific situation. Fellow doctors may also understand your financial goals better than a financial advisor who isn't familiar with the medical field.

1. **Potentially No Extra Costs**

When you take advice from a colleague, there's no added cost involved—unlike working with a financial advisor, where management fees or commissions are usually paid. This makes it an attractive option, particularly for doctors who may already feel financially stretched.

Additionally, a fellow doctor might provide insight on investment opportunities, such as real estate or tax-advantaged strategies, without charging you a fee for their time or knowledge. It can feel like a more cost-effective approach to getting advice without the added overhead.

1. **Trust in Peer Relationships**

Doctors typically have strong bonds of trust with their colleagues. When a trusted peer provides investment advice, you may feel more confident in their suggestions, believing that they have your best interests at heart. This level of trust can make you more comfortable acting on their advice, as you know they share similar values and goals.

1. **Real-Life Experience**

Fellow doctors may be able to provide firsthand experiences and lessons learned from their own investment journeys. This practical, anecdotal advice can be valuable, as it's based on real-life results and may help you avoid common pitfalls or mistakes.

Cons of Taking Investment Advice from Fellow Doctors

While the pros may seem compelling, there are several risks associated with relying on advice from doctors who don't use a financial advisor. These risks can significantly impact your long-term financial health.

1. Lack of Expertise and Objectivity

Doctors are trained to be experts in medicine, but this doesn't necessarily translate to expertise in financial planning or investing. Just because someone is successful in their medical career doesn't mean they have the necessary expertise to manage complex financial decisions. Medical training does not cover topics like tax planning, risk management, asset allocation, or retirement planning in the depth required to make well-informed investment decisions.

Additionally, without a financial advisor's objective guidance, there's a risk of making emotionally-driven decisions, especially when it comes to managing your wealth. A financial advisor offers a level of **objectivity** and helps you avoid biases that may arise from personal emotions or peer pressure. Fellow doctors, while well-meaning, may not provide that same level of impartial advice.

2. Limited Knowledge of Diverse Investment Strategies

Many doctors tend to invest in areas they are familiar with, such as real estate or stocks. However, these areas represent only a fraction of potential investment opportunities. Fellow doctors may be recommending investments that worked for them but may not be ideal for you, based on your specific financial goals, time horizon, and risk tolerance.

For example, a colleague who has invested heavily in real estate might suggest that you do the same, but without a thorough understanding of your overall financial plan. Similarly, doctors who are heavily invested in certain stocks or mutual funds might inadvertently encourage you to focus on a narrow range of investment options, missing out on more diversified opportunities.

3. Potential for Bias or Conflicts of Interest

Your fellow doctor might have certain biases or personal interests that could influence the advice they give you. For instance, if they've invested in a specific company, real estate development, or business, they may be inclined to recommend those investments to others, even if it's not the best fit for your situation. This conflict of interest could lead to you making decisions that are more aligned with their financial interests rather than your own.

Moreover, peer influence can be a powerful motivator, but just because a colleague has made money in a particular investment doesn't mean the same strategy will work for you. Doctors can be just as prone to "herd mentality" as anyone else, potentially leading to decisions based on the desire to "keep up with the Joneses" rather than sound financial principles.

4. Misunderstanding of Long-Term Financial Planning

Investment decisions should be aligned with your long-term financial goals, including retirement, tax planning, wealth preservation, and legacy planning. However, doctors who don't use a financial advisor may focus more on short-term gains (such as individual stock picking or flipping real estate) rather than comprehensive, long-term planning.

Investment strategies like tax-efficient retirement accounts, estate planning, and diversified asset allocation may not be prioritized if you're only receiving advice from peers who may not be focused on these broader, long-term strategies.

5. Missing Holistic Financial Planning

Investment decisions are only one part of a larger financial picture. To build a secure financial future, you need to take a holistic approach that includes retirement planning, tax optimization, insurance needs, debt management, and more. Fellow doctors, who may be focused on specific investments, often overlook these other crucial aspects of financial planning.

A **financial advisor** will provide a comprehensive financial plan that accounts for your income, expenses, assets, liabilities, goals, and risk tolerance. This holistic view can guide you in making more balanced decisions, whereas advice from peers may lack the broader context.

Rules of Thumb for Taking Investment Advice from Fellow Doctors

While seeking advice from fellow doctors can be valuable, it's important to approach it with caution. Here are some **rules of thumb** to keep in mind when considering investment advice from your colleagues:

1. **Assess the Source:**
2. Just because someone is a doctor doesn't mean they have a strong understanding of investments. Before acting on their advice, ask about their investment knowledge, experience, and success. If they are self-taught or only have limited experience in certain investments, their advice may not be well-rounded or suited to your specific financial goals.
3. **Diversify Your Sources of Advice:**
4. It's essential to get multiple opinions before making major financial decisions. If you're getting advice from fellow doctors, consider seeking guidance from other experts, such as certified financial planners, tax professionals, or investment managers. A diverse range of perspectives will help you make more informed decisions.
5. **Don't Imitate—Customize Your Strategy:**

6. Every individual's financial situation is unique. Just because a colleague has had success with a particular investment doesn't mean it's the right choice for you. Customize your investment strategy based on your own risk tolerance, financial goals, and time horizon.
7. **Consider the Long-Term:**
8. Focus on building long-term wealth and financial security rather than chasing quick gains. Short-term investment strategies can often lead to greater risks and volatility. Work with a financial advisor to develop a plan that ensures you're on track to meet your long-term goals, such as retirement and wealth preservation.
9. **Understand the Risk of "Following the Herd":**
10. Doctors, like everyone else, are susceptible to peer influence. Just because a fellow doctor recommends a particular investment doesn't mean it's the best choice. Make sure you understand the risks, potential rewards, and the broader context before following any advice.
11. **Use a Financial Advisor for Comprehensive Planning:**
12. While advice from fellow doctors may be useful for certain topics, working with a financial advisor can help you see the big picture. Financial advisors offer professional, objective advice and provide a holistic approach to your financial planning. They can guide you in creating a diversified portfolio, optimizing tax strategies, and planning for retirement.

Conclusion:

Taking investment advice from fellow doctors can offer valuable insights, particularly if they understand the unique financial circumstances of someone in the medical profession. However, there are significant risks involved in relying solely on this advice. Without the expertise and objectivity of a financial advisor, you may be vulnerable to poor decisions that could hinder your financial future.

Doctors should approach peer-driven investment advice with caution, ensuring that any strategy they follow aligns with their long-term financial goals and is based on sound principles. Diversifying sources of advice, customizing your investment strategy, and working with a financial advisor can help ensure you make well-informed decisions that will support your financial success for years to come.

Chapter 45: Student Loans – Strategies, Pitfalls, and Payoff Plans

Introduction: The Medical Degree Price Tag

Becoming a physician is one of the most noble, rewarding, and intellectually demanding paths a person can choose—but it comes with a steep financial price. The average medical school graduate leaves school with over $200,000 in student loan debt, not including undergraduate loans. Add in interest accrual during residency and fellowship, and many doctors are staring down balances closer to $300,000 or more.

The emotional toll can be as heavy as the financial one—anxiety, delay in major life decisions, and feelings of being financially "behind" despite a high-income profession. This chapter will help you navigate the maze of student loan repayment strategies, explain key terms, and guide you through decision-making at every stage of your medical career.

Section 1: Understanding Your Student Loans

Before we can talk about repayment or forgiveness, you must understand what you owe.

Federal vs. Private Loans

- **Federal Loans:** Most medical students borrow through the Direct Loan Program (Stafford and PLUS). These are eligible for income-driven repayment plans, Public Service Loan Forgiveness (PSLF), and deferment/forbearance.
- **Private Loans:** These are issued by banks or other private lenders and generally offer fewer protections or repayment options.

Loan Types

- **Direct Subsidized Loans** (rare for med students): Government pays interest while in school.
- **Direct Unsubsidized Loans:** Interest accrues during school and residency.
- **Grad PLUS Loans:** Higher interest rates and fees, but allow larger borrowing.
- **Perkins Loans:** Older, low-interest loans that are mostly phased out.

Section 2: The Residency Years – What to Do Early

The decisions you make during residency can have a lasting impact.

Do: Enroll in an Income-Driven Repayment (IDR) Plan

Most residents benefit from:

- **PAYE (Pay As You Earn):** 10% of discretionary income; forgiveness after 20 years.
- **REPAYE (Revised PAYE):** Also 10%, but includes an interest subsidy.
- **SAVE Plan:** Replaces REPAYE, lowers monthly payments, and enhances forgiveness.

Don't: Enter Forbearance Without a Strategy

Forbearance halts payments but interest still accrues. Many residents default into forbearance, but this delays progress toward forgiveness and causes balances to balloon.

Build PSLF Credit Early

If you work at a nonprofit hospital, get your loans certified and begin making qualifying payments. Even $0 payments during training count.

Start Living Below Your Means

Lifestyle creep is real. Avoid locking yourself into a car lease or expensive rent that makes it hard to tackle debt later.

Section 3: The Big Question – To Pursue Forgiveness or Not?

You must choose between two broad strategies:

- **Aggressive repayment** (paying off the loans yourself, quickly)
- **Forgiveness** (usually through PSLF or long-term IDR)

Option 1: Public Service Loan Forgiveness (PSLF)

- 10 years of qualifying payments at a nonprofit hospital.
- Tax-free forgiveness.
- Great for those staying in academics, VA systems, or nonprofit hospitals.

Do: Keep records and submit your Employment Certification Form annually.

Don't: Miss payment deadlines or assume all employers qualify.

Option 2: Aggressive Repayment

- Ideal if you go into private practice with higher income.
- Often involves refinancing after residency for lower interest rates.

Do: Refinance only once you're stable and have job certainty.

Don't: Refinance federal loans if you may qualify for PSLF.

Section 4: Refinancing and Consolidation – What's the Difference?

Consolidation

Combines multiple federal loans into one federal loan. Useful if:

- You need to qualify for IDR or PSLF.
- You want to simplify multiple loan types.

Pros:

- Simpler to manage.
- Access to forgiveness programs.
- Keeps federal protections.

Cons:

- May capitalize interest (increases balance).
- Resets some timelines if done improperly.

Refinancing

Replaces federal or private loans with a new private loan. Only do this if:

- You have high income.
- You don't need PSLF or IDR.
- You want a lower interest rate.

Pros:

- Lower interest rates.
- Can shorten repayment term.

Cons:

- Loss of federal protections.
- No access to IDR or PSLF.
- May not be reversible.

Section 5: Repayment Strategies – How to Pay Off Faster

1. The Avalanche Method

Pay off loans with the highest interest rate first. Saves money on interest.

2. The Snowball Method

Pay off the smallest loan first. Motivational progress, but may cost more long-term.

3. Hybrid Method

Pay minimums on all loans but aggressively tackle one loan at a time based on your priorities (interest rate, emotional satisfaction, etc.).

4. Lump Sum Payments

Use tax refunds, bonuses, moonlighting income, or signing bonuses to knock out debt.

5. Biweekly Payments

Make half-payments every two weeks. This adds up to one extra full payment per year.

6. Employer Repayment Assistance

Some employers offer student loan repayment benefits. Negotiate this in contracts.

Section 6: The Do's and Don'ts of Student Loans

Do:

- Track your loans at **studentaid.gov**
- Know your interest rates.
- Re-certify income yearly if on IDR.
- Keep documentation of payments.
- Explore forgiveness options.

- Maintain emergency savings before overpaying loans.
- Read the fine print of refinancing contracts.

Don't:

- Ignore your loans during residency.
- Refinance before exploring PSLF.
- Miss payments—this resets forgiveness clocks.
- Forget about taxes if pursuing long-term forgiveness (some may be taxable).
- Let lifestyle creep slow down debt payoff.
- Assume your friend's strategy works for you.

Section 7: Case Studies

Case Study 1: The PSLF Winner

Dr. J worked at a nonprofit hospital for 10 years and remained on the SAVE plan. After making 120 qualifying payments, she had over $220,000 in loans forgiven—tax-free. She never refinanced, certified employment yearly, and lived frugally during residency.

Case Study 2: The Refi Success

Dr. K graduated with $280,000 in debt. After matching into dermatology, he refinanced to a 5-year loan at 2.9% interest once he started private practice. He lived on $100K despite earning $350K and paid off his loans in 4.5 years.

Case Study 3: The "Uh-Oh" Path

Dr. M ignored her loans during residency, used forbearance, and didn't certify her nonprofit hospital employment. She lost 3 years of PSLF credit. She then refinanced after hearing friends talk about low rates—but later moved back to a nonprofit system. She missed out on forgiveness entirely.

Section 8: Advanced Strategies

1. Tax Filing for Loan Strategy

- If married, filing separately may lower your IDR payment.
- This could save thousands over time.

2. The "Double Doc" Plan

Two physicians married with debt? You may both qualify for PSLF. Optimize each spouse's payment strategy to maximize forgiveness.

3. Contract Negotiation for Repayment Assistance

Ask potential employers:

- Do you offer loan repayment?
- Can it be added to my sign-on bonus?
- Can it be structured over multiple years?

4. Business Ownership and Loan Strategy

If you plan to open your own practice, consider:

- Delaying aggressive payments until revenue stabilizes.
- Saving enough for operating costs before prioritizing student loan payoff.

Section 9: Pitfalls to Avoid

- **Failing to track deadlines** for IDR recertification or PSLF forms.
- **Choosing the wrong repayment plan**—some increase total interest.
- **Refinancing too early**—and losing forgiveness eligibility.
- **Letting debt delay investing.** Paying off debt is good, but don't forget to build wealth through retirement accounts.
- **Emotional burnout from focusing only on debt.** Your loans are a tool, not a punishment.

Section 10: A Word on Mindset

Debt doesn't define you—it's a tool you used to reach one of the most respected professions. Whether you choose forgiveness, refinancing, or a hybrid path, remember:

- Your degree is valuable.
- Your financial literacy is power.
- Your plan doesn't have to look like anyone else's.

This chapter is not about telling you the "right" way. It's about giving you tools, awareness, and confidence to take control.

Conclusion: Make the Decision, Then Move On

You didn't become a doctor to worry about loans forever. Pick your path, stay organized, and build wealth even while you repay. A well-structured loan strategy can free your mind—and your wallet—for more meaningful things.

Chapter 46: What Is the Market, the Economy, and Everything Else You See on TV? (Explained with Sports Analogies)

Understanding the Financial Game: A Physician's Guide to the Market

You've probably heard the headlines:

- "The market is crashing!"
- "The S&P 500 is on fire!"
- "The Fed hiked rates again!"
- "Inflation is spiraling!"

It's enough to make anyone want to ignore it and just focus on rounds, clinic notes, or finishing your next shift. But as a physician, you know better than to ignore the signs. You were trained to evaluate symptoms, diagnose the core issue, and prescribe a long-term solution.

Finance isn't that different.

Once you understand what's really happening under the surface, you'll realize that the financial world — like medicine — runs on data, systems, and behavior. And just like in medicine, success comes from long-term strategy, not emotional decisions in the moment.

Let's break it down with analogies that speak to both your professional training and the competitive drive that helped get you through residency.

What Exactly Is the Stock Market?

The stock market is where people buy and sell shares of companies. Owning a share means you own a small slice of a business — like holding equity in a clinic or surgery center. When the business grows and profits increase, the value of your share usually rises.

Doctor Analogy: Think of it like being a partner in a practice. You're not just working in the system — you own part of it. And when the practice thrives, your share becomes more valuable.

Why Do Markets Rise and Fall?

The market reacts to supply and demand. If more investors want to buy, prices rise. If more want to sell, prices fall. Emotions, news cycles, economic data, interest rates, and even global politics can influence these movements.

Doctor Analogy: Think of the market like patient vitals. Elevated heart rate or BP might reflect stress, infection, or a deeper issue. Market volatility is a symptom — not always the root cause. Your job is to look deeper and avoid overreacting.

Stock Market vs. Economy — What's the Difference?

The market reflects investor sentiment about the *future.* The economy reflects the real-time state of jobs, production, and spending. Sometimes they align. Sometimes they don't.

Doctor Analogy: It's like lab results versus a physical exam. One is perception; the other is reality. You need both to get the full picture.

Is Investing Risky? Can I Lose Everything?

Yes, if you invest in a single stock or gamble on trendy assets. But diversified investing — owning hundreds of companies through index funds or ETFs — dramatically reduces your risk.

Doctor Analogy: Treating one symptom doesn't guarantee a cure. You need a comprehensive treatment plan. Diversification is that plan — it protects your overall health even if one part of the system falters.

The Best Investment Strategy for Busy Doctors?

Keep it simple:

- Low-cost index funds or ETFs
- Automate monthly contributions
- Stick with it long-term

Doctor Analogy: It's like a preventive care protocol — consistent, boring, and highly effective. No need for financial heroics. Just consistent checkups and steady treatment.

When Should You Start?

Yesterday. But since time travel's not an option: now.

The earlier you start, the more time your money has to grow through compound interest.

Doctor Analogy: Think of it like starting a healthy lifestyle in your 30s versus your 60s. Both are helpful — but starting early gives you better outcomes with less effort.

Understanding the S&P 500

The S&P 500 is a list of the 500 largest U.S. companies — essentially a snapshot of the business world's most vital signs. If the S&P is doing well, the market in general is likely healthy.

Doctor Analogy: It's like a composite lab panel — no single result gives the full picture, but together, it gives you a strong diagnostic foundation.

Bull vs. Bear Markets

- **Bull Market:** Rising prices, optimism, growth
- **Bear Market:** Falling prices, fear, contraction

Doctor Analogy: A bull market is like a patient recovering well post-op — all signs point to strength. A bear market is like a flare-up in a chronic condition — it requires patience, discipline, and maybe a medication adjustment, not panic.

Should You Sell When the Market Drops?

Only if your diagnosis calls for it — not because of panic.

Selling when prices fall locks in losses. Historically, the market always rebounds.

Doctor Analogy: You wouldn't stop a medication after one bad lab result. You stay the course and adjust *only* if the patient's overall condition warrants it.

How Much Do You Need to Start?

$50. $100. Anything.

Most platforms now allow fractional shares and low-cost investing. Don't wait until you have "real money."

Doctor Analogy: You don't wait until Stage IV to start preventive care.

Start small, build the habit.

Day Trading vs. Long-Term Investing

Day trading is speculation. Long-term investing is strategy.

Doctor Analogy: Day trading is trying to treat every symptom individually with a new drug. Long-term investing is developing a holistic, evidence-based care plan.

What's an ETF?

An Exchange-Traded Fund (ETF) is a bundle of investments (like stocks or bonds) you can buy as one single product.

Doctor Analogy: It's like prescribing a combination therapy that targets multiple systems — efficient and effective.

Stocks vs. Bonds

- **Stock:** Ownership in a company
- **Bond:** A loan you give to a company or government

Stocks grow faster but are riskier. Bonds are slower but steadier.

Doctor Analogy: Stocks are like surgical intervention — high impact, higher risk. Bonds are like medication management — reliable and controlled.

Diversification

Diversification means spreading risk — not putting all your money into one asset or sector.

Doctor Analogy: You wouldn't base an entire treatment plan on a single test. Likewise, your portfolio needs multiple inputs to stay healthy.

Should You Invest During a Downturn?

Yes. That's when the best long-term opportunities often appear.

Doctor Analogy: You don't abandon treatment during a setback. You double down, monitor closely, and stay focused on recovery.

Financial Advisors: Do Doctors Need One?

You can start solo using platforms like Vanguard, Fidelity, or Schwab.

But once your income grows, taxes become complex, or you're balancing a practice and retirement planning — a financial advisor can serve as your quarterback.

Doctor Analogy: You can treat the common cold yourself. But for surgery? You want a specialist.

Final Thoughts: Build Your Financial Immune System

The market isn't magic. It's not rigged. It's not out to get you. But just like the body, it reacts to stress, adapts to change, and rewards consistent care.

- Diversify your investments like you would approach differential diagnosis
- Stick to your plan like you would a long-term treatment protocol
- Don't overreact to noise — base decisions on data
- Reassess annually — just like a physical exam

The best investors, like the best doctors, play the long game. They trust the process. They plan for setbacks. And they keep their eyes on the bigger picture — healing, growth, and long-term results.

Start today. And invest like your future depends on it — because it does.

Chapter 47: How to Start Investing

Don't Just Earn It—Build Something With It

You finally made it. After years of training, exams, late-night shifts, and loan deferments, you're earning real money. Whether it's your first attending paycheck, a signing bonus, or a practice buy-in distribution, the urge to *celebrate* is real.

New car? Weekend getaway? Maybe even a home upgrade? All valid.

But the real flex?

Financial independence.

Long-term wealth.

Getting your money to work as hard as you do.

That's what investing is about. And the sooner you start, the sooner you buy back your time, freedom, and peace of mind. This chapter is your playbook: how to start investing, which accounts make sense for doctors, and how to build a plan that turns income into wealth—whether you're earning \$100K, \$500K, or scaling toward seven figures.

Step 1: Understand What Investing Actually Is

Investing means putting your money into assets—stocks, bonds, ETFs, real estate—that grow in value over time and may generate income.

Instead of letting your earnings sit in a checking account (or vanish on Amazon and DoorDash), you're giving that money a job. It works 24/7 to build future wealth.

It's not about chasing "hot tips" or picking the next Tesla. It's about **consistency** and **compound growth**.

The earlier you start, the more your money can multiply—especially when reinvested over decades.

Step 2: Know Your Goals and Time Frame

Ask yourself:

- When will I need this money?
- Am I okay with short-term market fluctuations?
- Am I investing for retirement, lifestyle upgrades, or practice expansion?

If you won't need the money for at least 5–10 years, investing it is usually a wise move. But if it's for a down payment, tuition, or emergency fund, keep it in cash or low-risk accounts.

Pro Tip: You can—and should—invest *while* paying off student loans. Just don't use short-term money for long-term goals.

Step 3: Choose Your Investment Accounts

Not all investment accounts are created equal. Some have tax advantages, some have rules, and others give you total flexibility.

Here's a breakdown tailored for doctors:

Roth IRA

- Funded with after-tax dollars
- Grows *tax-free*
- Withdrawals in retirement are tax-free
- 2025 contribution limit: **$6,500**
- Must have earned income and fall under the income limit

Why it's great:

Doctors in residency or early in their career may qualify. You're likely in a lower tax bracket now than you will be later—paying taxes now means tax-free income later. That's a huge win.

Traditional IRA

- Contributions *may* be tax-deductible
- Grows tax-deferred
- Pay taxes when you withdraw in retirement
- Same $6,500 limit

Best for:

Mid-career doctors who want a tax break now. But note: deductions phase out if you also have a workplace retirement plan.

Taxable Brokerage Account

- No contribution limits or income restrictions
- Taxes on dividends and capital gains
- Full flexibility

Best for:

Doctors who want to invest beyond IRA limits, or who want access to funds *before* retirement. Also ideal for wealth building outside your practice.

401(k), 403(b), or 457 Plans

- Employer-sponsored plans
- 2025 employee contribution limit: **$23,000**
- Employer match (if available) is extra
- Pre-tax (Traditional) or Roth options

Best for:

Hospital-employed physicians. Use this to its full advantage—especially if your employer offers matching contributions (free money!).

SEP IRA (Simplified Employee Pension)

- Designed for self-employed individuals
- Contribution limit: **25% of compensation, up to $66,000** (2025)
- Tax-deductible contributions

Best for:

Doctors in private practice, locums, or side hustles (consulting, expert witness work, etc.).

Solo 401(k)

- For self-employed doctors with no employees
- Higher contribution limit than a Roth/Traditional IRA
- Can be Traditional or Roth

Best for:

Physicians who own their own practice or moonlight.

Step 4: What to Do With a $100,000 Windfall

Whether it's a signing bonus, inheritance, malpractice settlement, or side hustle success—here's how to turn $100K into momentum, not regret.

Step 1: Set Aside Taxes

If this is non-W-2 income (e.g., moonlighting, consulting, expert witness work), assume 30–40% for federal, state, and self-employment taxes.

$100,000 × 30% = $30,000

Move this into a separate account immediately. Do not touch it. Protect yourself from a surprise tax bill next April.

Step 2: Fund Your Roth IRA

Assuming you qualify (based on income or via a backdoor Roth), contribute the max:

$6,500 into a Roth IRA

Invest it in a diversified stock index fund (like the S&P 500). Let time and tax-free growth do the heavy lifting.

Step 3: Invest in a Taxable Brokerage Account

Still have room? Perfect. Let's grow that wealth.

Put **$35,000–$45,000** into a brokerage account

Pick low-cost ETFs or index funds. Keep it simple, consistent, and long-term.

Step 4: Establish an Emergency Fund

You never know when the furnace breaks, malpractice premiums spike, or you need to travel for a family emergency.

Set aside **$10,000–$15,000** in a high-yield savings account.

This is not investment money—it's *protection.*

Step 5: Enjoy a Little

You've worked hard. It's okay to enjoy a piece of your win.

Allocate **$5,000–$10,000** for something fun—vacation, car upgrade, new gear, whatever brings joy. Just make it intentional.

Recap: How a Doctor Breaks Down $100K

- **$30,000** – taxes
- **$6,500** – Roth IRA
- **$35,000** – brokerage investments
- **$15,000** – emergency savings
- **$8,500** – fun/discretionary

This is how doctors build not just income—but *wealth.*

Step 5: Set It and Stick With It

No six-figure windfall? No problem. The same strategy applies monthly:

- Save for taxes
- Max out retirement accounts
- Build your cash buffer
- Invest consistently
- Enjoy responsibly

Use auto-transfers. Automate investing. Pick simple funds. Don't overcomplicate.

Because the truth is, wealth isn't built from big wins—it's built from small, smart, consistent moves over time.

Final Thoughts: Don't Let a High Income Be a Missed Opportunity

Earning a lot doesn't mean building wealth.

You know colleagues who earn $400K+ and still live check to check.

You also know people who drive used cars, invest $3,000/month, and are financially independent by 45.

The difference isn't income—it's intention.

Start now. Even if it's $100 a week. Your future self will thank you.

Let your money work while you sleep.

Let it grow while you heal others.

Let it create the freedom medicine doesn't always give you.

Because the real win?

Not just making a good living—but building a great life.

Chapter 48: Helping Without Hurting – How to Support Loved Ones Without Going Broke

How to Set Boundaries With Family and Friends When You're the First to "Make It"

Let's talk about one of the most difficult, emotional parts of becoming a doctor and earning a high income—especially if you're the first in your family to do so.

You've worked hard. You've sacrificed years of your life, taken on student debt, and endured training most people can't even imagine. And now that you're finally earning real money… you're expected to *share* it.

Help your mom who raised you alone and sacrificed everything? Of course you want to.

Support your dad who never had much but always showed up for you? It feels like the least you can do.

Bail out a cousin, sibling, or friend who's in a bind and says, "You're a doctor now—you got it"?

You want to say yes.

You don't want to seem cold.

You feel responsible.

But if you're not careful, you'll spend the prime of your earning years putting out fires for other people—while your own financial foundation stays unstable.

This chapter is about love—with limits.

Support—with structure.

Generosity—without guilt.

Because your job is not to fund everyone else's lives. Your job is to *build* a life—and a legacy—that's sustainable.

You Are Not the Family's Retirement Plan

Here's the truth: when you're the first one in the family to "make it," people often look to you as the safety net. Some will ask directly. Others will just expect it.

But no matter how it shows up, remember this:

- You are not a bottomless pit of money.
- You are not the bank.
- You are not the family pension.

Even if you *choose* to help, that support must be structured, intentional, and limited.

Because if you let guilt write the checks, your future will bounce.

The Monthly Support Budget Strategy

Let's say you want to help regularly—whether that's with groceries, rent, or medical bills.

That's where a *monthly support budget* comes in.

Example:

You decide that $1,000/month is what you can afford to contribute to family or friend support—without compromising your own retirement, savings, or goals.

Break it up intentionally:

- $500 goes to your mother's rent
- $300 helps cover a sibling's tuition

- $200 is on a prepaid card for miscellaneous expenses

Once you hit $1,000, you're done for the month.

When someone else calls with an emergency?

You say:

> *"I've already hit my support budget this month. Let's talk again next month."*

That's not harsh—it's healthy.

That's not selfish—it's smart.

The One-Time Gift Strategy

Maybe you'd rather avoid ongoing requests altogether. In that case, a lump sum approach may be better.

Example:

You receive a signing bonus or end-of-year bonus and decide to give $5,000 to help your parents catch up on bills or pay down debt.

You say:

> *"This is a one-time gift. I wanted to do something meaningful, and I'm glad I can. But after this, I can't give more right now."*

You give. You communicate clearly. And you *don't reload the gift.*

This isn't a subscription. It's a one-time act of love.

What If Everyone Needs Help?

If it's more than just your parents—maybe your siblings, cousins, or a close friend who's struggling—the same rules apply.

Set a total **annual support budget**, and divide it accordingly.

Example:

You decide to allocate $12,000 per year ($1,000/month) toward helping others.

You break it down:

- Mom gets $500
- Dad gets $300
- Sibling gets $100
- Your best friend who's "just trying to get back on track" gets $100

That's it.

The number doesn't change because someone's story gets more emotional.

You're generous—but you're not unstable.

Say It Out Loud. Say It Early.

If you don't say anything, people will assume your resources are unlimited.

They'll keep asking. And when you finally say no, it'll come as a shock.

Avoid that by being upfront.

> *"I'm proud to be in a position to help. But I'm setting a boundary. I've got a monthly/annual support budget, and once I hit it, I can't go over. This is about protecting my long-term future."*

And when someone says:

> *"But just this once..."*
>
> *You say: "I love you. But I can't go past the number I've set. I'm sticking to my plan."*

Signs You're Enabling, Not Helping

Generosity becomes *enabling* when:

- They stop trying to help themselves
- They start expecting your support
- They guilt you when you say no
- You keep solving the same problem over and over
- You feel resentment instead of peace

To avoid this:

- Pay the bill directly—don't hand out cash
- Make your help short-term, not open-ended
- Offer job resources or connections instead of money
- Set clear boundaries: no loans, no "next time," no guilt

If someone's asking for help every month... what they need isn't your checkbook.

They need a **financial plan**.

If They Get Upset, Let Them

They might say:

- "You've changed."
- "You forgot where you came from."
- "You think you're better than us."

Let them say it.

You didn't work 10+ years in training to feel financially stuck, just in nicer scrubs.

You didn't endure med school, residency, call shifts, and burnout just to become everyone's personal ATM.

Let them be mad—for now.

They'll understand—*eventually*—when they see you financially stable years from now while others are still struggling and bitter.

Final Thoughts: Give With a Plan—Not Pressure

You're not wrong for saying no.

You're not heartless for having boundaries.

You're not selfish for wanting to protect what you worked for.

You can still help. You can still love deeply. You can still honor your roots.

But do it:

- With clarity
- With a budget
- With limits
- With peace

Because the best thing you can give your family isn't just money—it's the *example*.

Of strength.

Of structure.

Of someone who didn't just make it—but made it *last*.

That's how you shift generations.

That's how you build wealth that sticks.

That's how you give without giving *yourself* away.

That's legacy.

Chapter 49: Stupid Investments – Schemes That Trap Doctors

Introduction: When Smart People Make Dumb Money Moves

Doctors are highly educated—but not necessarily in finance. This makes them prime targets for bad investments, get-rich-quick schemes, and poorly vetted opportunities. Many physicians fall into financial traps not because they're careless, but because they trust the wrong people, chase status, or assume their high income means they can afford to take big risks.

In this chapter, we'll unpack some of the most common "stupid" investments doctors get involved in, why these traps are so tempting, and how to avoid losing money—and sleep—by staying grounded, skeptical, and strategic.

Why Doctors Are Prime Targets

1. **High Income, Low Financial Literacy:** A six-figure salary without six-figure financial training.
2. **Trust in Other Professionals:** If another doctor, lawyer, or advisor is doing it, it must be smart... right?
3. **Busy and Burned Out:** With long hours and little free time, many physicians outsource decisions—or invest without researching.

4. **Delayed Gratification:** After years of training and sacrifice, many feel entitled to enjoy the fruits of their labor—sometimes prematurely or recklessly.
5. **Status Pressure:** Big house, luxury car, prestigious investments—doctors often feel like they have to keep up with their peers, regardless of cost.

Investment Traps and Schemes: What to Watch For

1. The "Too Good to Be True" Private Deal

A former med school classmate or a patient's cousin approaches you with an "exclusive" opportunity to invest in a startup, film project, tech company, or app. You're promised high returns with little risk.

Red flags:

- No formal business plan or audited financials.
- You're being asked to invest "quickly" to secure your spot.
- You don't understand how the business makes money.

Reality: Most startups fail. Even legitimate ones take years to turn a profit. Without proper due diligence, you're just gambling.

2. Shady Real Estate Syndications

You're invited to invest in a real estate deal: "Just $50,000 and you'll earn passive income while owning part of an apartment complex." But you don't know the operators, and you're unsure how the returns are calculated.

Red flags:

- Complex LLC structures you don't understand.
- No transparency about fees or exit plans.
- "Guaranteed" returns in an unpredictable market.

Reality: Some syndications are solid, but many overpromise and underdeliver. Others are outright scams.

3. **Ponzi Schemes Masquerading as "Alternative Investments"**

You're pitched a foreign exchange (forex) trading program or a cryptocurrency mining operation that pays you 2-3% monthly. Returns are steady—until suddenly, they're not.

Red flags:

- You don't understand how the returns are generated.
- You're encouraged to recruit others.
- Your returns are paid from new investors' money—not actual profits.

Reality: If the pitch sounds like "make money while you sleep" with no downside, it's likely a Ponzi scheme.

4. **Restaurant and Bar Ventures**

"Doctor-owned steakhouse" sounds fun and prestigious—until you realize that 80% of restaurants fail within 5 years.

Red flags:

- Emotional attachment to the idea ("It'll be fun!").
- No operational experience on the team.
- Unrealistic profit projections.

Reality: Restaurants are high risk, high overhead, low margin. You're not investing—you're donating.

5. **MLMs and Direct Sales**

Yes, some doctors have been lured into selling supplements, essential oils, or "health" products via multi-level marketing companies.

Red flags:

- You're required to buy inventory upfront.
- You're pressured to recruit other sellers.
- The income structure rewards recruitment more than sales.

Reality: MLMs are designed to profit those at the top. Most participants lose money—or damage their credibility.

6. **"Insider" Medical Device Startups**

A device that will "change medicine"—and your colleague says it's the next big thing. You invest early and heavily. Years later, the FDA still hasn't approved it and the company burned through its seed money.

Red flags:

- No regulatory pathway.
- No reimbursement strategy from insurers.
- Science isn't peer-reviewed or independently validated.

Reality: Many medical startups are overhyped and underfunded. Most never make it to market.

Psychology Behind Dumb Decisions

Understanding why doctors fall into these traps can help prevent future mistakes.

1. Overconfidence Bias

"I'm smart, so I must be good at investing." Intelligence doesn't equal expertise in all fields.

2. Herd Mentality

"If other doctors are in it, I should be too." Groupthink often leads to shared losses.

3. Anchoring to Income

"I make $300,000 a year, so what's $50,000?" Losses are rationalized instead of evaluated.

4. Fear of Missing Out (FOMO)

You hear others talking about a hot investment and jump in without research. If it was a real opportunity, you'd have heard about it *before* it got hot.

What You Should Ask Before You Invest

1. **Do I understand how this investment works?**
2. **What is the risk of total loss?**
3. **Is this investment liquid—or will my money be locked up?**
4. **Who else is investing—and why?**
5. **Am I being emotionally swayed or peer-pressured?**
6. **Has this investment been vetted by a financial advisor or attorney?**
7. **What's the worst-case scenario? Can I afford it?**

Better Alternatives for Physicians

Instead of chasing big wins or flashy deals, doctors are better off sticking with proven wealth-building strategies:

- **Low-Cost Index Funds**
- Track the market with broad exposure and minimal fees.
- **Backdoor Roth IRA**
- Tax-advantaged retirement strategy for high earners.
- **Taxable Brokerage Accounts**
- Flexible investing with no income limits or withdrawal penalties.
- **Real Estate (Smartly Done)**
- Buy and manage properties directly or through REITs.
- **Paying Down Debt**
- A guaranteed return equivalent to the interest rate.
- **Investing in Yourself**
- Continuing education, certifications, and skills that increase income.

Case Studies: Smart vs. Stupid

Dr. B and the Crypto Mining Disaster

Dr. B invested $75,000 in a crypto mining company run by a friend of a friend. Promised returns of 25% annually. The website disappeared, and so did the operators. He never saw a dollar back.

Dr. C and the Steady Wealth Builder

Dr. C maxed out her 401(k), funded a taxable brokerage account, and bought a modest rental property after studying for a year. She ignored hot tips and built $500K in net worth over 5 years.

Dr. D and the "Doctor Bar"

Dr. D invested $100K in a trendy lounge near the hospital. He liked the vibe. The business folded in 14 months. He lost everything.

Pitfalls to Watch Out For

- **High fees, low transparency**
- **Promises of guaranteed returns**
- **Lack of a business plan or audited financials**
- **Pressure to act quickly or recruit others**
- **Emotion-based decision making ("It's my friend's idea")**
- **Lack of legal or financial review**

How to Say No

You'll be approached with "opportunities" because you're a doctor. Here's a script to shut it down professionally:

> *"Thanks for thinking of me. I have a strict investment policy and only commit after thorough due diligence and consultation with my financial advisor. Best of luck with your venture."*

Conclusion: Be Boring, Be Rich

The best investment strategy is often the most boring. Buy things you understand, stay diversified, and don't chase hype. The market rewards patience, discipline, and humility.

You don't need to invest in a steakhouse to feel successful. You already are. Protect your wealth by making smart, simple, and evidence-based decisions—just like you would for a patient.

Chapter 50: Conclusion: Doctor, Heal Thy Finances

The Prescription for Your Own Peace of Mind

You've spent a lifetime studying, sacrificing, and serving—putting patients first, responding to emergencies, and showing up on call, in the clinic, and in the OR. Your work has saved lives, soothed pain, and shaped communities.

But now, it's time to turn that same care inward.

Not for your patients—but for **yourself**.

You've earned a respected title, a strong income, and a place in the fabric of the healthcare system. But none of that guarantees financial security. In fact, too many physicians reach the peak of their careers still stressed about money, unsure about retirement, and unprepared for the next chapter.

This book was written to change that.

Because the truth is, you already have everything you need:

- The discipline to follow a long-term plan
- The intelligence to understand complex information
- The work ethic to take action when it matters

Now, it's about **applying those traits to your finances.**

Whether you're just starting out, in your peak earning years, or preparing to hang up the white coat, the message is the same:

Doctor, heal thy finances.

Not overnight. Not perfectly. But intentionally.

With the right tools, the right strategy, and the right support, you can:

- Eliminate the stress of debt
- Grow wealth that outlasts your working years
- Protect your family against the unexpected
- Leave a legacy that reflects not just your work—but your wisdom
- Experience freedom, flexibility, and purpose far beyond hospital walls

Money should never control your life. It should empower it.

Let this be the beginning—not the end—of your financial journey.

Thank you for the lives you've healed, the service you've given, and the future you're about to claim for yourself.

Your patients needed you at your best.

Now, your future does too.

This book was never meant to be the finish line. It's the **starting block**—a new phase of empowerment, one where you move from being reactive with money to being **deliberate, strategic, and confident**.

Because the same precision you apply in diagnosis, the same steadiness you bring to a procedure, and the same critical thinking you've used your entire career—**those skills are your superpowers in financial planning too**.

So what's next?

- **If you've read this book and still feel unsure—ask questions.**
- Reach out to a fee-only financial advisor, a CPA, or an estate attorney. You're not expected to do this alone.
- **If you feel behind—start where you are.**
- The best time to get financially organized was yesterday. The second-best time is today.
- **If you feel good—keep going.**
- Financial peace isn't a finish line. It's a practice, just like medicine.

And finally—share what you've learned. Talk about it with your spouse. Teach it to your children. Bring it up in the lounge. Advocate for it in medical schools. **Be the voice** that says: "Financial literacy matters just as much as clinical literacy."

Because here's the truth:

Physicians like you are pillars in society. You lead, you educate, you inspire. When you're financially stable, **you're free to practice medicine with integrity**, make decisions without pressure, and retire on your own terms—not out of necessity, but out of choice.

That's not just good for you—it's good for patients, families, and the future of healthcare itself.

So yes—doctor, heal thy finances. But more than that: **protect them, grow them, and use them to live the life you deserve.**

On your terms. With clarity. With purpose. With peace.

Questions for Professionals

Questions to Ask a Financial Advisor

1. **Are you a fiduciary 100% of the time?**
2. (Fiduciaries are legally required to act in your best interest.)
3. **Do you have experience working with physicians or other high-income professionals?**
4. **How do you get paid?**
5. (Fee-only, fee-based, or commission? Transparency is critical.)
6. **Do you help with student loan strategy, retirement planning, and insurance reviews?**
7. **Will you coordinate with my CPA, attorney, and other advisors?**
8. **What is your investment philosophy?**
9. (Ask for simple, jargon-free answers.)
10. **How do you handle risk management and asset protection strategies for clients like me?**
11. **Can you help me with financial decisions related to practice ownership or contract review?**

Questions to Ask a CPA (Certified Public Accountant)

1. **Do you work with doctors, practice owners, or other medical professionals?**
2. **Can you help with tax planning, not just tax filing?**
3. (Many CPAs only file taxes but don't offer proactive planning.)
4. **Are you familiar with how to file income from moonlighting,**

locums, or consulting?

5. **Do you offer guidance on multi-state taxation or self-employment income?**
6. **How do you help clients structure deductions, depreciation, and retirement contributions?**
7. **What tax-saving strategies do you recommend for high-income earners like physicians?**
8. **Can you review my employment contract for tax implications?**
9. **Do you offer audit support or representation if I'm ever audited?**

Questions to Ask an Estate Planning Attorney

1. **Do you specialize in estate planning for high-income professionals or medical families?**
2. **What are the essential estate documents I need in place (will, trust, power of attorney, etc.)?**
3. **Can you help protect my assets from potential lawsuits or malpractice claims?**
4. **What strategies do you recommend for tax-efficient wealth transfer to my heirs?**
5. **Do I need a revocable living trust, and what are the benefits for someone in my position?**
6. **Can you help plan for my minor children or a special-needs family member?**
7. **How often should I update my estate plan?**
8. **Can you work alongside my financial advisor and CPA to ensure my plan is fully integrated?**

Questions to Ask a Business Attorney (for Practice Owners or Partners)

1. **Do you have experience working with physicians, group practices, or healthcare startups?**
2. **Can you review or help negotiate my employment or partnership agreement?**
3. **What should I watch out for in non-compete clauses and buy-in/buy-out provisions?**
4. **What's the best legal structure for my practice (LLC, PLLC, S-Corp, etc.)?**
5. **Can you help me set up asset protection strategies, such as family trusts or holding companies?**
6. **What do I need to know about HIPAA, liability risks, and compliance from a legal standpoint?**
7. **Can you assist with succession planning if I want to sell or retire from my practice?**
8. **How do you charge—by the hour, flat fee, or retainer?**

Bonus: Questions to Ask Other Professionals

Insurance Agent (Disability, Life, Umbrella, Malpractice)

- Are you independent or tied to one company?
- Do you understand own-occupation disability coverage for physicians?
- Can you review all my current policies for gaps?
- Do I need an umbrella policy given my profession and liability exposure?

Practice Consultant or CFO (For Practice Owners)

- Can you help streamline my practice's cash flow and financial statements?

- Do you benchmark profitability compared to similar practices?
- Can you help with staff compensation models and bonus structures?

Disclaimer

Financial Literacy For Doctors is written with the intent to educate, empower, and encourage physicians at all stages of their careers to take control of their financial lives. The insights in this book are based on the author's personal experiences, professional training, and research gathered over more than two decades of work in financial services, physician education, and personal development.

That said, it's important to be clear on what this book *is*—and what it *is not*.

Educational Purpose Only

All content in this book is presented for general educational and informational purposes. It is designed to provide doctors—whether in medical school, residency, fellowship, or private practice—with foundational financial concepts, tools for responsible decision-making, and awareness of the common challenges and opportunities that come with a high-income medical career.

While this book shares strategies, insights, and real-world examples, it is *not* personalized advice, nor should it be used as a financial roadmap specific to your situation. Everyone's financial life is different. Your goals, specialty, employment structure, family needs, student loan burden, and risk tolerance are unique.

Before making any significant financial, legal, or business decisions, you should consult with qualified professionals licensed to provide advice in those areas.

No Legal Advice

Although many doctors eventually own practices, sign employment contracts, or enter into partnership agreements, this book does not offer legal advice. It is not a substitute for the counsel of a licensed attorney.

If you are:

- Negotiating a contract
- Starting or buying into a practice
- Creating estate planning documents
- Forming a legal business entity
- Navigating malpractice issues

…you should work directly with an attorney who specializes in healthcare law, business law, or estate planning. Legal obligations and liability risks can vary dramatically depending on your practice location, employment model, and personal structure. You are responsible for ensuring compliance with all laws and contractual terms that apply to you.

No Financial or Investment Advice

While this book discusses vital topics such as budgeting, student loans, investing, taxes, retirement planning, and wealth-building, it does so from an educational lens—not an advisory one.

This book is *not* written by a Certified Financial Planner™, Registered Investment Advisor, or broker-dealer. The ideas presented are general in nature and are not a substitute for the services of a licensed financial professional.

Before implementing any financial strategy, investing in a product, or making decisions related to your portfolio or retirement plan, consult with a financial advisor who understands your personal goals, income structure, and risk profile—especially one experienced in working with physicians.

The author makes no guarantee of financial success, investment returns, or specific outcomes as a result of applying any concept discussed herein.

No Accounting or Tax Advice

Although taxes play a huge role in physician wealth management, this book is not written by a CPA, enrolled agent, or tax preparer. Any references to deductions, filing strategies, or IRS policies are intended to raise awareness—not to replace the advice of a licensed tax professional.

If you:

- Work as an independent contractor or locum tenens
- Run your own practice or side business
- Contribute to multiple retirement plans
- Receive income from multiple states or countries
- Need guidance on student loan repayment tied to AGI

...then you should seek the help of a qualified tax advisor. Only a licensed accountant or tax preparer can determine your eligibility for deductions, structure your quarterly payments properly, and minimize your audit risk.

No Guarantees or Promises

Reading this book does not guarantee financial success, wealth accumulation, or long-term security. Personal outcomes vary greatly depending on discipline, decision-making, behavior, life circumstances, and market conditions.

This book was written to inspire and inform—not to predict or promise.

Any case studies, examples, or numbers provided are for illustration only. They do not represent actual investment results or guaranteed career outcomes.

Limitation of Liability

By reading this book, you acknowledge that the author, Pat Brown, MBA, and all affiliated brands or websites—such as FinancialLiteracyForDoctors.com, FinancialLiteracyForStudentAthletes.com, and others—are not responsible for any decisions you make or outcomes you experience based on the information provided herein.

Neither the author nor any associated entity shall be held liable for any financial loss, legal issue, tax consequence, or business-related outcome that results directly or indirectly from your use of this material.

Encouragement to Build Your Team

It is the author's firm belief that every doctor—whether a med student or a seasoned specialist—deserves access to a trustworthy team of professionals, including a financial advisor, attorney, tax expert, and insurance consultant. This book is intended to *complement* that team—not replace it.

If you do not yet have professional guidance, now is the time to begin. Early planning and informed decisions can dramatically affect your long-term financial health and personal well-being.

You've invested time, energy, and sacrifice into becoming a physician. Now it's time to make sure your money works just as hard for you as you've worked for your patients.

Annual Financial Calendar – Important Dates Every Doctor Should Know

JANUARY

- **January 1**
- New contribution limits for **401(k), 403(b), 457**, and **IRA/Roth IRA** go into effect.
- **Health Savings Account (HSA)** and **Flexible Spending Account (FSA)** limits reset.
- Begin **new year's budget and cash flow review**.
- Update **paycheck withholding (Form W-4)** if you've had life changes.
- **January 15**
- **4th Quarter Estimated Taxes Due** (for income earned October 1 – December 31 of previous year). Use IRS Form 1040-ES.
- **Late January**
- Begin receiving **W-2s, 1099-NEC, 1099-MISC, 1099-INT, 1099-DIV, and 1099-B** from employers, banks, brokerages, and clients.

FEBRUARY

- **February 1**
- Deadline for employers and payers to issue **W-2s and 1099s** to employees and contractors.
- **Mid to Late February**
- Receive **K-1s** from partnerships or S-corporations (may be delayed

into March or April).

- Start preparing documentation for **tax filing** or submission to your CPA.

MARCH

- **March 15**
- **Partnership and S-Corporation Tax Returns Due (Form 1065 or 1120-S).**
- (Can file extension using Form 7004.)
- **March 31**
- Last day to receive **electronic** Form 1095-A, 1095-B, or 1095-C (health insurance coverage documentation).

APRIL

- **April 1**
- Required Minimum Distributions (RMDs)** must begin if you turned **73 last year** and delayed your first RMD.
- **April 15 (or next business day if weekend/holiday)**
- **Personal Tax Filing Deadline (Form 1040)**
- **First Quarter Estimated Taxes Due**
- **Deadline to make prior-year contributions** to:
- Traditional IRA / Roth IRA
- SEP IRA
- HSA
- Coverdell Education Savings Account (ESA)
- **Last day to file for a 6-month tax extension** (Form 4868).
- **Last day to file FAFSA** in some states if applying for financial aid (for dependent children).

MAY

- **Early May**
- Review **property tax assessments** if applicable. Protest deadline usually mid-May depending on your state.
- **May 29 (5/29)**
- National **529 College Savings Plan Day** – Great reminder to review or open 529 accounts for children.

JUNE

- **June 15**
- **2nd Quarter Estimated Taxes Due**
- **U.S. Citizens Abroad** tax filing deadline (can extend to October 15).
- **Mid-June**
- Mid-year **retirement account performance review**. Adjust contributions if needed.
- Reassess **charitable giving** plans for the year.

JULY

- **July 1–15**
- **Mid-year financial check-in:**
- Review spending, savings goals, debt paydown progress.
- Rebalance portfolio if allocation is off by more than 5–10%.
- Schedule a **meeting with your financial advisor or CPA**.

AUGUST

- **August 1–31**
- Plan for **open enrollment** (usually starts in October or November).
- Review HSA/FSA balances and projected usage.
- **Review insurance policies**: life, disability, malpractice, and umbrella

coverage.

- Prep for **year-end charitable planning** (DAFs, appreciated stock, QCDs if age 70½+).

SEPTEMBER

- **September 15**
- **3rd Quarter Estimated Taxes Due**
- **Tax Deadline for Calendar-Year Partnerships and S-Corps (if on extension)**
- **Late September**
- Check for any **backdoor Roth IRA contributions** to convert before year-end.
- Consider **harvesting capital losses** to offset gains before Q4 ends.

OCTOBER

- **October 1**
- Deadline for **establishing a SIMPLE IRA** for current tax year.
- Medicare Open Enrollment preview window begins (important for you, parents, or retired patients).
- **October 15**
- **Extended Individual Tax Return Due Date** (Form 1040 with extension).
- **Deadline to fund SEP IRA** for prior year (if filed extension).
- **Deadline to recharacterize prior-year Roth IRA contributions**.
- **Late October**
- Review open enrollment options for employer-sponsored insurance.

NOVEMBER

- **November 1–30**
- **Health Insurance Open Enrollment** begins for ACA Marketplace.
- Employer benefits enrollment usually begins. Reassess:
- Health plans (HSA-eligible?)
- Life & disability insurance
- 401(k) contribution changes
- FSA/HSA elections
- Legal services or supplemental benefits
- **Black Friday Weekend**
- Consider timing large purchases with end-of-year spending and cash flow planning.

DECEMBER

- **December 1–15**
- **Last call to max out retirement accounts**:
- 401(k), 403(b), 457 contributions
- HSA contributions (if payroll deductions)
- Backdoor Roth conversion
- **December 31**
- **Last day for:**
- Charitable contributions to count for current year (check DAF cutoffs).
- **Tax-loss harvesting** (sell losers to offset capital gains).
- **RMDs for age 73+** (Required Minimum Distributions).
- **Gifting up to $18,000 per recipient** (annual exclusion for gift tax).
- Spend down **FSA funds** (check for grace period or carryover).
- Convert to Roth IRA (backdoor Roth deadline).
- Complete **year-end bonuses and profit-sharing contributions** for S-corps.

BONUS: Rolling & Event-Based Reminders

- **Every Paycheck:**
- Check 401(k)/403(b) deductions.
- Verify health/dental/vision premiums and HSA contributions.
- **After Major Life Events:**
- Marriage/divorce
- Birth/adoption of child
- New job or contract
- Disability or injury
- Change of primary residence
- Significant windfall/inheritance
- **Quarterly:**
- Revisit budget and spending.
- Make estimated tax payments if self-employed or have side income.
- Review investment performance and allocations.
- Meet with advisor if pursuing tax-loss harvesting or Roth conversions.

Final Tip: Automate What You Can

Set calendar reminders. Automate contributions. Set up recurring transfers. The less reliant you are on memory, the more consistent your wealth-building habits will become.

Financial Literacy Resources for Doctors

1. www.financialliteracyfordoctors.com

A dedicated platform created specifically for physicians at every stage of their career—from med school to retirement. Offers practical guides, book chapters, tools, and educational resources tailored to the financial lives of doctors.

2. White Coat Investor

www.whitecoatinvestor.com

One of the most popular physician finance blogs. Covers investing, insurance, debt management, and more. Founded by emergency physician Dr. Jim Dahle.

3. Physician on FIRE

www.physicianonfire.com

A physician-focused blog about financial independence and early retirement. Emphasizes intentional spending and lifestyle design for doctors.

4. Medscape Finance Section

www.medscape.com

Offers articles on physician compensation, debt, taxes, and investment strategies. Also provides specialty-specific salary reports annually.

5. American Medical Association (AMA) – Financial Resources

www.ama-assn.org

Provides financial planning resources, especially for early-career physicians, including budgeting, student loans, and retirement planning.

6. Doximity's Finance and Careers Section

www.doximity.com

This professional networking site for physicians includes articles and discussions on salaries, side hustles, and job contracts.

7. SoFi for Doctors

www.sofi.com/medical-professionals

Offers student loan refinancing, personal loans, and financial tools tailored to physicians and other high-debt professionals.

8. NerdWallet – Doctors & Medical Professionals

www.nerdwallet.com

Great for general financial literacy. Their physician-specific articles help with loans, credit, insurance, and budgeting.

9. Passive Income MD

www.passiveincomemd.com

A blog and course platform that teaches doctors how to build passive income through real estate, side gigs, and entrepreneurship.

10. Physician Side Gigs (Facebook Group)

www.facebook.com/groups/physiciansidegigs

A massive community of doctors sharing tips on side income, investing, and financial planning outside of clinical work.

11. Financial Residency Podcast

www.financialresidency.com

Hosted by a physician's spouse and financial planner. Covers money strategies, investing, and interviews with financially-savvy doctors.

12. Investing Doc

www.investingdoc.com

A practicing physician's blog about practice ownership, investing, and managing finances in private practice.

13. The White Coat Investor Podcast

Available on Apple, Spotify, and Stitcher

Weekly financial education in podcast form—perfect for busy doctors on the go.

14. Future Proof MD

www.futureproofmd.com

Focuses on early financial planning for residents and fellows, including real-world budgeting tips and loan management.

15. AAFP (American Academy of Family Physicians) – Financial Tools

www.aafp.org
Provides calculators, budgeting tools, and career finance guides tailored to family medicine physicians.

16. Journal of Medical Practice Management

www.greenbranch.com
A leading publication focused on the business side of medicine—great for practice owners and aspiring entrepreneurs.

17. Medical Economics

www.medicaleconomics.com
Long-standing magazine and online resource covering physician finances, billing, and practice management.

18. The DO (from the American Osteopathic Association)

www.thedo.osteopathic.org
Includes articles on physician finances, debt, and career growth for DOs and other medical professionals.

19. Docs Outside the Box Podcast

www.docsotb.com
Highlights doctors building careers and businesses outside traditional clinical roles. Includes finance, branding, and side hustles.

20. Earned Media for MDs

www.earnedmediaformds.com

Specializes in personal branding and media visibility for doctors. Includes advice on monetizing social influence and online presence.

21. Student Loan Planner – Physicians Section

www.studentloanplanner.com

Expert advice on managing and refinancing medical student loans, especially for high-debt borrowers like doctors and dentists.

22. PracticeLink – Physician Contracts & Compensation

www.practicelink.com

Besides job listings, they offer guidance on negotiating salaries, signing bonuses, and understanding physician compensation.

23. KevinMD

www.kevinmd.com

A physician blog platform with regular posts on money, business, side gigs, burnout, and the economics of modern medicine.

24. AMA Insurance – Physician Guides

www.amainsure.com

Provides physician-specific advice on disability, life, and malpractice insurance—critical parts of any financial plan.

25. Medscape Physician Compensation Report

www.medscape.com

An annual report detailing average incomes by specialty, region, and gender—great for benchmarking your earnings.

About the Author

Patrick Brown, MBA, is a former Division I football player turned wealth advisor, educator, and nationally respected voice in financial literacy. With over two decades of experience in financial planning, insurance, and investment strategy, Patrick has built a reputation for helping individuals and families build wealth with clarity, confidence, and purpose.

After earning his MBA and launching a successful career in wealth management, Patrick established a series of focused financial literacy platforms designed to serve communities often overlooked by traditional financial education. These platforms include:

- **Financial Literacy For NIL**
- **Financial Literacy For Student Athletes**
- **Financial Literacy For The Culture**
- **Financial Literacy For College Coaches**
- **Parents Of Student Athletes**

Now, through **Financial Literacy For Doctors**, Patrick extends his mission to the medical community—a group uniquely affected by student loan debt, delayed income accumulation, and the pressures of managing high earnings with little time or training in personal finance.

Patrick's passion for financial education is rooted in personal experience. Raised in a household where money was never discussed, he witnessed how financial insecurity and lack of guidance affected not only his own journey but those of countless peers and clients. His mission is clear: to bridge the gap between earning income and building sustainable, generational wealth.

Patrick has become a trusted advisor to a wide range of clients, including physicians, student-athletes, retirees, coaches, and young professionals. His guidance is known for being practical, culturally aware, and grounded in real-life scenarios—not financial jargon. Whether you're a medical student, resident, attending physician, or chief of staff, Patrick's goal is to equip you with actionable, judgment-free advice to help you thrive.

Beyond his financial work, Patrick is a dedicated community leader. He currently serves as a **Trustee on the Board of Lawrence Memorial Hospital (LMH)** and plays an active role on **several hospital board committees** focused on governance, patient care, and strategic planning. He also serves on **multiple other nonprofit and civic boards** across the region, advocating for improved healthcare access, financial literacy, and family support systems.

Patrick is a devoted husband and father, and when he's not helping others navigate their financial lives, he enjoys speaking at medical institutions, churches, and community events—bringing financial education to life through storytelling, empathy, and truth.

He believes financial literacy isn't just about numbers—it's about **freedom, peace of mind, and creating a legacy that lasts**.

Case Studies..

1. A Dual-Physician Couple: Managing Debt vs. Investing

Drs. Carter and Malik, both 34, are married internists. Together they earn $480,000 per year and have $420,000 in combined student loans at 5.8%. They're saving 10% to retirement accounts but debating whether to pay off loans aggressively or invest more.

Scenario A: Aggressive Debt Payoff

They decide to live on one income and use the other to pay off loans within 3.5 years. They delay investing in a taxable brokerage account but keep contributing to 401(k)s.

Scenario B: Balanced Strategy

They refinance their loans to 3.9%, maintain minimum payments, and divert extra cash into a taxable investment account, allowing compound growth to begin early.

Outcome:

After 10 years, the aggressive payoff strategy leads to zero debt but a lower investment portfolio. The balanced plan results in more investment gains—though debt lingers longer. The couple chooses based on **their emotional tolerance for debt vs. desire for liquidity**.

2. A Mid-Career Doctor Buying Into a Practice

Dr. Elaine, a 45-year-old dermatologist, has worked as an associate for seven years and is offered a 20% ownership stake for $250,000. The practice generates strong profits, but she's unsure how to evaluate the offer.

What She Does Right:

- Hires a healthcare attorney to review the **buy-in agreement**
- Requests a **third-party valuation** of the practice
- Negotiates a **five-year vesting schedule** with graduated buy-in payments
- Insists on visibility into financials and a **clear exit clause**

Result:

Dr. Elaine secures an equity stake, receives distributions averaging $65,000/year, and builds long-term value—without overcommitting financially or legally.

3. A Resident Sold a Bad Whole Life Policy

Dr. Jason, a 28-year-old PGY-2 anesthesiology resident, is approached by an insurance agent who convinces him to buy a $600/month whole life policy "as an investment." He's told it's better than term insurance and will build cash value.

What Goes Wrong:

- He has **no emergency fund or disability insurance**, but commits to high premiums
- The policy's cash value grows slowly due to **high commissions and fees**
- After four years, he's paid over $28,000 but can only surrender the policy for $8,000
- He can't afford to keep it—and regrets not getting **low-cost term insurance** and investing the difference

Lesson:

Insurance is for **protection**, not wealth-building. Young physicians should avoid mixing insurance and investing unless they fully understand the product.

4. An Attending Using a Financial Advisor vs. DIY Investing

Dr. Priya, a 39-year-old OB/GYN, is considering whether to manage her finances on her own or work with a fee-only financial advisor.

Scenario A: DIY Investing

She reads blogs and books, opens Roth and brokerage accounts, and builds a low-cost index portfolio. She makes solid progress but procrastinates on estate planning, insurance audits, and tax strategies.

Scenario B: Fee-Only Advisor

She hires a fiduciary advisor who charges $4,000/year. They help her:

- Optimize tax-loss harvesting
- Coordinate with her CPA on charitable giving
- Build a trust for her child
- Review disability and umbrella insurance coverage
- Project her path to financial independence by age 52

Outcome:

The DIY approach saves money on fees but leaves gaps. The advisor costs more—but provides holistic planning, especially during career transitions and family planning.

5. A Physician Mishandling Taxes After Moonlighting

Dr. Luis, a 36-year-old hospitalist, picks up extra shifts at an urgent care center, earning $55,000 in 1099 income—but he doesn't set aside taxes or track deductions.

What Goes Wrong:

- He files taxes in April and is shocked by a **$18,000 federal tax bill**
- Misses deductions for mileage, CME expenses, and scrubs

- Didn't make **quarterly estimated payments**, triggering IRS penalties
- Struggles to pay and ends up on a payment plan

Solution Going Forward:

- Opens a **Solo 401(k)** and begins deferring income
- Works with a CPA to track expenses and plan quarterly payments
- Keeps 30% of all 1099 income in a separate tax savings account

6. A Burnout Scenario and Financial Plan to Downshift Careers

Dr. Nina, a 43-year-old pediatrician, is burned out after two decades in practice. She wants to downshift—maybe move to part-time work or shift into teaching or telehealth.

Her Financial Plan:

- Assesses monthly needs and finds she only needs $7,000/month to support her family
- Cuts back to 3 clinic days/week and supplements with locums
- Starts drawing from a brokerage account while continuing minimal retirement contributions
- Works with a coach to build a **5-year plan** into medical education
- Maintains **disability insurance** in case burnout turns into a medical leave

Outcome:

With lower expenses and flexible income, Dr. Nina maintains financial stability, improves her mental health, and begins building a **second-act career** on her terms.

Pros and Cons of Working with a Financial Advisor

Working with a financial advisor can offer significant value—especially for busy professionals like physicians. But it's not the right choice for everyone, and understanding the trade-offs is essential before making the decision.

Pros of Working with a Financial Advisor

1. Expertise Across Multiple Areas

A qualified financial advisor brings experience across key areas such as investing, taxes, insurance, estate planning, retirement, and debt management. This can be especially helpful for physicians whose financial needs are more complex than average.

2. Saves Time and Reduces Stress

Between clinical hours and personal obligations, most physicians don't have the time to research investment strategies, review insurance coverage, or analyze tax moves. Delegating this to a trusted advisor frees up mental bandwidth and adds peace of mind.

3. Objective Decision-Making

An advisor helps you avoid emotional mistakes—like panic selling during a market downturn or making impulsive large purchases. They bring perspective and a long-term view to major financial decisions.

4. Accountability and Follow-Through

A financial advisor helps keep you organized and on track. Whether it's updating beneficiary forms, setting up 529 plans, or sticking to a budget, they help ensure action items are completed, not just discussed.

5. Customized, Holistic Planning

Rather than offering one-size-fits-all advice, a good advisor tailors recommendations to your specific situation. For physicians, that might include student loan repayment strategies, planning for practice buy-ins, or protecting income through specialty-specific insurance.

Cons of Working with a Financial Advisor

1. Cost

Financial advisors charge fees, either based on a percentage of your assets (typically 0.5% to 1%), as a flat fee, or hourly. For early-career doctors with high debt and limited savings, the cost may seem high—especially if you're not receiving comprehensive services.

2. Quality and Transparency Vary

Not all advisors are held to the same standard. Some are fiduciaries who put your interests first; others may be compensated by selling you products. It's critical to vet any advisor you consider working with and understand how they are paid.

3. You Still Need to Be Engaged

Even with a great advisor, you can't check out entirely. You'll still need to participate in key decisions, understand your plan, and stay informed about your goals and progress.

4. Risk of Generic Advice

Some advisors offer templated plans or model portfolios that don't reflect your unique situation. If an advisor doesn't ask about your values, priorities, or professional risks, the advice may be too generic to be effective.

5. DIY May Work for Some

If you're financially literate, enjoy personal finance, and have the discipline to stay consistent, you might successfully manage your own finances. With the rise of low-cost investing platforms and planning tools, DIY is more accessible than ever—especially for physicians in early career stages with straightforward needs.

Should You Hire a Financial Advisor?

To decide whether working with an advisor is right for you, ask yourself:

- Do I have the time and desire to manage my finances myself?
- Am I confident in my current investment, tax, and protection strategies?
- Am I facing complex decisions about student loans, buying into a practice, or tax planning?
- Do I feel financially overwhelmed or uncertain about what to prioritize?

A good financial advisor can act as your coach, quarterback, and accountability partner—helping you avoid costly mistakes and maximize your opportunities. The key is finding someone who listens, educates, and acts in your best interest.

Let me know if you'd like to follow this with a sample worksheet: "How to Interview a Financial Advisor" or a comparison chart for DIY vs. professional advice.

Made in United States
Orlando, FL
04 November 2026

90201046R00216